The Philosophy of Language in Classical Indian Tradition

Hyderabad Studies in Philosophy, no. 2

The Philosophy of Language in Classical Indian Tradition

Edited by

K.S. Prasad

Suryodaya Books
New Delhi

Published and Printed by:
Suryodaya Books
D-36-A/1, Mohan Garden
Najafgarh Road
New Delhi - 110059
Ph.: 98713 94811

Distributed by:
D.K. Printworld (P) Ltd.
Regd. office: Vedasri, F-395, Sudarshan Park
New Delhi - 110015
Ph.: 98713 94815
e-Mail: indology@dkprintworld.com
Web: www.dkprintworld.com

ISBN: 978-81-86921-20-3

First Published in India in 2002
Second impression in 2023

Acknowledgements

The present volume contains some of the papers presented in a National Seminar on 'Classical Indian Philosophy of Language' held in 18-20 October, 2000. The seminar was organised under the UGC Special Assistance Programme of the Department of Philosophy, University of Hyderabad. We are grateful to Indian Council of Philosophical Research (ICPR), New Delhi for sponsoring the seminar.

The present volume entitled *Philosophy of Language in Classical Indian Tradition* is the second under the series **Hyderabad Studies in Philosophy**. We are grateful to the University Grants Commission (UGC) for providing funds for publication of this volume under the Special Assistance Programme.

We take this opportunity to place on record our gratitude to our Vice-Chancellor and the Chairman of the SAP Advisory Committee, Professor P. Rama Rao for encouraging us in all our academic pursuits. We are extremely indebted to Professor Amitabha Dasgupta, co-ordinator of the SAP and the then Head, Department of Philosophy, for his keen interest and assistance in the publication of this volume and for extending all help in organising the seminar. On this occasion, we feel it to be our duty to express a deep sense of gratitude to our senior colleague Professor A. Ramamurthy for his valuable suggestions in connection with the publication of this volume. We are grateful to Professor R.C. Pradhan, Member Secretary, ICPR, New Delhi for his support in numerous ways in bringing out this volume. We are thankful to Professor Chinmoy Goswami, Head, Department of Philosophy, for his suggestions in the publication of this volume.

We are thankful to Dr. S.G. Kulkarni, one of the co-ordinators of the seminar on 'Classical Indian Philosophy of Language' for his help in bringing out this volume. Publishing a volume of this sort is a community project. With a profound sense of gratitude we acknowledge the assistance of our colleagues: Dr. A. Raghurama Raju, Dr. Prajit Kumar Basu and Mr. Anand Vidyadhar Wazalwar in making this publication possible.

We are thankful to Mr. Rajendra Agarwal of Decent Books, for bringing this volume in a record time. We are thankful to Mr. Gupta for processing the manuscript on to the computer efficiently.

Hyderabad
2002

K.S. Prasad

Contents

Introduction

LANGUAGE is essentially a social phenomenon, for it is through language we share our experiences. We use language to describe past, present or future events and to express desires, wishes, emotions, commands, statement of facts, etc. Thus, the basic function of language is 'communication'. Human beings have at their disposal various means of communicating with one another, not all of which require language in an articulated form. A wave of a hand, a nod, or sometimes even a well-placed cough, for instance, can each convey a different meaning to the hearer though no words are explicitly involved. However, it is language, which is at the back of these gestures. There exists, thus, a close relation between thought and language. Even thinking about language makes use of language. Hence, an insight into the working of language can be and must be the beginning of philosophical inquiry.

In India, there is a rich tradition of debate on philosophy of language. It may be recalled that the importance of language is acknowledged as early as in the Vedic period. In *Ṛgveda* several hymns are devoted to *vāk.*[1] The central feature of philosophy of language in classical Indian tradition is that it maintains a congruous relation between language and Reality. In Indian tradition, language is never separated from metaphysics. Prof. T.R.V. Murthi expresses this fact in the following words,

> Every system of philosophy had to consider language at some stage or other, and each one had to ponder over ultimate

---

1. *yāvad brahma viṣṭhītam tāvatī vāk* — *Ṛgveda, X.10.114.8.* Quoted by R.C. Pandey in *The Problem of Meaning in Indian Philosophy,* Motilal Banarsidass, Delhi, 1963, p. 5.

questions concerning the relation of the word to reality, of the modes of meaning and the validity of Verbal Knowledge (*śabda-pramāṇa*). Their metaphysical bias determined their answers to these questions.[2]

A word about the thematic organisation of the book: Papers have been arranged in four groups according to their thematic composition. The book begins with the general issues relating to language as figured in classical schools of Indian philosophy. This is followed by the papers dealing with the semantic structure of language. Bhartṛhari, being one of the principle exponents of the Grammarian School, made a significant contribution on the issues relating to philosophy and the structure of language. Hence, papers falling under this group are all concerned with *Vākyapadīya* of Bhartṛhari. The next set of papers is related to some of the important semantic notions of Nyāya philosophy of language. In this respect notions like sense, reference, proper names, meaning, etc., have been figured for discussion. The last set of papers is concerned with the nature and role of action sentences. In this connection, papers dealing with Pūrva-Mīmāṁsā have been discussed.

I

In the tradition, we find two diametrically opposed views regarding the relation between language and reality. According to the first view, language has the competence to describe everything that is there. Whatever exits is knowable and whatever is knowable is nameable is the view of the Nyāya-Vaiśeṣika.[3] On the other hand, the opposed view is that language has no competence to express the nature of the real is held by the Mādhyamika School of Buddhism

2. T.R.V. Murthy, in his foreword to *Sphoṭa theory of Language* by H.G. Coward, Motilal Banarsidass, New Delhi, 1986, p. viii.

3. *sāṇṇām api padārthānām astitvābhidheyatvajñeyatvāni* — *Padārtha-dharmasaṁgraha*, III.11. Quoted in S. Radhakrishnan and Charles A. Moore, eds., *A Source Book in Indian Philosophy*, Princeton University Press, Princeton, 1957, p. 399.

and the Advaita Vedānta.[4] By this, it follows that there are facts or state of affairs, actual or possible, which cannot be linguistically expressible. The tasted sweetness of a mango for instance, cannot be linguistically expressible.

V.N. Jha in his paper **'Language and Reality: Some Reflections from Indian Philosophy of Language'** has highlighted the above controversy. He begins his paper by tracing Bhartṛhari's philosophy in *Ṛgveda*. In this context, he exposes the basic distinction between the philosophy of Nyāya and the philosophy of Bhartṛhari on problems related to language. According to the former, as Jha observes, cognition is followed by language, while for the latter no cognition is possible without language. Besides illustrating the various theories of sentence-meaning in Indian philosophy, Jha finally goes into the problem of the relation between language and reality as conceived in Indian philosophy of language.

Language in Indian philosophy is usually referred as *śabda*. *Śabda*, in a broad sense means sound (*dhvani*), both in its articulated and inarticulate forms. The articulated forms of sounds can also be termed as 'verbal'. The term 'verbal' stretches itself from a single articulated letter (*varṇa*) to sentential structure (*vākya*) as modes of expression. Broadly, the term 'linguistic utterance', where the main concern is presumably with words and meanings than with the sounds associated with these words, is regarded as *śabda-pramāṇa* in Indian philosophy, which constitutes a major source of our knowledge. However, the Cārvākas, the Buddhists and the early Vaiśeṣikas rejected *śabda* as a *pramāṇa*. While the Buddhists and the early Vaiśeṣikas reduced *śabda* to inference, the Cārvākas with their exclusive emphasis on sense experience denied all other methods of

4. Indescribability (*anirvacanīya*) is the nature of Reality according to Mādhyamika School of Buddhism and Advaita Vedānta of Śaṅkarācārya. For Advaita Vedānta, *Brahman* is the Reality and it cannot be defined, as there is nothing beside it. Description of *Brahman* is not possible for any description presuppose something other than *Brahman* in terms of which *Brahman* may be described. *Brahman* is to be realised.

knowledge except perception. John Vattanky in his paper **'Word — A Separate Means of Valid knowledge'** examines in detail the arguments of the Naiyāyikas in support of their claim that *śabda* is an independent and irreducible means of valid knowledge in the context of the counter arguments of the Vaiśeṣikas.

With the preoccupation of philosophy with language in recent times, the philosophers of religion and theologians have shown considerable interest for understanding the problems related to the meaning of religious language. Conventionally, religious language has the same structure as that of ordinary language used in common parlance with the exception of certain oral or written religious expressions, which are not part of a linguistic system but only symbolic sounds and signs. Religious language serves many purposes. A religious statement can be historical, descriptive, definitional, invocative, persuasive, emotive, etc. However, the main challenge for the philosophy of religious language comes from the logical empiricists, whose criterion of empirical verification excludes the religious statements as meaningless. A. Ramamurthy in his paper **'Religious Language'** argues that the ordinary methods of knowing the objective meaning of religious statements will be of no use, for the domain of the religious language is not empirically verifiable reality. What distinguishes a religious interpretation of the world or the meaning given to it from other interpretation and meanings, according to Murthy, is that the religious interpretation of the world is more integral as in a non-religious interpretation we interpret world of facts and human existence independently of each other. Murthy concludes that the aim of religious language is not to communicate factual information about the world or reality or to describe it but to inspire or influence people to participate and live in the world of meaning.

II

The contribution of the Grammarians in general and Bhartṛhari in particular to the study of language is highly significant. Bhartṛhari in his celebrated work *Vākyapadīya* identifies language with the ultimate reality which has neither beginning nor end.[5] He understands the world through language[6] and believes that there is an inseparable relation between language and thought. To him language is not to be acquired but is to be realised which is there as an inherent constituent of our awareness through learning process. In each significant linguistic utterance, there are two aspects; one is *sphoṭa*, which is the cause of the real word and the other *nāda* (sound), which is used to convey the meaning.[7] The relation between *nāda* and *sphoṭa* is of the nature of revealer and the revealed. As *sphoṭa* is one, indivisible and remains unaffected all the time, plurality is superimposed on it by the revealer. The *sphoṭa* being an indivisible whole, according to Bhartṛhari, reveals itself in various ways at various stages without sacrificing its indivisibility.[8] Instead of the absolute holism attributed to the theory of *sphoṭa* propounded by Bhartṛhari, R.C. Pradhan in his paper **'Grades of Holism: Bhartṛhari Reconsidered'** has suggested that there are different grades of holism in Bhartṛhari's theory. Pradhan has identified two ways in which holism could be understood as a theory of meaning; horizontal holism, where meaning is spread across the whole language and vertical holism which pushes meaning back into deep structure of grammar. According to Pradhan, Bhartṛhari's holism is of the latter type. Further, the idea of different grades of holism such as global

---

5. *anādinidhanam brahma śabdatattvam yadakṣaram* ।
   vivartate'rthabhāvena prakriyājagatoyataḥ ॥

   — Bhartṛhari, *Vākyapadīya*, I.1, tr. K.A. Subramaniya Iyer, Deccan College Postgraduate Research Institute, Poona, 1966.

6. *na so'sti pratyayo loke yaśśabdānugamād ṛte* ।
   anuviddhamiva jñānam sarvam śabdena bhāsate ॥
   — *Ibid.*, I.123

7. *dvāvupādānaśabdeṣu śabdau śabdavido viduḥ* ।
   eko nimittam śabdānām aparo'rthe prayujyate ॥
   — *Ibid.*, I.44

8. *nādasya kramajanmatvāt na pūrvo nāparśca saḥ* ।
   akramaḥ kramarūpeṇa bhedavāniva jāyate ॥
   pratibimbam yathānyatra sthitam toyakriyāvaśāt ।
   tatpravṛttimivānveti sa dharmaḥ sphoṭanādayoḥ ॥
   — *Ibid.*, I.48-49

holism and local holism, for Pradhan, is implicit in Bhartṛhari's philosophy of language. Viewed from an absolute metaphysical standpoint, meaning is an indivisible whole and is the foundation of all language. Such a view is termed as global holism. On the other hand, when language is spoken, the sentences can be endowed with meaning without breaking it into parts. The idea that is implicit here is that the meaning of a sentence is a whole, which cannot be broken into pieces. Local holism may be, thus seen as sentential holism. Bhartṛhari, according to Pradhan, 'brings in the idea of the levels of language only to ward off the view that he accepts only a monistic view of meaning'. At the end, Pradhan relates Bhartṛhari's notion of *sphoṭa* with modern mentalistic theory that defines the content of consciousness in terms of meaning. Pradhan claims that Bhartṛhari anticipates this theory because *sphoṭa* though considered to be a linguistic entity very much belongs to consciousness. Hence, *sphoṭa* is the ground where language and consciousness become indistinguishable. In this connection, Pradhan further argues that Bhartṛhari's theory of *sphoṭa* supports what he calls content holism, which says that contents of consciousness as a whole can be represented in the mechanism of language of thought. According to Pradhan, content holism is possible only when we can bring all the contents of consciousness into one single system. In other words, content holism speaks for the unity of contents. *Sphoṭa* is the unifying principle that brings all contents into one whole. The problem with modern content theorists is that they fail to suggest any such unifying principle and as a result, they only talk about local holism. *Sphoṭa* theory of Bhartṛhari on the other hand according to Pradhan could able to provide the ground that unifies locally conceivable contents into one single system. Pradhan ascribes this holism as global holism.

P.R. Bhat in his paper **'The Problem of Meaning in Vākyapadīya'** has criticised *Vākyapadīya* for lack of coherence on certain issues. He argues, for instance, that if we take use as the criterion for determining the meaning as suggested at some places in *Vākyapadīya* then the distinction between *mukhyārtha* and *lakṣyārtha* cannot be maintained coherently. As he argues, what is considered *lakṣyārtha* at one point of time becomes *mukhyārtha* at a different point in time due to usage. Further, this leads to the admission of non-eternal character of the meaning of words, which according to Bhat, is not consistent with the basic position of *Vākyapadīya*. In his words, 'either the thesis of eternal relation is over statement or dynamism in language is not properly acknowledged in *Vākyapadīya*'. In addition to this, Bhat also pointed out the incoherent stance taken by Bhartṛhari on various issues in *Vākyapadīya*.

The various theories of meaning in Indian philosophy in general derive from the basic concept of language as the only means of communication. Linguistic utterances are made with a view to communicate information to the listener. This leads to the construction of theories of meaning solely as explanations of how the listener obtains knowledge from the spoken words of a reliable person. The theories of meaning are simply the explanations of knowledge which a listener acquires from the words of a speaker, and in this sense it is basically a theory of understanding. Thus, in developing the theories of meaning, Indian philosophers in general deal exclusively from the listener's point of view. It is a fact that at times the listener has to take into account the intention of the speaker as determinant factor in understanding the meaning of the sentence. Yet the intention of the speaker cannot create new meanings of expressions, he can only choose one of the meanings already ascribed to them. Knowing the intention of the speaker is what the listener has to do to acquire knowledge. Thus, the theory of meaning in Indian philosophy is primarily an epistemic enterprise, chiefly concerned as one of the sources of valid knowledge. However, Tandra Patnaik in her paper **'Intention and Linguistic Communication: The Bhartṛharian Perspective'** has drawn our attention to the fact that Bhartṛhari approaches the theory of meaning from speaker's point of view as well. According to Tandra Patnaik, the problem of transferring meaning from speaker to hearer is crucial. She identifies that it is always the 'sense' of the whole expression that is communicated and not isolated meanings of the constituent words uttered by the speaker. There must be a common ground for the transmission of the 'sense'. Bhartṛhari, according to her, locates it in the concept of *sphoṭa.*

III

It is generally believed that the concept of sense as a component of the meaning of an expression as understood in the analytic tradition of philosophy in the West is missing in Indian philosophy of language.[9] Amitabha Dasgupta in his paper **'Śābdabodha and the Epistemic Primacy of Sense: An Exercise in Comparative Philosophy of Language'** argues that the Nyāya concept of *śābdabodha* may be roughly understood as the concept of sense introduced by Frege in the West. However, he made it clear that *śābdabodha* is not a variant of Frege's doctrine of sense. It offers an alternative model — a different framework of understanding in terms of which the primacy of sense can be established. In this respect, the issue that matters here is the epistemic priority of sense. Accordingly, the main focus of the paper is to show how the concept of sense is posited in Nyāya, as a part of its epistemological concern. In Nyāya, the significance of sense derives its entire justification from its epistemic counterpart. It is due to the epistemological rendering of sense; it can avoid many of the difficulties of the Fregean model of sense. Based on this consideration, Dasgupta concludes that the model of *śābdabodha* in Nyāya can successfully account for the primacy of sense which Fregean model lacks.

According to the philosophy of Nyāya, the relation between a word and meaning may be either *saṅketa* (primary) or *lakṣaṇā* (secondary). *Saṅketa* is the direct relation between word and meaning, such that the cognition of the word immediately leads to the knowledge of its relation to that meaning. *Saṅketa* may be eternal or non-eternal. When it is eternal, it is called *śakti* or inherent potency of the word. For instance, the relation between the word 'jar' and the object 'jar' is a direct and eternal relation called *śakti*. On the other hand, when *saṅketa* is non-eternal, it is called *paribhāṣā*, whose

9. Mark Siderits, 'The Sense-Reference Distinction in Indian Philosophy of Language', *Synthese, 1986.*

meaning is established by convention. Brinda Sen in her paper **'A Nyāya Interpretation of Proper Names'** clarifies that *pāribhāṣika* words of the Naiyāyikas are the so-called proper names. She is of the opinion that proper names refer to objects by virtue of the properties that inhere in those objects. The properties of the object constitute the ground for the application of the word. This is known in Nyāya as *pravṛtti-nimitta.* In this context, she has discussed in some considerable detail the role of *pravṛtti-nimitta*. Finally, she comes to the notion of sense and concludes that proper names are loaded with sense. Her argument is that a proper name is always connected with certain definite characteristics of the object to which it refer. Thus, when a proper name is uttered, it generates in the mind of the hearer the associated characters of that object. This, according to Brinda Sen, constitutes the sense of a proper name.

When the primary meaning of word does not consist with the other words of the sentence or the context, we generally take recourse to *lakṣyārtha* (secondary meaning).[10] Raghunath Ghosh in his paper **'In Search of the Seed of Lakṣaṇā'** undertakes a full-length study in locating the root of *lakṣaṇā* in the context of Nyāya theory of meaning. His line of argument may be summarised in terms of the three following propositions. First, he considers whether the non-realisability of the relation among the words can be regarded as the seed of *lakṣaṇā (anvayānupapatti*). Second, whether the non-realisability of the semantic competency can be regarded as the seed of *lakṣaṇā* (*yogyatānupapatti*). Third, whether non-realisability of intention can be regarded as the seed of *lakṣaṇā* (*tātparyānupapatti*). Based on his enquiry into these three issues, he concludes that the non-realisability of intention in the given sentence is the seed of *lakṣaṇā* through which the intention of the speaker is realised because it accommodates the other two issues namely, non-realisability of relation and non-realisability of semantic competency.

It is commonly held that *abhihitānvayavāda* is the view of the

---

10. *lakṣaṇā śakyasambhandastātparyānupapattiḥ*, Viśwanātha Nyāya-pañcānana, *Bhāṣāpariccheda* with *Siddāntamuktāvalī*, tr. Swami Madhavananda, Advaita Ashrama, Calcutta, 1977, p. 158.

Naiyāyikas with regard to the cognition of the meaning of a sentence. According to *abhihitānvayavāda*, the meaning of a sentence is due to its syntactically interrelated meanings of the words. Prabal Kumar Sen in his paper **'Abhihitānvaya, Anvitābhidhāna and Ananvitābhidhāna: Some Basic Problems'** elucidates in detail the views of the Grammarians, the Mīmāṁsakas and the Naiyāyikas on sentence and sentence-meaning. In this connection, he argues against the popular view of associating *abhihitānvayavāda* with the Naiyāyikas. According to Sen, *ananvitābhidhānavāda* is regarded as the view of the Naiyāyikas. To defend his position, he draws support from *Nyāyamañjarī* of Jayantabhaṭṭa, *Nyāyabhūṣana* of Bhāsarvajña, *Nyāyakusumāñjali* of Udayana and *Tattvacintāmaṇi* of Gaṅgeśa Upādhyāya.

IV

It is well known that the central concern of the philosophy of Pūrva-Mīmāṁsā is to explain and interpret the Vedic practices. In this sense, Pūrva-Mīmāṁsā is essentially a book of rituals dealing with commandments prescribing injunctions or prohibitions. Due to this fundamental concern, the notion of action becomes the focal point of their enquiry. Accordingly, language in Pūrva-Mīmāṁsā is viewed in relation to action. Even a simple statement of fact, for Pūrva-Mīmāṁsakas, may be construed as statement of action. For instance,

> in the case of identity statements like 'This (is) a pot' (*ayam ghaṭa*) the copula (is) (*bhavati* or *asti*) which denotes the most comprehensive genus of activity (*bhavasti para jātiḥ*) being (*sattā*) or existence is understood.[11]

The meaning of a sentence, for Pūrva-Mīmāṁsakas, thus arises through the verb (*kriyā*). The verb, which expresses the action, connects all the meanings of the words occurring in that sentence together.[12] In view of this, we find that in Pūrva-Mīmāṁsā the role of

---

11. Veluri Subbarao, *The Philosophy of a sentence and its parts*, Munshiram Manoharlal, New Delhi, 1969, p. 31.

12. Kumārilabhaṭṭa, *Ślokavārttika*, tr. into English by Ganganath Jha, Sri Satguru Publications, 1983, *Vākyādhikaraṇam*, 267, p. 534.

verb is crucial in understanding the meaning of an expression. It may be said that the position of Pūrva-Mīmāṁsā subscribes to what may be called verb semantics. As against the language-action nexus of the Pūrva-Mīmāṁsakas, S. Panneerselvam in his paper **'Can Action Be the Import of all Sentences? — A Dialogue with the Prābhākaras'** subscribes to the position that not all sentences are action oriented. Taking clue from Advaita Vedānta, Pannerselvam argues that the Prābhākara School of Pūrva-Mīmāṁsā fails to distinguish between statement of facts and injunctions and as result; they consider language is always action oriented. As against this view, Panneerselvam illustrates that there are statements such as 'This is a cow', which fails to generate any action in the hearer. The reason is that it is a simple statement of fact conveying certain information. Hence, this cannot be confused with injunction. Note that this is not acceptable to Pūrva-Mīmāṁsakas as mentioned earlier. Panneerselvam maintains that the well-known Upaniṣadic statement *tat-tvam-asi* is also a statement of fact and not an injunction for Advaita Vedānta. Mīmāṁsakas do not accept this Advaitic position, because for them the said statement is subsidiary to injunction. The response of the Advaita Vedānta is that *tat-tvam-asi* is an independent statement which in no way can be associated with injunction. The reason is that the purport of this Upaniṣadic statement is directed to the realisation or *mokṣa*. *Mokṣa* is not a state of action. Moreover, it renounces all actions. This provides the basis for Panneerselvam's claim that all sentences may not be related to action. In fact, in language there is a place for non-action oriented expressions.

Mohini Mullick in her paper **'Word and Act: Pūrva-Mīmāṁsā's Prescriptions for Heaven'** tries to bring out language-action nexus in Pūrva-Mīmāṁsā. According to Mullick, indicative sentences can have persuasive force. In view of this persuasive character of language, the distinction between indicative sentences and injunctions may not be tenable. According to the Mīmāṁsā, the purposefulness of the sentence converges on the action word, the verb (*kriyā*). The verb is the word, which expresses *bhāvanā*, the efficient means of actualising. For instance, in the sentence, *svargakāmo yajeta*, *yajeta* is the word that implies the action of 'performing sacrifice' to achieve the desired goal (*svarga*).[13] This is *bhāvanā* consisting of two stages; *arthi-bhāvanā* and *śābdi-bhāvanā*. The former is to make possible the realisation of the desired object and the latter is to instigate one two perform an action. This establishes the position that language is action oriented. According to Mullick, action is defined in terms of purpose. So long as a single purpose is served by an expression, that expression is considered as grammatically well-formed expression. Thus, a well-formed sentence becomes co-extensive with single purpose that it serves. Based on her general argument regarding the inseparable nexus between language and action, Mullick makes an important distinction between *mokṣa* and *svarga*. This distinction, as she argues, can be maintained at a mundane level where more than *mokṣa* we look for *svarga*, 'extreme happiness, complete fulfilment, in a word bliss'. If language is action oriented, then what role does language play in our search for bliss? Mullick's reply is that it 'successfully instigates the "right" kind of *arthi-bhāvanā* in us — quite literally *arthi*'.

The issues on language in classical Indian tradition have not been sharply kept apart from metaphysical, ethical and religious considerations. The controversy over the relative primacy of word-meaning and sentence-meaning among different schools of Indian philosophy in connection with *śābdabodha* may be seen to be sequel to their metaphysical outlook. However, if we look at language against the background of common sense, i.e., against the background of empiricistic or pluralistic beliefs, probably we may appreciate the spirit of the theory of *anvitābhidhānavāda*, proposed by Prābhākara School of Pūrva-Mīmāṁsā as a reasonable explanation of sentential meaning. In my paper, **'In Search of a Sound Theory in Indian Semantics'**, I have argued a case for *anvitābhidhānavāda*. While doing this, I have critically examined *akhaṇḍa-vākyārthavāda* and *abhihitānvayavāda*. *Akhaṇḍa-vākyārthavāda*, adopted by the Grammarians, maintain the sentence as the basic indivisible semantic unit and consider words and word-meanings as unreal

13. *Ślokavārtika, Vākyādhikaraṇam*, 248-55, pp. 531-32.

abstractions of the sentence and sentence-meaning respectively, is empirically weak, for we do find sentence as a whole consisting of words as parts. *Abhihitānvayavāda*, adopted by the Bhāṭṭa School of Pūrva-Mīmāṁsā puts premium on the constituent words and their meanings relegating to the background their mutual relationship. Consequently, the sentence-meaning does not form the primary meaning, it is the secondary one, which is arrived at by a process of relating the different word-meanings. Such view is untenable as we resort to secondary meaning only when there is incompatibility regarding the syntactical combination of the primary meanings or with the intention of the speaker and not always. While granting independent status to words, *anvitābhidhānavāda* deny an independent meaning to the word outside the sentential frame. The fact that words are never used in isolation suggests that words are meaningful only in sentence and thus the word-meaning is always a related word-meaning. The sentence is a reality over and above the constituent words. However, unlike *akhaṇḍa-vākyārthavāda*, *anvitābhidhānavāda* is less insistent on the absolute indivisibility of a sentence. What is immediately grasped to start with is the primary meaning of a sentence as a whole and the meanings of the constituent words are located is necessary, although their functional value would be insignificant. This is obvious from the way people learn language and use language. Thus, gauging from an empirical standpoint, *anvitābhidhānavāda* seems to be the most convincing theory of semantics in Indian philosophy.

The present volume seeks to explore the various debates in classical Indian philosophical tradition concerning the structure of language and meaning. In this connection, one important feature of this volume is that some of the issues and problems of Indian philosophy of language have been approached from the contemporary Western perspective with a view to explicate and evaluate them in a better way.

K.S. Prasad

1

Language and Reality
Some Reflections from Indian Philosophy of Language

V.N. Jha

RIGHT from the Ṛgvedic time we find that Indians have directed their enquiry on two basic issues: (1) How do we speak?, and (2) How do we understand a sentence? The first is an enquiry from a speaker's point of view and the second is an enquiry from a listener's or reader's point of view. The Ṛgvedic *ṛṣi*-poets discovered the answers to these two questions in their own characteristic way. Thus, when we read the following *mantra* of the *Ṛgveda*, I.164.45.

> *catvāri vākparimitā padāni*
> *tāni vidurbrāhmanā ye manīṣinaḥ* ।
> *trīṇe guhā nihitā naṅgyanti*
> *turīyam vāco manuṣyāḥ vadanti* ।।

It is obvious that this *mantra* is the result of an enquiry: how do we speak? The *ṛṣi* says that there is a process of evolution of language in four stages. The fourth stage of manifestation is what we all speak (*turīyam vāco manuṣyāḥ vadanti*); but below this final manifestation, there are three stages of manifestations of language (*vāk*) which are unmanifest (*trīṇī guhā nihitā naṅgyanti*). Hardly one can resist comparing this *mantra* with the findings of Bhartṛhari in his *Vākyapadīya*. For Bhartṛhari in tradition the unmanifest forms of language are *para, paśyantī* and *madhyamā*. Thus, the source of Bhartṛhari's philosophy of Language can be found in this very *mantra* of the *Ṛgveda* quoted above.

Now look at the findings of the Pāṇinīyaḥ śikṣā —

ātmā bhudyā sametyarthān
mano yuṅgte vivakṣyā
manaḥ kāyāgnimāhanti ।
sa prerayati mārutam
mārutastūrasi caran
mandram janayati svaram ।।
sodīrṇo mūrdhanyabhihato
vakratṛmāpdya mārutaḥ
varṇān janyate teṣām ।
vibhāgaḥ pañcadhā smṛtaḥ
svarataḥ kalataḥ sthānāt
prayatnānupradhānataḥ ।।

Here is a clear psychological analysis of the process, which a speaker adopts. A speaker acquires knowledge (*jñāna*) through some process of knowing and desires (*icchā*) to express that knowledge through language; he prepares (*kṛti*) his mind to take up the act of uttering and the process of communication begins. The instrument (*karaṇa*) of speech production namely, the tongue gets activated. The lungs pump the pulmonic air; it goes into the oral cavity and at various places of articulation of linguistic sounds and it is stopped by the *karaṇa* to give effect to various linguistic sounds involving places of articulation and manner of articulation.

Coming down to Vātsyāyana's *Bhāṣya* on *Nyāyasūtra*, I.1.4, we find that the tradition is aware of the fact that language encodes a cognition. Vātsyāyana, while commenting on the word *avyapadaśya* of the *sūtra* I.1.4, writes

yadidamanupayukte śabdārthasambandhe'rthajñānam na tannāmadheyaśabdena vyapdiṣyate. gṛhītepe ca śabdārthasambandhe'asya arthasya ayam śabdo nāmadheyamiti. yadā tu so artaḥ gṛhate tadā tat pūrvasmāt arthajñānat na viśiṣyate tadartha vijñānam tādṛgeva bhavati. tasya tu arthajñānasya anyaḥ samākhyāśabdo nāstīti

> *yena pratīyamānam vyavahārāya kalpet. na ca apratīyamānena vyavahāraḥ. tasmād jñeyasya arthasya saṁjñāśabdena itikaraṇayuktena nirdheṣyate rūpamiti jñānam rasa iti jñānamiti. tadevam arthajñānakāle sa na samākhyāśabdo vyāpriyate vyavahārakāle tu vyāpriyate. tasmād aśabdam arthajñānam indriyārthasannikarṣotpannamiti.*

This is a clear position taken by Vātsyāyana in the sense that he thinks that language plays a role after cognition is generated. In other words he thinks that language encodes knowledge.

As against this view, Bhartṛhari takes a stand that no knowledge is possible without language, when he says —

> *na so'sti pratyayo loke yaśśabdānugamād ṛte*
> *anuviddhamiva jñānam sarvam śabdena bhāsate*
> — *Vākyapadīya*, I.123

For Bhartṛhari, therefore, there is only one variety of knowledge and that is verbalisable (*savikalpaka-jñāna*).

We are not going to examine who is wrong or who is right here. What I wanted to point out is this, that right from the Ṛgvedic time there is a serious enquiry as to the process of verbalising one's cognition or knowledge.

Similarly, there is a serious enquiry as to how one understands the meaning of a sentence. The *Ṛgveda*, X.71.4 says —

> *uta tvaḥ paśyan na dadarśa vācam*
> *uta tvaḥ śruṇvan na śṛṇotyenām* ।
> *uto tvasmai tanvam viśastre*
> *jayeva patya uṣati suvāsaḥ* ।।

I take this *mantra* to be the finding of the *ṛṣi*-poets with regard to the second question, namely, how do we understand a sentence? *Ṛṣi* says language (*vāk*) presents herself to the listener or reader. In other words, language unfolds and the listener or reader decodes it. This *mantra* may be treated as the source of the attempts to build theories on the *śābdabodha-prakriyā*. The very imagery of unfolding of language must have provided clues to build different theories. All the *śābdabodha-granthas* are to be treated from this point of view of listener or hearer or reader. These texts provide us a clear description of the epistemology of a verbal understanding.

Before we take up the issue of Language and Reality, it will be in order to present a general universal picture of the process through which one understands the meanings of a sentence. Suppose, there is a sentence (*vākya*) *a+b+c+d* consisting of four morphemes (*padas*), *a*, *b*, *c*, and *d*. The process of understanding begins as follows:

Step I: Hearing or reading the sentence *a+b+c+d*.

Step II: Remembering the word-meanings *a'* from *a*, *b'* from *b*, *c'* from *c* and *d'* from *d*.

But, how can one remember *a'* from *a*, *b'* from *b* and so on unless he knows the relationship between *a* and *a'*, *b* and *b'*, *c* and *c'*, *d* and *d'*? This relationship is called *vṛtti*, which is of two types *śakti* (primary) and *lakṣaṇā* (extended). If one has the knowledge of this *vṛtti* he can remember the respective meanings from the respective *padas*. Therefore, the knowledge of *vṛtti* is said to be the auxiliary factor for arriving at Step II above from Step I.

Thus, the Step II may be re-written as

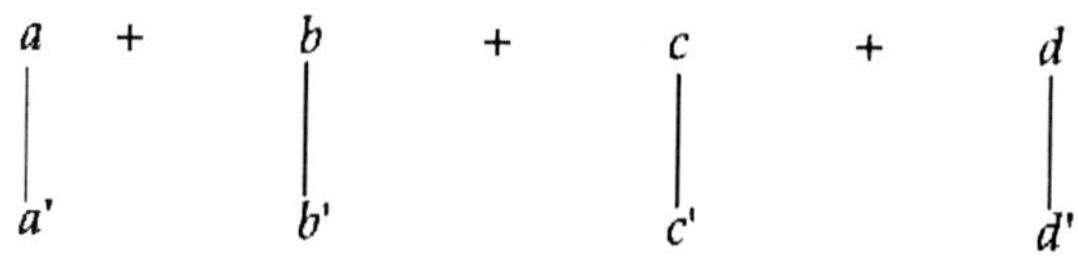

Now, another issue emerges. May be, in a sentence there is a polysemous word, which has more than one meaning. The listener of the *pada*, therefore, may remember more than one meaning. But it is also a fact that, the speaker does not intend all the meanings of the *pada* at a time. Language behaviour is an intentional act and so in order to convey a particular meaning, the speaker has uttered that *pada*, not all. Therefore, in order to understand the sentence-meaning it becomes necessary to know the intention of the speaker. Mostly, it is the context that provides us the ground to know the speaker's intention. Thus, in this process of understanding the sentence-meaning, it is necessary to accept the knowledge of the intention of the speaker as an essential factor.

Let us rewrite step II twice to illustrate the point made above

Step II

Where there is a possibility that the *pada a* has more than one meaning.

This situation will force the hearer or reader of the sentence to know the intention of the speaker. And once he knows that the speaker has uttered *a* to convey *a'* the other meanings will be easily eliminated. Then, finally the step II will appear as follows:

Step II

In the next step III, the relationship among word-meanings (*a'*, *b'*, *c'*, and *d'*) will be established. In that case the picture will emerge as follows:

Step III *a* + *b* + *c* + *d*

a' _ _ _ _ _ _ _ _ _ *b'* _ _ _ _ _ _ _ _ _ _ _ *c'* _ _ _ _ _ _ _ _ _ _ _ *d'*

Here, *a'* _ _ _ *b'* _ _ _ *c'* _ _ _ *d'* is the content (*viṣaya*) of the verbal understanding.

Thus, *a'* _ _ _ *b'* _ _ _ *c'* _ _ _ *d'* is the verbal understand or *śābdabodha* arising from the sentence *a* + *b* + *c* + *d*.

Note, that *a*, *b*, *c* and *d* are called *pada*, *a* + *b* + *c* + *d* is called a *vākya*, the vertical lines are called the *vṛtti*; *a'*, *b'* , *c'*, and *d'* are called *padārtha*, and the horizontal lines between two word-meanings are called *vākyārtha*.

The *vākyārtha* is of the nature of a relation (*anvaya, saṁsarga*) and therefore, *śābdhabodha* is also called *anvayabodha* or *saṁsargabodha*.

Now, it is true that each *padārtha* appearing in the *śābdabodha* can be understood to have appeared from the respective linguistic unit in the sentence. But, wherefrom, does the *anvaya* or *saṁsarga* appear in the *śābdabodha*? There have been diverse answers to this question resulting into various theories of verbal understanding.

The Bhāṭṭa School of Pūrva-Mīmāṁsā came out with the theory of *abhihitānvayavāda* according to which the *padārthas* are conveyed by the respective linguistic units of the sentence and the sentence-meaning, i.e., the *anvaya* or *saṁsarga* is obtained by *lakṣaṇā*. Therefore, according to this view, a *vākyārtha* is a *lakṣyārtha*.

Prābhākara School of Pūrva-Mīmāṁsā cannot support the above views because their prime concern was to develop a theory in the context of the Vedas. They pleaded that even *anvaya* or *saṁsarga* appearing in the *śābdabodha* of a Vedic sentence must be derived from the element of Vedic sentence itself. Thus, they proposed a theory called *anvitābhidhānavāda*. Thus, according to this theory *anvaya* or *saṁsarga* is an expressed sense *vācyārtha* or *śākyārtha*.

Jayantabhaṭṭa of Kashmir identified the source of such *anvaya* or *saṁsarga* in the intention of the speaker. This theory is called *tātparyavāda*. The relationship between two meanings must be understood, as it is intended by the speaker.

In the medieval period after the advent of Navya-Nyāya a fresh thought was given to this problem and it was Gadādhara Bhaṭṭācārya of Navadvīpa who added another theory of verbal understanding in his *Vyutpattivāda* by saying that *śābdabodhe ca ekapadārtha apar padārthasya saṁsargaḥ saṁsargamaryādā bhāsate*. According to this theory which is known as *saṁsargamaryādāvāda* the *anvaya* or *saṁsarga* is brought into reality by juxtaposition of two meanings. In this way several theories emerged to account for the *anvaya* or *saṁsarga*, i.e., the *vākyārtha* appearing in the verbal understanding. This model of epistemological analysis is more or less acceptable to almost all the Indian philosophical systems with some alternations here and there.

The next question that arises in our mind is about language and Reality. On this issue too we have divergent views ranging from saying that what language says is True, up to saying that the Reality is beyond the reach of language, through saying that language speaks of Reality as well as non-Reality. According to the Indian logic (*Nyāya śāstra*), the world is said to be the referent of Language, i.e., *padārtha*. According to this system language maps the Reality. That which is knowable and nameable is alone a Reality. According to the Buddhists, a verbalisable cognition (*savikalpaka-jñāna*) is false. Only a *nirvikalpaka-jñāna* (non-verbalisable cognition) is true. It amounts to saying that language cannot touch Reality. The same is the case with the Advaitins according to whom there is one and only one ultimately real and that is the *Brahman* and that *Brahman* is beyond the range of language (*a-vāṅ-manasoḥ gocaram* beyond language and mind).

The Indian logicians, however, hold that as language encodes a true cognition, so also it encodes a false cognition. But at no cost they are ready to accept a category of meaning over and above a reference.

In other words, the Indian logicians are not ready to accept sense as a conceptual entity. There is a reason behind this. If a sense is accepted as a conceptual entity, it will imply that there can be a conceptual World, which will open the door for Idealism and in that case the Realists will loose their distinct identity. An entity cannot be both inside and outside simultaneously and if it is inside, its outside appearance is to be declared a mental projection and hence unreal. The logicians opted for the referent of any word to be an external referent so that their realism is not disturbed.

Bhartṛhari, however, accepted that there can be a category of meaning called conceptual meaning (*artha-sphoṭa*). Not only that he further accepted that the meaning-carrying form of language is also conceptual and the relationship between a form and meaning is that of an identity. If expanded, this becomes a rectangular theory of meaning and not the triangular theory of meaning of Ogden and Richard (*Meaning of Meaning*). Bhartṛhari did this because he was elaborating his theory of *Śabdādvaita*. This theory also is based on Indian Idealism.

In this way, one can find that almost each philosophical system has something to say on language as per the basic frame-work of the respective philosophical system adding thereby to the richness of the Indian Philosophy of Language.

Bibliography

Jha, V.N., *Logic of Intermediate Causal Link*, Indian Books Centre, New Delhi.

———, *Philosophy of Injunction*, Pratibha Prakashan, New Delhi.

———, *Visayatavada* (Eng. tr. and Notes), University of Pune.

———, *Language, Logic and Epistemology*, Pratibha Prakashan, New Delhi

———, *Indian Philosophy of Relations*, Indian Books Centre, New Delhi.

———, *Śabdakhaṇḍa of Nyāyasiddhānta muktāvalī* (Exposition in English) Sanibhasa, Nagoya University, Japan.

———, 'Indian Philosophy of Language', *International Journal of Communication*, New Delhi.

2

Word — A Separate Means of Valid Knowledge

John Vattanky

It is well known that Nyāya admits four means of valid knowledge, Perception, Inference, Comparison and Word. While the status of Word as a separate means of valid knowledge has been accepted by Mīmāṁsā, Vedānta and the Sāṅkhya, the Vaiśeṣikas and Buddhists deny it. According to the latter Perception and Inference are the only two means of valid knowledge. They hold that Word and Comparison are not to be considered as separate means of valid knowledge; the Vaiśeṣikas argue that they be included in Inference. This is because the purpose of Word (viz., Knowledge of the intended mutual relation of meanings recollected by words) and the purpose of Comparison (viz., Knowledge of denotative function of words like *gavaya* and so on) are accomplished by Inference. *Kārikāvalī* rejects this opinion and establishes that both Word and Comparison are to be accepted as separate means of valid knowledge. This is because knowledge of invariable concomitance is essential to inferential knowledge. But even without the knowledge of invariable concomitance after hearing words, there arises verbal knowledge. Similarly after the perceptual knowledge of the similarity of cow in *gavaya*, even without the knowledge of invariable concomitance, there arises the knowledge of the denotative function of the word *gavaya*. Our purpose in this essay is to examine in detail this basic argument of the Naiyāyikas in support of their claim that Word is a separate means of valid knowledge in the context of the counter-arguments of their opponents, especially the Vaiśeṣikas.[1] In this attempt we will chiefly base ourselves on *Kārikāvalī, Muktāvalī, Dinakarī, Rāmarudrī*[2] and other works of the Nyāya School will also be referred to according to the need.

Let us examine the argument of the Vaiśeṣikas denying Word as a separate means of valid knowledge. The Vaiśeṣikas do not accept Word as a separate source of valid knowledge because the knowledge of relation of meanings of words that arises from words is valid but it can be reduced to inferential knowledge since the methods of Inference are also operative here. Just as a person who has the perception of the reason and has the knowledge of invariable concomitance infers through the recollection of the invariable concomitance the thing which is not directly experienced, so also a person has valid knowledge of the relation of meanings through the reason of being a group of words having syntactic expectancy, etc. In this way, the Vaiśeṣikas point out that after hearing the words there arises the apprehension of their meanings; after this one takes the words themselves or their meanings as the subject of the Inference and the relation of their meanings can be inferred by the listener. Hence, knowledge of the relation of meanings of words is not an instance of verbal knowledge but as instance of inferential knowledge.

---

1. *Kārikāvalī, Muktāvalī, Dinakarī* and *Rāmarudrī* do not consider the Buddhist arguments. *Tattvacintāmaṇi* briefly refutes the Buddhist position: The assertion of the Buddhists that 'Word is not a means of valid knowledge' is itself a sentence either producing or not producing valid knowledge. If it produces valid knowledge, then Word is a means of valid knowledge. If it does not produce valid knowledge, then the assertion of the Buddhists is not valid. (*nanu śabdo na pramāṇam. tathāhi, karaṇaviśeṣaḥ pramāṇam, karaṇam ca tat yasmin sati kriyā bhavatyeva, na ca śabde sati pramā bhavatyeveti nāyam śabdaḥ pramāṇam, na ca śabdo na pramāṇam iti vākyasya prāmāṇyayor vyāghātaḥ, asyāprāmāṇye pi etadutthāpyamānāvisaṁvādād iti cet, na. ākāṅkṣādimataḥ padārthasmaraṇādivyāpāravataḥ pramāṇatvena tathābhūtāt pramotpatter āvaśyakatvāt, atathābhūtatve ca phalājanakatvasya karaṇāntarasāṁyāt — Tattvacintāmaṇi*, p.14,1.1 — p.22, 1.1).
2. The relevant passages in *Kārikāvalī, Muktāvalī, Dinakarī* and their translations are given in my work *Nyāya Philosophy of Language*, pp.513-30.

Muktāvalī presents the arguments of the Vaiśeṣikas in order to establish that Word is included in Inference: They argue that Word is a means of valid knowledge in the capacity of being Inference (*anumānavidhayaiva śabdasya prāmāṇyam*). The argument itself is in the form of an Inference as follows: Secular words such as 'bring the cow with a stick' or[3] Vedic words like 'one who is desirous of heaven should perform sacrifice' are preceded by the valid knowledge of the relation of recollected meanings which (i.e., relation) is the object of the intention of the speaker, because they are group of words having syntactic expectancy, etc., like the group of words 'Bring the jar' (*daṇḍena gāmānayetyādilaukikapadāni yajetetyādivaidikapadāni vā tātparyaviṣayamārita padārtha-saṁsargapramāpūrvakāṇī ākāṅkṣādimat-padakadambakatvāt ghaṭamānayeti padakadambakavāt*).

Dinakarī explains this Inference in detail. First of all, it should be

3. *Dinakarī* points out that according to the Prābhākaras secular words convey only meaning of words which are already known. That is why *Muktāvalī* gives an example from the Vedas. The reason why the Prābhākaras assert that *laukika-padāni* are only *anuvādakāni* is the following:

'It is only the Veda that can be called *śabda-pramāṇa* and that also only when containing an injunction; ordinary words cannot be so; because the cognitions afforded by them are purely inferential; when we hear a man saying something, our mind goes through the following reasoning "This man speaks of such a thing — this he must be speaking of after having known what he speaks of — so what he says must be true;" the speech of the man is an effect of his knowledge; and hence from the effect we infer the cause. Thus, all ordinary verbal cognition is inferential; that afforded by the Veda alone is purely verbal. It is true that all words are endowed with an inherent denotative potency; but in the case of ordinary speakers of the world, this potency of the word is obscured by suspicions with regard to the trustworthy character of the persons; in the case of the Veda, there being no speaker, and hence no grounds of suspicion, the potency remains unobscured'. — Ganganath Jha, *The Prābhākara School of Pūrva-Mīmāṁsā*, pp. 65-66; See also Sālikanātha, *Prakaraṇapañcikā*, pp. 29-42. According to Prābhākaras *anādhigatabādhitaviṣayajñānaṁ pramāṇam*. They contend that in the knowledge arising from the ordinary sentences (*loka-vākya*) there is no *anādhigatatvam*, since these words used in ordinary sentences are already found in the Vedas. (cf. *Nyāyakusumāñjali, Kārikās* 3.14, 4.1).

noted that the subject of the Inference is words or sentence. Such a sentence is not to be taken as sentence in general, but as particular sentences such as 'bring the jar', 'one who is desirous of heaven should perform sacrifice', etc.; therefore, the knowledge of a particular semantic relation is intended. Next *Dinakarī* explains the purpose of the qualifications in the enunciation of the *sādhya*. The *sādhya* in the Inference is 'being preceded by valid knowledge of the relation of recollected meanings which (i.e., relation) is the object of the intention of the speaker' (*tātparyaviṣaya-smaritapadārthasaṁsarga-pramāpūrvakatvam*). Here the qualification 'the object of the intention of the speaker' (*tātparya-viṣaya*) is given to 'relation' (*saṁsarga*). Otherwise, there would be the following difficulty: Someone utters the sentence *brāhmaṇevidyā;* this sentence can be understood in two ways: 'The brāhmaṇa has knowledge' (literally, there is knowledge in brāhmaṇa, i.e., *adhikaraṇasaptami*) or 'someone else has knowledge of which the brāhmaṇa is the object' (*viṣaya-saptami*). The speaker, however, intends the first meaning. In order that the hearer also may infer the semantic relation of 'being the substratum' (*adhikaraṇatva*) and not of 'being the object' (*viṣayatva*), the qualification of 'object of the intention of the speaker' (*tātparya-viṣaya*) is given to 'relation' (*saṁsarga*).

If the qualification of 'recollected' (*smārita*) is not given to 'meanings' (*padārtha*) in the enunciation of the *sādhya*, then from the expression *ghaṭam* the inferential knowledge of the relation of meaning as meaning only would arise and not the relation of meaning as recollected from the expression 'jar' and so on. Further, the meaning should be recollected by means of the significatory function (*vṛtti*) of the word. Otherwise, by the word 'jar', one can recollect also ether by means of the relation of inherence and infer the relation of ether. Hence, there would not be the inferential knowledge of the relation of jar with the state of being the object of action.

Further, in the enunciation of the reason the qualification of syntactic expectancy is to be added. Otherwise, there would be deviation in such ambiguous sentence as *ayam eti putro rājñaḥ puruṣo pasāryatām*. Here in the part of the sentence *rājñaḥ puruṣaḥ*, the speaker does not intend the relation of the meanings of words *rājan* and *puruṣa*. Therefore, there is no *sādhya* because the speaker has no intention to convey the knowledge of the relation of the meanings of the words *rājan* and *puruṣa*. But here there is the reason in the form of the state of 'being a group of words' (*padakadaṁbatva*). Hence there is deviation. In order to avoid this fault, the qualification of 'syntactic expectancy' (*ākāṅkṣā*) is given to the reason. According to the old Naiyāyikas, syntactic expectancy is *tatpade samabhivyāhṛtatat-padaviśiṣṭatvam*, and *samabhivyāhāra* means only mentioning of a word immediately after the other word; but *samabhivyāhāra* as *ākāṅkṣā* should be according to the (*pada-tātparya*) in the form that a particular word as connected with another word should produce the knowledge of its meaning as connected with the meaning of the other word by a particular relation. Only this part of the definition of syntactic expectancy (i.e., *padatātparyakatvam*) is given as a qualification to the reason of the present Inference, since the other part (i.e., *tatpadviśiṣṭatvam*) of the definition of syntactic expectancy does not serve to prevent deviation.[4]

Further, the qualification of 'semantic competency' (*yogyatā*) is also to be given to the reason. Otherwise, in such sentences as 'he waters with fire' (*vahninā-siñcati*), there is the absence of the *sādhya* (i.e., *tātparyaviṣayasmāritapadārthasaṁsargapramāpūrvakatva*), but there is the reason (i.e., *ākāṅkṣādimatpadakadaṁbatva*). Hence there is deviation. Therefore, the qualification of *yogyatā* is given to the reason and then in the sentence *vahninā-siñcati*, there would be no reason and so there would also be no deviation.

Further, the qualification of 'contiguity' (*āsatti*) is to be given to

4. Where *ākāṅkṣā* is taken as only *samabhivyāhāra* in the expression *ayam eti putro rājñaḥ puruṣo'pasāryatam* there is *ākāṅkṣā* both between *putra* and *rājan; rājan* and *puruṣa*. However, when *ākāṅkṣā* is taken as *padatātparyakatva* then there would not be any *ākāṅkṣā* between *rājan* and *puruṣa* since the speaker does not intend the relation between these meanings. Hence, in the inference of the Vaiśeṣikas trying to establish verbal knowledge *ākāṅkṣā* is to be taken as only *padatātparyakatva* and not merely as *tatpade tatpadasamabhivyāhṛtatvam*.

the reason. Otherwise, there could be deviation in the following way: Take the sentence 'blue pot substance cloth'. Here the part of the sentence 'blue cloth' has no *sādhya* because the speaker does not intend the connection of the meanings of these words, but it has the reason 'being the group of words having syntactic expectancy etc.' (*ākāṅkṣā-yogyatā ghaṭitapadakadambatva*). Therefore, there is deviation. In order to prevent this fault, the qualification of 'contiguity' (*āsatti*) is given to the reason and since there is no contiguity between the words 'blue' and 'cloth' because they are not juxtaposed together, there is no reason in the part of the sentence 'blue cloth'.

The last expression in the enunciation of the reason is *kadamba* which means 'group' (*samudāya*). Now it may be objected that since the word 'group' does not help to prevent deviation, it is useless to include it in the enunciation of the reason. This objection is answered by pointing out that there would be deviation, if the word 'group' is not a part of the enunciation of the reason. As for example, someone utters the expression *ghaṭam* with the intention of conveying the relation of 'jar' (*ghaṭa*) and 'the state of being object of an action' (*karmatva*). Here, if the reason is only (*ākāṅkṣādimatpadatva*) in a general way, then there would be deviation. This is because in such expressions as *paṭam* and so on, there is no *sādhya* in the form of *ghaṭakarmatvayoḥ saṁsargapramāpūrvakatvam*. When the word 'group' is also used in the enunciation of the reason such a deviation is avoided. This is because in the *sādhya* the meanings of certain words are included. By the use of the word 'group' in the enunciation of the reason the syntactic expectancy of those very words is intended. Here, therefore, in the instance of *paṭam*, there is no syntactic expectancy because these words, *paṭa* and *am*, do not convey the meanings which are included in the *sādhya*, namely, 'the jar (*ghaṭa*)' and 'the state of being the object of an action' (*karmatva*).

Similarly, the use of the word 'group' also shows that the very word which indicates syntactic expectancy should indicate also semantic competency, etc. Otherwise, there would be deviation in such sentences as *ayam eti putro rājñaḥ puruṣo pasāryatām*, since there is the reason of syntactic expectancy and contiguity between the words *rājan* and *putra* and there is semantic competency between the words *rājan* and *puruṣa* (through their meanings), but there is no *sādhya* in the form of *tātparya-viṣaya-saṁsarga-pramā-pūrvakatva* in the part of the sentence *rājñaḥ puruṣaḥ*. But when it is stated that the very word which indicates syntactic expectancy should indicate also semantic competency, etc., in the sentence mentioned *ayam eti*, etc., although there is semantic competency in the word *rājan* indicated by the word *puruṣa* there is no syntactic expectancy indicted by the word *puruṣa* in *rājan*. Therefore, in the part of the sentence, *rājñaḥ puruṣaḥ* there is no reason and so there is no deviation. It should be noted here that the point of the argument is that 'syntactic expectancy', etc., which are included in the enunciation of the reason must mutually indicate. (*Subodhinī*, pp. 309-10)

However, such an Inference establishing just 'being preceded by the valid knowledge of relation (of meanings)' (*saṁsarga-pramā-pūrvakatva*) does not lead to any activity. This is because, the cause of activity is the knowledge in which the qualificand is the object of activity and the qualifier is the determinant of the state of being desired (*iṣṭatāvacchedakaprakārakapravṛttiviṣayaviśeṣyakajñānam eva pravartakam*). As for example, in 'silver is desired by me' (*rajatam madiṣṭam*), silverness (*rajatatva*) is the determinant of the state of being desired (*iṣṭatāvacchedaka*) and silver (*rajata*) is the object of activity the qualifier of which is the state of being desired (*iṣṭatāvacchedakaprakārakapravṛttiviṣaya*). Further, by means of the Inference mentioned earlier, we can establish only *saṁsarga-pramā-pūrvakatva* as *saṁsarga-pramā-pūrvakatva* since in every Inference the qualifier is the determinant of the state of being the pervader.[5]

5. In every Inference, the determinant of the state of being pervader is the qualifier of that particular instance of inferential knowledge. As for instance in the inferential knowledge *parvato vahnimān*, *vahni* is *prakāra* but *vahnitva* which is the *vyāpakatāvacchedaka* is also *prakāra* in the knowledge of *vahni*. In the present instance since *saṁsarga-pramā-pūrvakatvatva* is the *vyāpakatāvacchedaka* we can establish *saṁsarga-pramā-pūrvakatva* as determined by *saṁsargapramā-pūrvakatvatva*. In this way in the present instance of the words *idam rajataṁ* even if there is the valid knowledge that the meanings of these words are related to →

Therefore, such an Inference does not give rise to the knowledge in which the qualificand namely silver is that which is in front of the person concerned and the qualifier is the determinant of the state of being desired, namely silverness, etc. Hence, the proposed Inference does not lead to any activity. Therefore, to gain the knowledge that leads to activity one has to admit Word as a separate means of valid knowledge.

The Inference of the Vaiśeṣikas to reject the argument of the Naiyāyikas as well as the reason of the Naiyāyikas to refute the Inference of the Vaiśeṣikas may be explained in ordinary life situation as the following: Someone utters the sentence 'Bring me a cup of tea'. One who hears this sentence can easily infer that this sentence actually expresses an instance of valid knowledge of the speaker. This valid knowledge of the speaker is brought about by the remembrance of the meanings of these words as intended by him. The contention of the Vaiśeṣikas is that because the hearer can in this way infer that the speaker has such an instance of valid knowledge of the connection of the meanings of the words used by the speaker, verbal knowledge is only an instance of inferential knowledge. Obviously this is wrong because the nature of verbal knowledge is different. The form of verbal knowledge is not that the speaker has the knowledge of the proper connection of the meanings of words of the sentence he utters but in the form 'This is silver', etc. It is only such a kind of knowledge that gives rise to activity, i.e., if only a person has such a knowledge it is possible for him to act in order to get silver, etc. And mere knowledge of the connection of the words 'this' and 'silver' does not bring about activity. Therefore, Word is to be considered as a separate means of valid knowledge.

These objections of the Naiyāyikas are answered by the Vaiśeṣikas by proposing another Inference in the following manner to show that Word is a means of valid knowledge only as Inference.

→ one another no activity can arise with regard to *rajata*; i.e., even if we can establish *saṁsarga-pramā-pūrvakatvatva* in these words there would be no activity with regard to *rajata*. Therefore in order that activity may arise verbal knowledge in the form *idam rajataṁ* is necessary. This is the idea.

These meanings have mutual relation, which is the object of the intention of the speaker, because they are recollected by words having semantic competency, etc., like another meaning of a similar nature (*ete padārthā mithaḥ saṁsargavantaḥ yogyatādimatpadopasthāpitatvāt tādṛśapadārthantaravat*). Nor can it be objected against this Inference that in the example there is no sure knowledge of *sādhya* and so invariable concomitance cannot be grasped. This is because, in the example, the *sādhya* is to be established by means of another example. Therefore, this Inference is valid and the knowledge which this Inference produces leads certainly to activity. As for example, someone utters the sentence *idaṁ rajataṁ*. Here the Inference produces the knowledge in which 'this object' (*idaṁ padārtha*) is connected as the qualificand with 'silverness' (*rajatatva* which is the *iṣṭatāvacchedaka*) as the qualifier and activity necessarily follows. It may be noted here that in this Inference the subject (*pakṣa*) is meanings (*padārthaḥ*) and *sādhya* is relation (*saṁsarga*) between them whereas in the previous Inference, the subject is the words (*padāni*) and *sādhya* is the state of being preceded by the valid knowledge of the relation of meanings (*saṁsarga-pramā-pūrvakatva*). Therefore, in the previous Inference what is known by the hearer is that the speaker has the knowledge of the relation of meanings of the words. But such a knowledge does not produce any activity in the speaker. On the contrary, in the present Inference what is known by the speaker is the actual relation of the meanings of words (e.g., *idaṁ* and *rajataṁ*) and therefore the form of the knowledge is 'this is silver' and hence activity necessarily follows.

Further, the argument by which the Vaiśeṣikas try to establish that Comparison could be reduced to Inference is as follows: After the perception of an individual *gayal* (it is possible to infer) that the word *gavaya* indicates the denoted meaning the determinant of which is the universal *gavayatva* because while it does not have any other significatory function (i.e., implication) elders use the word with reference to that (*gayal*). When there is no other significatory function (i.e., implication) for a word, a word which is used by elders in a particular meaning indicates denoted meaning, the determinant of which is that (particular universal) just as the word 'cow' has the universal *gotva* as the determinant of the state of being the denoted meaning (*gavayavyaktipratyakṣānantaraṁ gavayapadaṁ gavayatvapravṛttinimittakam, asati vṛttyantare vṛddhais tatra prayujyamānatvāt, asati ca vṛttyantare vṛddahair yatra yat prayujyate tatra tatpravṛttinimittakaṁ yathā gopadaṁ gopravṛttinimittakam*).

Another Inference to show that Comparison is included in Inference is as follows: The word *gavaya* indicates some characteristic as its *pravṛtti-nimitta* (i.e., the reason for its particular application to a particular meaning) because it is a correct word. Here, by means of the force of the reason existing in the subject, it can be established that the word *gavaya* indicates the universal *gavayatva* as the determinant of its state of being denoted meaning which is the same as its *pravṛtti-nimitta* (*yadvā gavayapadaṁ sapravṛttinimittakaṁ sādhupadatvāt ityanumānena pakṣadharmatāblād gavayatvapravṛttinimittakatvam sidhyati*).

Such a view of the Vaiśeṣikas cannot be admitted, because it is our experience that there arises verbal knowledge even without the knowledge of invariable concomitance, which is essential to Inference. And in fact, after hearing words we do not have always the knowledge of invariable concomitance. Thus, after perceiving similarity of cow in *gayal*, even without the knowledge of invariable concomitance (i.e., whatever is a correct word has the determinant of its state of being denoted), there arises the knowledge of the denotative function of the word *gavaya*. Hence, both Word and Comparison have to be considered as separate means of valid knowledge.

It may now be objected that since there is the effect in the form of inferential knowledge after every instance of the hearing of the word, its cause, viz., the knowledge of invariable concomitance is to be postulated. The answer to this objection is that, by a similar argument, it could as well be shown that every instance of inferential knowledge can be reduced to verbal knowledge in the following way. An instance of inferential knowledge like mountain has fire, has as object certain meanings like fire, etc. From such meanings one can have the recollection of words like 'fire', etc., through the relation of the state of being that which denotes (*vācakatva-sambandha*). Further, one can postulate also such causes of verbal knowledge as knowledge of syntactic expectancy, etc. Now all the causes of verbal knowledge are present and so the inferential knowledge that mountain has fire can as well be considered as verbal knowledge.

Gaṅgeśa, the author of *Tattvacintāmaṇi,* refutes the opinion of the Vaiśeṣikas in another way. The Inference of the Vaiśeṣikas to establish that Word is a means of valid knowledge in the capacity of Inference is as follows: These meanings have mutual relation because they have the state of being conveyed by words having semantic competency, etc. Here, semantic competency is a qualification to the reason. But in order to have instance of inferential knowledge, there should be definite knowledge of the reason. Therefore, there should be the definite knowledge of the qualification of the reason also. Here, in the Inference of the Vaiśeṣikas semantic competency (*yogyatā*) is a qualification of the reason, viz., 'the state of being conveyed by the words having semantic competency, etc.' (*yogyatādimatpadopasthāpitatva*). Therefore, in order to have the inferential knowledge, there should be definite knowledge of semantic competency which is a qualification of the *hetu,* since a doubt of the qualification leads to the doubt of the qualified. On the contrary, even if there is doubtful knowledge of semantic competency, verbal knowledge arises. Hence, Word has to be considered as a separate means of valid knowledge.[6] By the expression 'so they say' (*iti vadanti*) Dinakara implies that he prefers his own way of refuting the arguments of the Vaiśeṣikas as given earlier.[7]

---

6. This is the summary of the argument in *Tattvacintāmaṇi,* vol. IV (p. 77, 1.3 — p. 79, 1.2): *vayaṁ tu brūmaḥ-bādhakapramāṇābhavo yogyatā, sā ca na liṅgaviśeṣaṇaṁ, bādhakapramāṇamātravirahasya sarvatra niścetum aśakyatvāt, tatsaṁśaye'pi śabdānvayabodhācca, śabdaprāmāṇye tu yogyatāyāḥ saṁśayaniścayasādhāraṇaṁ jñānamātram prayojakam iti śabdaḥ pramāṇam iti.*

7. The reason for this is given by Prīksit Tampurān (*Subodhinī,* 312. II.13ff). Even in the absence of definite knowledge of *yogyatā* Inference is possible by means of *parāmarśa* where *tātparya* of the speaker is the reason. And in this way it is possible to include Word in Inference, i.e., →

Jayadeva Miśra (Pakṣadhara Miśra) however, refutes the opinion of the Vaiśeṣikas in still another way. According to both Vaiśeṣikas and Naiyāyikas, sentences like 'bring the jar' and so on are capable of producing knowledge while expressions like 'jar the state of being object of action act of bringing effort', etc., are not capable of producing knowledge. If the opinion of the Vaiśeṣikas that words produce knowledge in the capacity of Inference is accepted, then even sentences such as 'jar the state of being object of action act of bringing effort' can produce knowledge because it is possible to have Inference in the case of these sentences also. As for instance, in the present case, we can have the Inference that the meanings conveyed by the words 'jar', 'the state of being object of action', 'act of bringing', 'effort' have mutual relation because they have the state of being conveyed by words having semantic competency, etc. Nor can it be objected that the reason does not have syntactic expectancy and so there is no inferential knowledge. This is because through the erroneous knowledge of syntactic expectancy there could be inferential knowledge. And the object of such an inferential knowledge is not contradicted in our experience; hence, such an inferential knowledge is also valid.

Therefore, in order to avoid such a possibility of knowledge from sentences like 'jar the state of being the object action act of bringing effort' we have to admit that word is a separate means of valid knowledge. And now from such sentences, no verbal knowledge arises by their very nature because of the absence of syntactic expectancy between the words 'jar', 'the state of being the object of action', etc. Hence, it is also possible to assert that sentence like 'bring the jar', etc., are capable of producing knowledge and sentences like 'jar the state of being object of action act of bringing effort', etc., are not capable of producing knowledge and such an assertion would be impossible in the opinion of the Vaiśeṣikas. By the expression 'so they say' (*ityāhuḥ*), Dinakara implies that he

→ word need not be accepted as a separate means of valid knowledge (*yogyatāyās tadghaṭitahetor vā sarvatra niścayāsaṁbhave'pi tadaniścaya-daśāyām kḷptahetutākaniścayaviṣayatātparyaliṅgakaparāmarśād eva anumitisaṁbhavena na śabdasya pramāṇāntaratvasiddhiḥ*).

prefers his own way of refuting the opinion of the Vaiśeṣikas which was mentioned earlier namely, verbal knowledge arises even without the knowledge of invariable concomitance without which inferential knowledge is impossible.[8]

There are some other Naiyāyikas who refute the opinion of the Vaiśeṣikas in another way. They point out that from the sentence 'separate from jar' it is experienced by all that there is the verbal knowledge in the form of the substratum of separateness which has jar as its limit (*ghaṭāvadhikapṛthaktvaprakārakāśrayaviśeṣya-kaśābdabodha*). In this verbal knowledge the qualificandness resides in the substratum and it is not determined by any characteristic. Separateness (*ghaṭāvadhikapṛthaktva*) is the qualifier. In the opinion of the Naiyāyikas such a verbal knowledge can easily be explained from the fact that it is produced by the knowledge of words having such a sequence (*gaṭāt pṛthak*). Vaiśeṣikas try to reduce this verbal knowledge into an instance of inferential knowledge in the following way. Separateness has jar as its limit because it is recollected by the word 'separate' which has syntactic expectancy with the word 'jar'. Such an Inference gives rise only to the knowledge that separateness has jar as its limit (*ghaṭāvadhikaṁ pṛthaktvam*) and not to the knowledge that the substratum of separateness which has jar as its limit (*ghaṭāvadhikapṛthaktvāśraya*). The reason for this is that although separateness is the object of inferential knowledge as the subject of Inference, the substratum of separateness becomes in no way the object of the same inferential knowledge.[9]

---

8. The reason for this preference of Dinakara is that the expressions 'Bring the jar', etc., are capable of producing verbal knowledge (*śābdabodhaṁ prati svarūpayogya* for verbal knowledge), whereas expressions like 'jar the state of being the object of action, act of bringing effort', etc., are not capable of producing verbal knowledge (*śābdabodhaṁ prati na svarūpayogya*) because they do not have a particular sequence of words which alone is capable of producing verbal knowledge. See *Rāmarudrī*, ed. Krishnadas Sanskrit Series, 1951, p. 500, 1.32ff; and *Subodhinī*, p. 313, II. 10-11.

9. Here Prīksit Tampurān gives further arguments also to show that words are separate means of valid knowledge. First of all the objection →

Now, the Vaiśeṣikas bring forward another inferential knowledge to show that even the substratum of separateness can become its object, viz., cloth is the substratum of separateness having

→ is raised that the sentence *ghaṭāt pṛthak* does not produce any verbal knowledge because there is no proof about such a verbal knowledge in which the qualificand is not determined by any characteristic since such an instance of knowledge is not negated by the knowledge of its contradiction. It cannot further be argued that the instance of knowledge *ghaṭāt pṛthak* is contradicted by the instance of knowledge *pṛthaktvaṁ na ghaṭāvadhikam*. This is because even then there is no possibility of its being contradicted because the qualificandness existing in the substratum of separateness is not the determinant of the state of being contradicted by the knowledge of contradiction. (*pṛthaktvāśrayaniṣṭhaviśeṣyaṁ na bādhabuddhiviśeṣyaṁ*).

This argument cannot be admitted. The reason is that there is no proof for the rule that all instances of qualificandness belonging to verbal knowledge have the state of being the determinant of the state of being contradicted by the knowledge of contradiction. In other words all instances of the *viśeṣyatā* of *śābdabodha* need not be the determinant of the state of being prevented by the knowledge of contradiction. Otherwise it is not possible to have verbal knowledge from such sentences as *caitro gacchati* where *caitratvaniṣṭhaprakāratānirupita-viśeṣyatā* is *niravacchinnā*.

Here it may be objected that in the case of the sentence *cairo gacchati*, *caitratvaniṣṭhaprakāratānirūpitaviśeṣyatā* is identical with *kṛtitva-niṣṭhaprakāratānirūpita-caitratvavacchinnaviśeṣyatā*. Hence, *nirāvacchinna-viśeṣyatā* in *caitro gacchati* can also be the determinant of the state of being contradicted by the knowledge of contradiction. Hence, there is no exception to the rule mentioned above and so from the sentence *ghaṭāt pṛthak* there arises verbal knowledge.

Prīksit Tampurān refutes this stating that when the causal complex like the knowledge arising from the words and the like is present, verbal knowledge from the sentence *gaṭāt pṛthak* necessarily arises.

Further, the argument to show that Word is a separate means of valid knowledge is the following. After the verbal knowledge in the form 'I hear' we have the reflective knowledge in the form 'I have heard this' and not in the form 'I have inferred this'. This shows that verbal knowledge is different from inferential knowledge. Therefore, the means, which bring about these instances of knowledge, are also different.

By this argument the following objection of some others also is rejected. According to them just as the word *pidhehi* is to be supplied to the →

jar as its limit. In this case, it is true that the substratum of separateness becomes the object of inferential knowledge. Still the form of this inferential knowledge is not the same as the form of the verbal knowledge in question. This is because in the verbal knowledge, the qualificandness residing in the substratum is not determined by any characteristic, but in the proposed inferential knowledge, the qualificandness residing in the substratum is determined by clothness, which is the determinant of subjectness. Therefore, the conclusion is that verbal knowledge can in no way be reduced to inferential knowledge and that Verbal testimony is to be considered as a separate means of valid knowledge.

→ expression *dvāram* in order that there may arise verbal knowledge, so also in the expression *ghaṭāt pṛthak, paṭa* is to be supplied. Therefore, from this sentence there can be inferential knowledge since the *viśeṣyatā* is *sāvacchinnā*.

Besides nowhere *ekadeśānvaya* is accepted. And so in the expression *ghaṭāt pṛthak* the meaning of the fifth case cannot be semantically connected with separateness. The reason is here *pṛthak* means *pṛthaktvāśraya* and therefore the meaning of the ablative case cannot be semantically connected with separateness, which is a part of the meaning of the word *pṛthak* here. Therefore, the meaning of the ablative case should be semantically connected with the substratum of separateness. Thus in this instance of verbal knowledge there is a *dharmī* and so it can be reduced to inferential knowledge.

By the expression *dik* in *Dinakarī*, other arguments to establish that words are separate means of valid knowledge are indicated. Prīksit Tampurān gives one such argument. The verbal knowledge, which arises from the sentence *vahnivyāpyabhāvavān vahnimān*, can never be reduced to inferential knowledge. This is because the *parāmarśa* necessary for this Inference would be *vahnivyāpyābhāvavān vahnivyāpyavān*, which is a contradiction, and therefore Word has to be accepted as a separate means of valid knowledge.

Bibliography

Gaṅgeśa Upādhyāya, *Tattvacintāmaṇi*, vol. IV, parts 1 and 2, *Śabdakhaṇḍa* with the commentaries of Mathuranatha Tarkavagisha and Jayadeva Mishra and Raghunatha Shiromani's *Nañjvāda* and *Ākhyātavāda*, ed. by Prīksit Tampurān, Kamakhyanath Tarkavagish, Vrajajivan Prachyabharati Granthamala, 47, Delhi, 1990.

Ganganatha Jha, The *Prābhākara School of Pūrva Mīmāṁsā*, Motilal Banarsidass, Allahabad, 1911.

Rama Varma Pareekshith Thampuram, *Subodhinī* — a commentary on *Bhāṣāpariccheda, Muktāvalī, Dinkareeya and Rāmarudreeya*, Sree Rama Varma Government Sanskrit College, Tripunithura, Kerala, 1987.

Sālikanātha Miśra, *Prakaraṇapañcikā* with the commentary *Nyāyasiddhi*, ed. by A. Subrahmanya Sastri, Benaras Hindu University Darsana Series, 4, Benaras, 1961.

Udayana, *Nyāyakusumāñjalī* with the commentary *Nyāyavāsanā*, Srimadannayaryamahadesika Vidvatsabha, Tamil Nadu, 1979.

Vattanky John, *Nyāya Philosophy of Language*, Sri Satguru Publications, Delhi, 1995.

Viswanatha Nyayapanchanana Bhattacharya, *Kārikāvalī with Muktāvalī, Dinakarī and Rāmarudrī*, ed. with foot-notes, etc., by Atmaram Narayan Jere, Krishnadas Sanskrit Series 22, Varanasi, 1988.

3

Religious Language

A. Ramamurthy

SHORN of all jargon the problem of religious language is whether the religious statements have any objective meaning or is there any cognitive value to religious beliefs expressed through religious statements. Ever since philosophy turned its attention to analysis of language with a view to understanding its meaning most of the philosophers of religion and some of the theologians have shown concern for understanding the problems related to the meaning of religious language. While most of the philosophers of religion tend to see only subjective or emotional meaning to religious language, majority of theologians assert that religious language has an objective meaning though the method of knowing the objective meaning of religious statements is not open to all. Their main argument is that since the religious language is not about empirically verifiable reality the empirical methods of knowing the objective meaning of religious statements will be of no avail. Only a few of the gifted or spiritually awakened persons can know and appreciate the objective validity of religious claims, and for them the religious claims are as objectively true and meaningful as any empirical claim. The cognitive value or objectivity of meaning of religious language is a problem only for us or for those who are not equipped internally to know the cognitive value of religious statements. However, if those who have known directly the reality that is represented or described by religious language are basically human then there is no reason why other human beings, like us, cannot know the reality that is represented by religious language. On the other hand, if those who are supposed to know the real or objective meaning of religious statements are not human in the ordinary sense but are divine then the problem of intelligibility of what they have known and spoken arises. If they are divine or are specially or divinely gifted or inspired, which others are not, implying thereby that the former are extraordinarily equipped to know the reality represented by religious language then that language may have no meaning to us as it will not be intelligible to us. On the other hand, if it is admitted that the difference between them and us is not radical or is not one of kind but of degree then only we can at least claim to have the capacity to understand what they speak. And if this is denied we cannot say that what they speak is intelligible to us, or we understand their language which is a pre-requisite for knowing and judging the meaning of their language. Whatever a human being says the others can understand and appreciate on the presupposition that humanity is common to all the human beings or human beings have the capacity to understand what is human. For instance, if we take the case of certain geniuses though we have not attained the same level of creativity as they have still we can understand them, or what is said by them will be intelligible to us as we have something in common with them, call it rationality or creativity. If, on the other hand, divine is something alien to human nature what is spoken by a supposedly divine person will not be intelligible to others, who are not divine, unless they read their meanings into the language of the former. In other words, if divine is a category which is completely different from and other than human, what is divine will not be intelligible in terms of what is human. It is only when the divine and the human do not exclude each other or are not opposed to each other what is divine will be intelligible in terms of what is human, and vice-versa. In addition, if we admit that divine is also a quality or dimension of what is human then every human being will be able to know and understand what others, who are more clearly aware of or have realised their divine nature, have known or experienced.

Now, the religious people often claim that the mystical or revelatory experiences, which some persons have, are the real means of knowing the objective meaning of religious statements or in knowing their cognitive value. The religious statements have objective meaning because they express what is experienced objectively by the mystics, and we have to have faith in what they say or describe to know the meaning of religious statements. Now, I am not asking the question, which is usually raised in relation to mystical experiences, namely, that they are not objective because they are not universal; they are not commonly experienced by all. And to admit that what has been known or experienced by someone cannot be repeated or experienced by all is to admit that it is not an experience or knowledge in the ordinary sense. Therefore, the statements that express such experiences cannot be said to have objective meaning, as that fact itself is not intelligible to us. They lack objective meaning in the sense we understand the sense of objective meaning. Nevertheless, the mystical experiences are intelligible to us as otherwise we cannot make any kind of judgement about them. Even to say that they are objectively meaningless is possible as well as meaningful only when we have some understanding of them and know what they speak about. The mystical experiences are intelligible to us as they are fundamentally about the basic human situation, or about certain states of human consciousness, or about certain facts of man's inward life, and their significance to man.

However, even supposing that one has a mystical experience it may not be sufficient to justify a religious claim he makes or is made by a religion on its basis. All the mystical experiences are not acceptable to all the religions, as all the religions do not accord the same value and significance to all the mystical experiences. All the religions do not recognise the authority of all the mystics. And all the mystical experiences are not regarded as equally significant in justifying the religious claims. The revelatory experience of Jesus did not have the same significance and value to all the Jews, and the experience of the Buddha was not acceptable to most of the Hindus. That is to say, the experience of the Buddha was not regarded by most of the Hindus as evidence either to prove or disprove some of their religious beliefs and doctrines, and the revelation of Jesus was not considered significant in relation to Judaism by most of the Jews. In our own times, the experiences of Śrī Rāmakṛṣṇa do not have the same value and significance to all the religions. We can give any number of examples, but the point I want to stress is that it is not the mystical experience as such but its interpretation that is considered to be objective and meaningful by the religions as otherwise the objective or cognitive value of a mystical experience must have been accepted by all the religions. If a mystical experience is really objective, it should have the same value to all, which, however is not the case with regard to any mystical experience. The reason why no religious or mystical experience is really objective and hence universally valid is that it is not basically about any reality that is objectively there which all the mystics can experience and describe in the same manner. Now, to say that there is a core element in all the mystical experiences which is objective though it is interpreted differently by different religions is a different problem. However, if we are to depend on the accounts of the mystics to know the nature and object of mystical experience then there will be no way of knowing the core or objective element in a mystical experience as the descriptions of mystical experiences differ, at times very significantly, and even radically. And to think that the experience must have been already interpreted while describing it is not so much significant as we have no means of knowing the objective content of a mystical experience independently of its description by a mystic.

All the mystical experiences are primarily about man and his inner life. Even the divine or God they speak about is experienced within as a state of being or consciousness. These experiences which are really states of human consciousness, or states of his being such as love, compassion, moral purity or perfection, inner peace or tranquillity, or a flush of creative energy or power, or a sense of transcendence in relation to ordinary mode of human existence, help man in knowing or understanding in depth the nature and meaning of human existence which in turn will influence his understanding of the nature and meaning of the world. These are facts of man's inner life though the value and significance attached to them distinguish a religious person from a non-religious person or a theist from an atheist. These are experienced in different degrees by all of us though the value and significance we give them or the way we interpret them is not the same. A non-religious person or an atheist also experiences them as he is also human but the meaning he gives to them distinguishes him from a religious person.

Similarly, the world in which both the religious and non-religious persons live is objectively the same, but the meanings they give to it are not the same. Similar is the case with different religions. The meaning one religion gives to the world of facts is not the same as that is given by another religion, though objectively speaking all of them live in the same world, and speak about the same world. They view it differently and interpret it differently. What is basically important for a religion is not the objective world of facts but the meaning or significance it has for it or the way it is interpreted. In other words, what distinguishes a religious person from a non-religious person, or one religion from another is not the world of facts but the meaning it has for them. The same facts, either of man's inner life or of the world, are interpreted differently by different religions. Though it is a fact that we all live and share the same objective world, the meaning-world in which we live and participate is not the same to all of us. It is the meaning-world which distinguishes one religion from other religions, as well as a religious person from a non-religious person.

What distinguishes a religious interpretation of the world or the meaning given to it from other interpretations and meanings is that the religious interpretation of the world is more integral. That is to say, in a non-religious interpretation we view and interpret either the human existence or the natural world of facts independently of each other. The meaning we give to human existence is seen as having nothing to do with the meaning we give to the natural world of facts. They are not viewed together or integrally, and therefore the meaning given to human existence is not seen as related to and integrated with the meaning given to the world. It is also a fact that we seldom try to find out the meaning of human existence or interpret it as a whole. Instead, we view and give meaning to different facts and aspects of human life independently of each other. For instance, the meaning we give to our emotional life is not related to the value and meaning we attach to our intellectual life, and vice-versa, as they are not viewed and interpreted in terms of a meaning which is total and comprehends the whole of human existence. But in the case of religion the meaning given to the world is integral in the sense that the natural world of facts is not viewed and interpreted independently of human existence, and its basic concerns, more particularly man's inner life. In other words, whenever the world is viewed and interpreted integrally a religion is born. A religious view of the world is comprehensive or integral in which though a particular aspect or fact of human life is given supreme importance all other things are viewed integrally and interpreted in terms of a single value and meaning. This is not the case with other interpretations. But when the meaning or interpretation given to the world is confused with causal or rational explanation of the world the religions come into conflict with each other, and also with science and philosophy or metaphysics. This is not, however, the case with all the religions and religious people. Those who really live or have faith in a religious world-view seldom come into conflict with other religious world-views or with empirical sciences as for them religion is basically living and transforming the life in the light of a meaning given to it by a religious world-view. When one so lives, one feels that his existence is fulfilled, and his life helps in revealing the meaning of religious language.

Now the question whether a world-view or a world of meaning is objective or not is basically a wrong or an irrelevant one. There are no different worlds corresponding to different world-views or worlds of meaning. People having faith in different world-views live in the same world, objectively speaking, but what does the world mean to them differs from religion to religion. Since what is the real or objective nature of the world has no one simple or straightforward answer as there is no universally valid knowledge of the world as a whole, which is definite and final, we cannot compare the various world-views with what may be regarded as the objective picture of the world. What has been once regarded as the objective picture of the world is seen in course of time as only a view of it. But we have to admit that the various world-views cannot be objectively true and

3

Religious Language

A. Ramamurthy

SHORN of all jargon the problem of religious language is whether the religious statements have any objective meaning or is there any cognitive value to religious beliefs expressed through religious statements. Ever since philosophy turned its attention to analysis of language with a view to understanding its meaning most of the philosophers of religion and some of the theologians have shown concern for understanding the problems related to the meaning of religious language. While most of the philosophers of religion tend to see only subjective or emotional meaning to religious language, majority of theologians assert that religious language has an objective meaning though the method of knowing the objective meaning of religious statements is not open to all. Their main argument is that since the religious language is not about empirically verifiable reality the empirical methods of knowing the objective meaning of religious statements will be of no avail. Only a few of the gifted or spiritually awakened persons can know and appreciate the objective validity of religious claims, and for them the religious claims are as objectively true and meaningful as any empirical claim. The cognitive value or objectivity of meaning of religious language is a problem only for us or for those who are not equipped internally to know the cognitive value of religious statements. However, if those who have known directly the reality that is represented or described by religious language are basically human then there is no reason why other human beings, like us, cannot know the reality that is represented by religious language. On the other hand, if those who are supposed religious world-view is that in so far as human creativity plays an important role in shaping it, and as human creativity is a free expression of human spirit, the nature and meaning of a world-view cannot be determined. There can be no causal or deterministic explanation of it.

Since a religious world-view is more a matter of creative imagination or a vision, which cannot be well defined and articulated in clear-cut and straightforward propositions, no single religious statement can express the vision adequately. Though a world-view is about the world and man in active interaction with each other, it is more meaningful in terms of man's inner life, feelings, his hopes, and aspirations. Therefore, if the language expressing a world-view represents anything it is the state of being of the person who has that vision. It is a vision or feeling or view about the world, the main concern of which is not to know, for the sake of knowledge, the nature of the world objectively. As human existence is fully involved in the formation of religious world-view human feelings, hopes and aspirations are not kept aside in knowing or understanding the meaning of the world. They are seen as most significant in understanding the meaning of the world. A religious view of the world is more a human world in which neither man is abstracted from the world nor the world is abstracted from human reality in understanding the meaning of either or both of them. Man and his inner life are not insignificant in understanding the meaning of the world, and the world is not indifferent to the inner experiences and feelings of man. It is a different problem as to how far the inner experiences of man are significant in understanding the nature of reality. But if we admit that they are significant in understanding the nature of reality then that reality is more human than the reality that is revealed to dispassionate understanding of man. This is what is expressed by the idea of God who stands as a symbol to express the nature of reality. To think that God is the source of the world, and the world is purposive is to say that the world is more artistic and human rather than mechanical. It is not therefore indifferent to human feelings and values. Such a view of the world gives rise to an ontological position in which the reality is conceived in more and more personal terms. As in the formation of a religious world-view both the natural world and human reality are involved, and act and interact on one another neither the facts of the natural world nor the facts of man's inner life are independently sufficient to understand and judge the meaningfulness of the world-view. On the other hand, when we try to understand the world more and more objectively or scientifically we assume that the human reality with all that it means is irrelevant and insignificant or rather as a hindrance to understanding the world. And why is it so is more a matter of assumption or prejudice, and lacks justification ultimately, which is also the case with a religious world-view. Only one who is fully aware of human reality and its possibilities can live a religious world-view, and appreciate it. And as philosophy and science try to exclude human reality in understanding the world and its meaning the religious way of looking at the world or its interpretation of the world or its world-view may look bizarre and meaningless.

II

A religious world-view can express itself in various forms of language. However, religious language consists mostly of myths, stories, parables, etc., and is mostly meaningful in its indirect usage. The mythical mode of expression seems best suited to express a world-view rather than the propositional form of language. In the mythical mode or form of expression, the language is plastic, and is capable of being interpreted differently by different people depending upon their receptive capacity and the level of their understanding and maturity. The object of religious language is not primarily to convey factual information about the world or reality or to describe it but to inspire or influence people to live and participate in the world of meaning. It is to transform hearer's existence totally or to generate faith in him in the meaning of the world, including human existence, which the world-view expresses. It is to influence the hearer and affect a total change or transformation in him.

The religious language is not representative as the purpose of a religious person in expressing himself and his state of being is not to describe something that is other than his state of being. And the state of one's being or existence is not something that can be objectified. As a creative expression of one's state of being or state of faith or devotion, which is inspired or evoked by the meaning-world or the world-view, the object of religious language is to make the hearer experience the same state of being or consciousness. As the *Vedāntins* maintain the meaning of religious statements consists in their capacity to help one remember or recollect the true state of his being, but not to convey factual information about the world or reality.

The evocative power of religious language is evident when we read a scriptural text or religious or devotional literature. We try to imbibe those feelings which they intend to evoke or instill in us. The feelings or devotion or faith or the state of consciousness which is evoked or inspired in us by the religious language may be fleeting or short-lived in certain persons but may have a lasting influence on others, and transform their lives. On the other hand, if we read a religious text or any devotional literature with a view to getting some knowledge either about the world or about human existence we may be disappointed as it is not the intention of a scripture to give us objective information or knowledge of the world or what is there. It is to make us realise or feel for ourselves or evoke in us a meaning that transforms our existence; and that is the main purpose or object of religious language. In other words, it is to make us religious or to generate faith in us. In this regard, the influence or impact of religious language on us is similar to that of music and poetry, which we are able to enjoy and appreciate though all cannot clearly and adequately express what music and poetry mean to them. Music is meaningful when it evokes the mood in the hearer, and poetry when it inspires one to participate in the vision of the poet and appreciate it. Similar is the case with religious language.

Since a religious world-view is basically human, it has the capacity to evoke in man the feelings or to instill in him the meaning it intends to express. When once the feelings are evoked and faith is generated in man he lives and participates in the meaning world, the object of religious language. That is to say, the object of religious language is to transform a person or affect a change in the state of his existence, which it does by evoking in him a state of consciousness or a world of meaning. Certain feelings or states of consciousness are common to all as they are basically human, just as a rational idea is universal as rationality is intrinsic to man, and the object of religious language is to evoke or inspire those feelings or states of consciousness in the hearer, and to make him live and participant in the world of meaning or the world-view which it tries to accomplish most creatively by adopting all kinds of creative devices.

All other problems about the meaning of religious language arise basically when we try to understand the meaning of religious language in terms of facts it is supposed to represent or describe. If, on the other hand, we see that the object of religious language is not to describe the world of facts but to evoke in us a meaning or affect a change in our being, an ordinary analysis of religious language to understand its meaning will be misleading. Since a religious world-view is not a representation of what is there or a description of factual world, but a world of meaning, it would be wrong and highly inappropriate to equate the meaningfulness of religious language with factuality.

4

Grades of Holism

Bhartṛhari Reconsidered

R.C.Pradhan

HOLISM has many forms and is of different kinds. One of its forms can be traced back to Bhartṛhari,[1] the Indian grammarian and the philosopher of language. Bhartṛhari's philosophy of language and meaning can broadly be called holistic because he, unlike other Indian philosophers of language belonging to the schools of Nyāya and Mīmāṁsā, has argued for the view that language and meaning can be treated as integral wholes rather than as consisting of independent parts. Holistic theories of meaning and language in general press for the view that language can be treated as a system of meaningful symbols[2] such that no word or sentence can be taken in isolation for its meaningfulness. This argument for holism is underlying much of the writings of contemporary philosophers of language and mind in the West.[3]

---

1. See B.K. Matilal, *The Word and the World: India's Contribution to the Study of Language*, Oxford University Press, Delhi, 1990. See also S. Bhattacharya, *Language, Testimony and Meaning*, ICPR, New Delhi, 1990.

2. See W.V. Quine, 'Two Dogmas of Empiricism' in *From a Logical Point of View*, MIT Press, Cambridge, Mass., 1959. See also his 'Five Milestones of Empiricism' in *Theories and Things*, Harvard University Press, Cambridge, Mass., 1981.

3. See Jerry Fodor and Ernest Lepore, *Holism: A Shopper's Guide*, Blackwell, Oxford, U.K. and Cambridge, USA.

My aim in this paper is to trace out holism in Bhartṛhari's philosophy of language and to argue that there may be grades of holism in his theory instead of the absolute monism attributed to the theory of *sphoṭa* propounded by Bhartṛhari. It is true that Bhartṛhari dovetails his theory of *sphoṭa* to the metaphysical doctrine of *śabda-brahman*. In this paper I will not deal with Bhartṛhari's metaphysical doctrine as I intend to highlight his semantics and other related issues.

The semantics of sphoṭa: Bhartṛhari's plea for holism

Two ideas emerge as fundamental in Bhartṛhari's philosophy of *sphoṭa*, namely (a) that language or *śabda* is basically a unitary phenomenon, and (b) that meaning is implicit in the symbol which manifests it as its inner content. Language has both its external and internal structures or forms: the external form manifests the internal form. For Bhartṛhari, the internal form is the same as the internal content which is the *sphoṭa* having no determinate structure[4] of its own. It is the indivisible and unitary meaning-content that lies deep in the womb of the language as the embryo.[5] The metaphor of embryo does suggest that the meaning-content or the *sphoṭa* manifests gradually into a full-fledged linguistic expression only when utterances (*nāda*) are produced embodying meaning. Thus the production of meaningful expressions is an event in space and time whereas *sphoṭa* itself is a non-spatial and non-temporal entity like a Platonic form or essence. As Matilal puts it:

> For the grammarians, the *sphoṭa* is a whole and it is a metaphysical entity, neither an object of construction, nor an abstraction.[6]

That is, the meaning-content called *sphoṭa* is a non-physical and non-empirical entity very much like the Fregean sense[7] that is neither

4. Cf. Bhartṛhari, *Vākyapadīya*, I.1-10.
5. *Ibid.*, I.51.
6. B.K. Matilal, *The Word and the World*, p. 90.
7. Frege, 'On Sense and Reference' in *Translations from the Philosophical* →

a physical nor a psychological entity. However, the Bhartṛharian *sphoṭa* unlike the Fregean sense, is in the mind (*buddhi*)[8] of the speaker ready to manifest itself in the speech-utterances. The mind-embeddedness of the *sphoṭa* does not detract from the fact that the meaning-content is an eternal entity.

Bhartṛhari's main effort is to explain how the meaning-content expresses itself in language. That is, he is concerned with the relationship between the *sphoṭa* and the *nāda* to explain how the former arises from its latent stage in the mind (*paśyantī*), passes through the intermediate stage (*madhyamā*) and settles down in the last and the final stage (*vaikharī*). That the *sphoṭa* passes through all these stages is itself an interesting phenomenon and needs explanation. The explanation offered by Bhartṛhari is that the meaning-content, being a whole or an indivisible entity, manifests itself in various ways at various stages without losing its indivisibility and holistic character.

There are two explanations available in Bhartṛhari about this. One is that the meaning-content is itself a metaphysical and transcendent reality such that it retains its identity in spite of the many changes that take place in the outward forms of expression. The second is that meaning is a formal and logical entity does not get meshed up with the means of expression which is some particular language with its contingent symbols. The essence of all symbols, which is the universal form, cannot be corrupted by the contingent symbols. Thus the semantic content can remain the same even if the symbols that express it are contingent. Bhartṛhari here appeals to the notion of semantic universal to overcome the difficulty in explaining how meaning remains the same when languages may differ. Meaning or *sphoṭa* is itself the unitary semantic universal that underlies all linguistic changes.

Bhartṛhari depends much on both the metaphysical and

→ *Writings of Gottlob Frege*, tr. Peter Geach and Max Black, Basil Blackwell, Oxford, 1956.

8. *Vākyapadīya*, I.46-75.

semantic explanations to show that a metaphysical entity like the *sphoṭa* needs a medium for its expression. The medium consists of the symbols as well as sounds which together constitute the linguistic expression that manifests the *sphoṭa*. Here one may ask, how is the invariable meaning-content preserved by the symbols and the sounds that are empirical and ephemeral phenomena? Bhartṛhari is well aware of the idea that the *sphoṭa* or the meaning-content is unitary, invariable and eternal (*nitya*),[9] and so has to be kept so even while it is being expressed in the empirical language. This makes him turn to the idea that the *sphoṭa* or *śabda* is manifested by sound (*dhvani/nāda*) without the former changing at all. The temporal sequence found in sound or the utterances is only superimposed[10] on the *sphoṭa* without being real at all.

Bhartṛhari's explanation sounds primarily metaphysical, though it is also semantically relevant that the characteristics of the sound produced by the speaker cannot be logically associated with the meaning which is articulated by the utterances. Therefore, it is true to say that meaning is logically independent of the symbols used because meaning cannot be produced in the way the sounds are produced. Bhartṛhari's *sphoṭa* theory takes care to dissociate the empirical characteristics of the sound from the *sphoṭa* in order to preserve the transcendent character of the latter. The *sphoṭa* remains the real semantic entity in spite of the vicissitudes suffered by the symbols used for making utterances.

Sphoṭa as a unitary whole

The main argument which the Bhartṛharian must offer is regarding how the meaning-content is to be treated as a whole as contrasted with the parts. It is so far clear that for the grammarian there is nothing called meaning which can be composed out of the parts scattered throughout language. The sentence being the carrier of meaning is itself an indivisible entity, and so the meaning it carries is also indivisible. That is, both the sentence and the meaning which

9. *Vākyapadīya*, I.46-75.

10. *Ibid*.

it expresses are wholes which have no parts or which cannot be divided into parts without destroying the whole itself. This argument depends on the premise that meaning is not a spatio-temporal entity which can be divided at all.

There are two ways in which holism could be understood as a theory of meaning: first, it can be horizontal in approach taking meaning as spread across the whole language; second, it can be vertical laying meaning deep in the structure of language. Bhartṛhari's holism is of the latter kind which pushes meaning back into the deep-structure of grammar. *Sphoṭa* lies deep in the structure of what Bhartṛhari calls the *śabda* or language which is not the language as it appears in the surface-structure. The latter is associated with the production of sound and other phonetic features. Horizontal holism does not take into account the deep-structure of language as it is solely concerned with how language functions as a whole rather than with how language evolves out of a grammatical core.[11] Vertical holism, however, takes the grammatical core as the source of meaning which spreads across language. Meaning is holistic because it accrues to the whole of language as the latter has evolved out of the grammatical core.

Bhartṛhari takes language as consisting of sentences which themselves are the indivisible entities. These sentences are the carriers of meaning in the sense that they alone express the meaning-content through the elaborate surface-structure of language. But the way meaning is expressed is holistic in the sense that the whole sentence expresses it rather any part thereof. The following is an approximate formulation of the holistic thesis of Bhartṛhari:

> Meaning is an undivided whole that is expressed in a sentence: It is the sentence and sentence alone that expresses this undivided whole.

---

11. Quine, 'Two Dogmas of Empiricism'. See also for a discussion my 'Two Perspectives of Meaning Holism: Wittgenstein and Bhartṛhari' in *Tattvanidhi: A Felicitation Volume in Honour of Professor C. Ramaiah*, Professor C. Ramaiah Felicitation Committee, Tirupati, 1999.

This thesis carries the quintessence of the holistic thesis of Bhartṛhari in the sense that meaning is no more treated as a composite entity to be explained either as a result of combination of words or as the result of the conventional and empirical association of language with human actions. Meaning in this sense is autonomous and is revealed only in the language-use under the strict grammatical regimentation.

Bhartṛhari's approach to meaning is logically connected with his approach to grammar. Grammar alone is the home of meaning and not the actual language-use. It is because the grammatical structure of the sentence which is a unified whole, e.g., 'The cow is white' expresses the meaning. The sentence is one grammatical unit having no parts though for all practical purposes there are words in it. But the words themselves have no independent existence; hence there is no meaning associated with them. This seems to be contrary to what we believe to be true according to common sense. But the grammarian's argument is that what is true ordinarily is not true according to grammar. Grammar does not take note of the diversity of the linguistic expressions; it searches for the unity of the linguistic expressions in the *sphoṭa* underlying all languages. The sentence carries the whole meaning in the network of the language to which it belongs.

Now the question arises: if the words have no independent existence, how can there be a sentence at all for a sentence is by definition a combination of words? Besides, how can the sentence have meaning if the words have no meaning of their own? These are the questions which are likely to disturb anybody not thinking within the framework of the Grammarians. The fact of the matter is that words have no reality for the grammarians from the transcendental point of view, though they have existence for all practical purposes. The grammarian argues for the view that we fall back on sentences to express full meaning but not on the words which have meaning only in the network of the sentences. The primacy of the sentences over words has been recognised in semantics by the Prābhākara-Mīmāṁsākas in India and the philosophers like Frege and Wittgenstein in the West.[12] Therefore it is not surprising if the grammarians argue for the primacy of the sentences and deny altogether the role of words in semantics.

Why contextualism is not enough

Contextualism as we know it in Frege has not gone a long way in explaining meaning because the Context Principle[13] has not very clearly defined the relation between the sentence and the words. Frege definitely does not deny the independent existence of the words and their meaning. He fully recognises that the logical words like the logical connectives and quantifiers have their independent meaning. Besides, the proper names themselves as saturated terms have their independent sense. It is only the predicative expressions which are incomplete symbols which do not have independent meaning. Therefore Frege's Context Principle does not show that all words have to depend on sentences to have meaning. Besides, the Context Principle itself needs a Compositionality Principle to operate since unless the sentences are composed out of the words, it is difficult to talk of the sentence-meaning or sense at all. It seems Frege is more committed to the Compositionality Principle than to the Context Principle itself.

The Prābhākara's *anvitābhidhānavāda*, which is the theory of connected designation and meaning comes closer to the Context Principle mentioned above.[14] It holds that all word-meanings depend on a connection already established in the sentence. That is to say, the sentence-connection is presupposed by the words themselves. This leads to the assertion by the Prābhākara-Mīmāṁsākas that the sentences have a pragmatic priority over the words so far as expression of meaning is concerned. But this theory also fails to

12. Frege, *op.cit.* Also see Wittgenstein, *Tractatus Logico-Philosophicus*, tr. D.F. Pears and B.F. McGuinness, Routledge and Kegan Paul, London, 1961.

13. Frege, *The Foundation of Arithmetic*, tr. J.L. Austin, Blackwell, Oxford, 1950, Introduction, p. x.

14. B.K. Matilal, *The Word and the World*, Chapter 10.

explain how this connection itself is possible. If it is eternal, then it is as good as saying that the words have no independent meaning because the words have to depend on the eternal bond already established. This leads to holism as it cannot sustain the independence of words any more. But if it retains the independence of words, then it cannot explain how there can be any prior connection of words at all. The prior connection will be nothing but a conventional bond between words which can take place even without a sentence, e.g., yellow flower, blue sky, etc.

Contextualism fails because it presupposes rather than explains that there is already an intimate bond between words in a sentence. So a consistent contextualist will have to say that sentences are themselves indivisible entities and words are carved out of them by analysis. But this leads to holism even of a milder kind. The road from contextualism to (holism) is very short. Quine's and Davidson's holism[15] is of this kind because both admit that the Context Principle is basically true. Bhartṛhari, however, goes further in search of the semantic unity in the form of *sphoṭa*, which according to him is a primordial unity of meaning lying deep within language and human consciousness.

Holism in Bhartṛhari takes a radical turn precisely because he has to contend with the extreme atomism of Nyāya and the Bhāṭṭa-Mīmāṁsakas. Semantic-atomism is a commonsensical doctrine in the sense that it explains how words have meaning and then how they make a sentence possible. The atomists all believe that words are the primary units of meaning and only when we make a sentence we bring the words together according to some semantic rules. Thus sentence formation is a matter of logical and empirical conventions which make the communicational languages possible. Now the question arises: if the words are primary, then why do we feel the necessity of sentences at all? Why is it that for communication the words are not enough? Besides, the sentence-meaning itself is not a mere conglomeration of word-meanings at all. The sentence-meaning

15. Davidson, *Inquiries into Truth and Interpretation*, Clarendon Press, Oxford, 1984.

stands on its own because of the new meaning which the sentence brings into existence. Thus if the sentence-meaning is new, how can it be a product of composition?, asks the grammarian. Thus, there is little that the atomists have to offer as an explanation of the meaning of the sentences. Therefore holism comes forward to tell us that sentence meaning is itself an autonomous entity.

The autonomy of meaning can established only if we can prove that it is an indivisible entity that cannot be derived from any other source. This has been Bhartṛhari's contention that meaning is eternal and that it is there even if we do not express it in words. Especially the sentence-meaning which has been the bone of contention between the holists and the atomists can never be the product of human composition. Therefore, according to Bhartṛhari, meaning must be an eternal and indivisible entity. Holism takes off where atomism fails to explain how sentence-meaning is possible. The strength of holism lies in making meaning independent of the human conventions and the empirical conditions of language-use. It brings a transcendental perspective to account for the eternity of meaning or *sphoṭa*.

Grades of holism

The most important aspect of Bhartṛhari's holism is that he does not foreclose the possibility of language-learning as the atomists are worried about. Dummett,[16] for example, in this critique of Davidson's holism is worried that language as a whole cannot be learned, nor can the whole meaning be grasped by anybody. This worry issues from the idea that meaning at any given time or context has to be presented as a whole and that a single speaker or hearer has to contend with a large mass of language to learn and master. But this is a misunderstanding of the holist's position. The holist argues that meaning in principle is presented as a whole and that it is in the whole that the true nature of language is unfolded. So from the transcendental point of view meaning is one and indivisible and

16. Dummett, 'What is a theory of Meaning?' in *Mind and Language*, ed. S. Guttenplan, Oxford University Press, Oxford, 1975.

that it can be presented as a single entity. But from a practical point of view there are meanings of expressions which are not a part of whole, e.g., 'cat', 'dog', 'cow', etc. Thus the parts are not wished away by any holist much less by Bhartṛhari.

The idea of grades of holism is implicit in Bhartṛhari in the sense that at different stages holism takes different forms. Seen from the absolute metaphysical standpoint, meaning is one seamless whole — an indivisible entity. It is the one at the foundation of all language, it being the real language or the pure language. But the moment it enters into an impure stage, it shows division within itself. Meaning appears plural and diversified as it descends into the arena of speech. When language is spoken and utterances made meaning gets scattered and becomes multiple and diversified. There are sentences and words all vying with one another for meaningfulness. This cacophony of speech is the *vaikharī* that presents the multiplicity of meaning. This is the reason why language as it is used is never presented as a single whole.

Thus there is not only global holism of language and meaning from the wider point of view but also local holism. When we see meaning as a universal reality in the way Bhartṛhari sees it, one is bound to be a global holist. That is, one is bound to be a holist in the sense that nothing short of the whole language can be the bearer of meaning. But a local holist can be satisfied with the fact that sentences can be endowed with meaning without breaking it into parts. In this situation, the local holist accepts the fact that meaning even on a small scale is a whole and need not be divided into pieces. Nevertheless, holism is the only option available because there is no way we can go back to the words and start the process bottom up. There is only a top bottom analysis possible which fragments the universal whole into local wholes and so on. We must remain with some sort of the whole. Meaning in a sense is global at one point of time and local at another but at both stages it is holistic nonetheless.

Bhartṛhari brings in the idea of the levels of language only to ward off the notion that he accepts only a monistic view of meaning. He accommodates the plurality of language and meaning through his metaphysical doctrine that reality is one but it has many manifestations or appearances. Semantically speaking, there is one meaning whole which appears as many meanings in many contexts. Thus there is reason to believe that meaning or the *sphoṭa* is one reality but it has many manifestations. Therefore holism stands intact because at every level the whole is in sight, though the parts appear as manifestations of the whole. From the stage of pure language to that of the local or colloquial languages, there is a gradual development of language and meaning. At the level of pure language, the essential core of grammar remains in the pure form which takes shape as it descends to the level of the speech. This progress from pure to the impure is a gradual process of development. This explains how grades of meaning holism are available.

Meaning, content and consciousness

Bhartṛhari anticipates the modern theory that meaning pervades consciousness and that the contents of consciousness are linguistically structured. For him, meaning is the content of consciousness and is also linguistic in character. That is to say, *sphoṭa* is the linguistic entity that remains seated in the domain of consciousness. This leads further to the idea that language and consciousness at the highest level are one. Besides, it entails that consciousness has a syntactic structure reminding us of the Fodorian thesis that there is a language of thought (LOT).[17] The LOT thesis suggests that thought itself has a syntactic formal structure that can be mapped into a language of representations. Bhartṛhari also tells us that our consciousness is fully pervaded by the *sphoṭa* that represents the essence of language.

Bhartṛhari is in favour of what is known as content-holism for the reason that the contents of consciousness are represented as a whole in the mechanism of the language of thought. Contents are internally organised into the network of thought and are separable only when we fail to see the unity of the contents. *Sphoṭa* is the unifying principle that brings all the contents of consciousness into

17. Jerry Fodor, *The Language of thought*, Crowell, New York, 1975.

one single system. Modern content theorists insist that contents be only locally networked[18] and that they be causally identified. But the Bhartṛharian suggestion is that the contents are internally networked and that they are globally connected with the rest of the system of contents. Thus global holism follows as a result of the internal networking.

The difference between the global holists and the local holists appears only on the ground that what is locally networked has significance only with reference to the demand of the context and the speaker. But global holism applies to all cases of content irrespective of the speaker and the context. Thus, global holism is more acceptable as a solution of the problem of content and consciousness. Bhartṛhari's account seems acceptable because there is a gradualist approach to consciousness in his theory which resolves the conflict between local holism and global holism. In this sense we can very well argue that contents have a tendency to be affiliated to, or connected with, other contents in our consciousness.

Bhartṛhari's framework is well designed to accommodate the conflicting claims of the content theorists and to accommodate the various types of contents within the domain of consciousness. From the narrow contents to the wide or broad ones, there is a continuous process of integration of the contents into a wider whole. But the advantage with the Bhartṛharian theory is that ultimately all contents merge into the *sphoṭa* as the transcendental source of all contents. The single *sphoṭa* becomes the multiple contents all connected with the former. Thus a global holism prevails throughout the space of the contents. The logical space of the contents is cemented through the connecting link of the *sphoṭa*.

---

18. Fodor, *Psychosemantics: the Problem of Meaning in the Theory of Mind*, MIT Press, Cambridge, Mass., 1987.

5

The Problem of Meaning in Vākyapadīya

P.R. Bhat

Introduction

VĀKYAPADĪYA deals with the problem of language in all its aspects in an exhaustive manner. One would find that there are major themes and sub-themes running through the text with certain autonomy. No doubt, Bhartṛhari was responding to several issues raised in the context of language and meaning by his predecessors and the contemporary thinkers. What is his thesis and what is the thesis of his opponents that he intends to refute after critical examination is not always clear in the text of *Vākyapadīya*. We suspect, some of the difficulties that we see later in this essay are due to this reason.

We find in *Vākyapadīya* that there are remarks due to his own metaphysical compulsions. Quite a few remarks on *śabda-brahman* are due to this. Some of the remarks on grammar are necessitated because of his opposition to Grammarians. Some of the remarks on word-meaning seem to be due to this. One would find some remarks on phonetics as well. Conventional and pragmatic elements too enter the text while dealing with specific and controversial examples. Remarks on some of these themes are not directly relevant to the issue of meaning. However, his remarks on holism, word and sentence-meaning, primary and secondary meaning, use and usage's of words, etc., are directly relevant to the discussion on meaning.

Even with respect to meaning, we find several theses that are expressed in *Vākyapadīya* some of which have supporting arguments and some of them seem to be working hypotheses or thumb rules. What we shall do here is to reconstruct some of the arguments in support of central and uncontroversial themes of *Vākyapadīya* and point out some of the philosophical difficulties pertaining to them in the end.

The Main Arguments

In this context we mention only three theses:

(1) Holistic nature of meaning: *Vākyapadīya* has lengthy discussion on sentence and word-meaning. A sentence is the primary unit of meaning. Several arguments are advanced in favour of sentence-meaning as against word-meaning. Analysing a sentence into its parts such as words are done for better comprehension. But that does not mean that words are the units of meaning. Since communication is possible only through a sentence, the unit of meaning is considered to be a sentence.

(2) Grasping meaning often requires interpretation: Meaning cannot be read off from a symbol. Even perception of a word as word requires linguistic training. Each technical word will have a unique feature and its domain of operation. A word on colour belongs to the language of vision, and a *rāga* belongs to the language of sound. We need to know enough about a tradition to make right kind of linguistic inference to understand the cultural dimension of the speech. Long usages and the cultural habits give insight into the working of words.

(3) Authentic interpretation ought to refer to the use and usages of words: Not all interpretations can be taken as authentic. In fact, grammarians are said to be trained scholars who know both the etymological significance of the terms and their current usages in the society. Any controversy with

regard to the application of words is referred to such scholars. With their wisdom, they would be in a position to resolve the controversies about the correct use of terms taking context and tradition into consideration.

THESIS 1: MEANING IS HOLISTIC

Let us put forth several arguments that figure in the *Vākyapadīya* which support the thesis that meaning is grasped a whole.

1. A sentence is constituted of words. Both spoken and written sentences have sequencing of constituent words. When we speak or write a sentence, we follow certain order in uttering or writing the words of the sentence. We may first utter or write the subject of the sentence and then the verb. If meaning were to be grasped as and when we utter the constituent words, then we would have grasped the meaning of the subject term first followed by the predicate term and so on. In this analysis, we are required to visualise a process of progressive integration of meaning from subject term to predicate term of the sentence. If the sentence is constituted of several terms, then this process of integration would continue progressively till the sentence is terminated by a period. But this process visualised is counter intuitive. For instance, consider the sentence 'Touch me not'. This sentence has opposite meaning when only first two words are uttered in comparison to the full sentence when uttered. In fact, the last word 'not' negates what is asserted when the first two words 'touch me' are uttered or written. Obviously, either we have to give up the progressive integration theory of meaning of a sentence or admit such absurd things that opposite meanings can be integrated in a sentence. That is the reason why it is said that when you grasp, you grasp the meaning as a whole in a flash. (*Kāṇḍa* II, 143, 217, 220) You do not make the progress in understanding the sentence meaning word by word according to *Vākyapadīya*. (*Kāṇḍa* II, 410, 421, 424)

2. Individual words do not have intrinsic value; they acquire importance because of the role they play in the formation of a sentence. But, it is possible to divide the sentence into parts arbitrarily. (*Kāṇḍa* I, 85-92) We divide a sentence into its parts for convenience. (*Kāṇḍa* II, 343) It is also possible to divide a word into further sub-parts artificially (*Kāṇḍa* II, 13, 224, 225-26, 236) by those who insist on dividing any unit of understanding. We do speak of word-meaning, but that is in the sense of general meaning. (*Kāṇḍa* I, 60; II, 123, 156) The general meaning of words would give us the idea about their potential use. This is the reason why the meaning of the whole sentence is different from the meaning of the individual words. (*Kāṇḍa* II, 55, 206, 239, 246, 247, 248, 326, 398, 440) The concept of organic whole as opposed to the notion of aggregation may be invoked here. A sentence-meaning is not the aggregate of its constituent words is already stated. However, the meaning of the sentence cannot be totally unconnected to the meaning of the constituent words as well. (*Kāṇḍa* II, 391, 394, 465, 466) If that were the case, we could utter any sentence to communicate anything whatsoever. In a manner of speaking, the meaning of the whole sentence is present in each of the constituting words. (*Kāṇḍa* II, 115) A word in a sentence organically participates in the sentence than taken it individually. Thus, the meaning of a sentence is indefinable, (*Kāṇḍa* II, 145, 439) it is neither totally determined by the constituent words nor is it totally new.

Communication is the basic purpose of uttering a sentence or writing it down. (*Kāṇḍa* II, 423, 424) One cannot communicate anything simply by uttering a word or writing it down. Therefore, from the point of view of successful communication, words do not have independent meaning apart from the sentence-meaning. Thus, the word-meaning gives us the general idea about the usages of words and their specific role in a sentence is collectively and organically decided by the sentence-meaning in a communicative situation. It is the application of the word in a sentence that gives the meaning to the words. (*Kāṇḍa* II, 399-400, 437) Moreover, it is possible to have a compound sentence or a passage constituted of several sentences. It is possible to recognise them as separate entities. (*Kāṇḍa* II, 112) *Vākyapadīya* does not recognise a paragraph or a 'discourse' as one unit. A paragraph or a discourse could consist of several sentences each having independent meaning.

3. A word appears in several sentences, and these sentences do communicate different meanings. If words were the primary units of meaning, the identity of the words occurring in these different sentences would have been lost. For instance, 'Touch me not' and 'Touch me not is a plant' are the two sentences such that the three words of the first sentence occur in the second as well. If the primary unit of meaning were words, then the two sentences would have failed to have independent meanings for the simple reason that the meaning of the first sentence would have been partially the same as the meaning of the second sentence. Our linguistic intuition says that the two sentences have entirely different meanings. A word may be used in different sentences with different meanings, yet the word remains the same. (*Kāṇḍa* I, 61)

4. If words are the units of meaning, then there would have never been an unintelligible sentence if we knew the words. For instance, a self-contradictory sentence too would have been intelligible to us if we knew the constituent words of the sentence. A typical self-contradictory statement would be one where what is stated in the subject is denied by the predicate. 'A bachelor is not an unmarried man', would be a self-contradictory sentence. The sentence is unintelligible to us since it fails to communicate anything despite our knowing each and every word in the sentence. In similar vein *Vākyapadīya* states that even if we are unfamiliar with some words in a sentence, the whole sentence becomes

unintelligible to us. (*Kāṇḍa* II, 91) If words were units of meaning, we should have been in a position to understand the meaning of the sentence partially, if not fully. Similar analysis could be extended to cover contradictory statements as well. One cannot understand what is stated in a contradiction even if the two constituting sentences can be understood independently. Meaning of a sentence cannot be divided, (*Kāṇḍa* II, 75) and that is the reason why we do not have partial meaning.

5. Ambiguous sentences indicate that meaning is grasped as a whole. A sentence which is ambiguous leads to certain interpretation. (*Kāṇḍa* II, 471-75) One meaning of that sentence is grasped in a context in one particular manner and another meaning of the same sentence is grasped in another context. In any case, while grasping one meaning of the sentence one does not mix it up with another meaning of the same sentence. However, some sentences may be uttered with the intention of communicating both the meanings simultaneously. (*Kāṇḍa* II, 369-70, 472) For instance, one may crack a joke intending to mean both the meanings of a sentence together: 'Flying aeroplanes are dangerous.' Yet even in such cases, we grasp the two meanings of the sentence holistically and separately. If the holistic understanding of meaning of sentences were not quite natural, ambiguous sentences would have lead us to total chaos and confusion making the sentences unintelligible. The confusion might still remain, but this is not due to the lack of meaning of the sentence, rather it is due to the uncertainty about the application of the sentence. Context often clears the meaning that ought to be attached to the sentence. (*Kāṇḍa* II, 330-35)

6. We admit that there are one word sentences. Some thinkers tend to take such one-word sentences as incomplete. But how is it that we recognise a sentence as incomplete? The simple answer to this question is that we know how to

complete the sentence. Thus, incomplete sentences express the meaning of a complete sentence and we are able to complete the sentence on that basis. For instance, *dvāram* or 'water' can be an incomplete sentence. In a context where an individual is rushing hurriedly, the word *dvāram* would be the same as 'give way' and similarly, in a context where a person is highly thirsty, 'water' would be the same as 'give me water'.

7. A grammatical correction of an ungrammatical sentence could be done by a competent user. (*Kāṇḍa* I, 14) And this correction is possible only when the person is able to grasp the meaning of the sentence despite its wrong grammatical formulation. This also indicates, syntactical properties of sentences can be altered to suit semantical properties of sentences according to *Vākyapadīya*.

THESIS 2: INTERPRETATION IS ESSENTIAL ASPECT OF MEANING

Understanding without interpretation seems to be next to impossible. We shall develop the relationship between meaning and interpretation on the basis of the remarks made in *Vākyapadīya*.

1. According to *Vākyapadīya*, a word has a perceivable part. Though words can be in written form, the spoken form of them is considered to be more basic and hence phonemes are important in the context of the discussion of words. Articulated sounds lead to difference in perception says *Vākyapadīya*. Perception of *sphoṭa* is supposed to take place before this articulated perception takes place. (*Kāṇḍa* I, 76-77) Any sign, something that is perceivable, is not a word till it is a part of the language.

   What is note worthy is that there is no natural and automatic meaning coming out of words. (*Kāṇḍa* I, 57) That is to say, a person needs to set his mind to perceive the meaning of a sentence. (*Kāṇḍa* I, 53, 121-22) Moreover, the same word may communicate different meanings in different contexts (*Kāṇḍa* I, 60; II, 250-55, 333)

2. Inferring the correct form of words from incorrect ones and inferring the complete sentence from incomplete ones are possible because we are able to interpret what we hear. One is able to infer the correct word from the corrupt forms. (*Kāṇḍa* I, 148-50) For instance, *amba* is inferred from *mma* in the case of a child. (*Kāṇḍa* I, 152-53) This indicates that interpretation of the word when required is permitted. Similarly, one word sentence *dvāram* in a context can be interpreted as 'open the door'. (*Kāṇḍa* II, 333) The incomplete sense that is communicated by the one word sentence is completed by supplying additional words while interpreting it. 'Water' in a context can mean, 'Give me water', for instance.

3. Interpreting the meaning of certain sentences is not just possible without attributing certain intention to the speaker. Taking literal meaning of these sentences would be really absurd. For instance, when someone asks you to 'save the butter from crows' you should not protect it only from crows and allow the dogs to eat it away. (*Kāṇḍa* II, 312) Similarly, when someone says 'one has to go, look at the sun' the sentence is not about the sun, but it is about the time. (*Kāṇḍa* II, 310) We are able to grasp the far-fetched meaning of the intended meaning than what is apparent in a context. (*Kāṇḍa* I, 137; II, 251) That is to say, literal meaning is different from the interpreted meaning. (*Kāṇḍa* II, 135)

4. If a controversy arises because commonly known meaning is hindered by the intended meaning, experts use their own standard to interpret the meaning. Experts have long training and have perfected themselves. Moreover, they know the grammar of these terms and their etymological origins. Therefore, interpretation of experts would be taken

as standard and the issue would be resolved. (*Kāṇḍa* I, 33-35)

5. If a sentence is ambiguous, it is resolved by referring to the context (*Kāṇḍa* II, 250, 268, 317-18) it is said. There is mention about the suitability, propriety, place, time, gender and accent, etc., are the parameters using which one moves towards the definiteness of meaning. (*Kāṇḍa* II, 314-16) These considerations indicate that grasping the right meaning requires linguistic labour.

6. Certain presuppositions and implications are part of the understanding. For instance, if someone asks you to feed the guest, certainly feeding would involve washing the dishes, plates, spoons, etc., are understood. (*Kāṇḍa* II, 313) Similarly, it is understood by enlightened hearer that praise is meant to promote the action and blame is meant to abstention from action. (*Kāṇḍa* II, 319)

7. The role played by the concepts and the theories on understanding something cannot be undermined. For instance, the same word may be a noun or a verb or an adjective. Taking it as a noun would give us one meaning and taking it as a verb would give us different meaning. (*Kāṇḍa* II, 318, 326) For example, the word 'picture' occurs as verb in the first occurrence and occurs as a noun in the second occurrence in the sentence 'picture the duck-rabbit picture'. If the first occurrence of the word is taken to be the noun, then the sentence could be taken as incomplete, and if both the occurrences are taken as occurrences of verb form, then also we would consider the sentence to be grammatically erroneous. In a sentence, the word 'long' can be understood as a verb or as an adjective. For instance, 'I long a long banana' the first occurrence of the word in the sentence would be a verb, whereas the second occurrence of it would be taken as an error if it is taken as a verb, but would be taken grammatically correct if it is taken as an adjective.

Similarly, the perspective from which we look at things can matter much. (*Kāṇḍa* I, 8) For instance, when there is an error in perception, the words do not mean the same. 'Water' in a mirage cannot mean the same as water in the real world. (*Kāṇḍa* II, 287) A 'mountain' in a picture and a 'fort' in an imaginary world do not have the same meaning as is the case in the actual world. (*Kāṇḍa* II, 290, 292) The same sacred hymn can have many meanings depending on the perspective of ***ātman***, that of **gods,** or of **the ritual.** (*Kāṇḍa* II, 254, 474) One and the same term, for instance, Sāṅkhya, can have technical meaning or an ordinary meaning depending on the context. (*Kāṇḍa* II, 369) Similarly, there could be certain profound sentences that have fixed meaning which is understood by all and could have hidden meaning that can only a careful trained listener can discover it. (*Kāṇḍa* I, 54)

THESIS 3: CRITERIA OF MEANING

The importance given to grammar, tradition and social norms is immense in *Vākyapadīya*. Let us consider the reasons why scholars like Bhartṛhari gives such an importance to convention and rituals.

1. Word and meaning: The relationship between the word and the meaning is said to be the eternal and everlasting. (*Kāṇḍa* I, 23; II, 364) However, this is not to say that there are no differences in the manner in which we speak the words. With all the variations of spoken form, we understand the word correctly. (*Kāṇḍa* I, 47) *Nāda*, the sound, may vary in length, or loudness and yet the word expressed could be the same. (*Kāṇḍa* I, 47, 49-52) We achieve more exactness through written forms of words. The written forms, which involve laws regarding them are called *smṛtis*. (*Kāṇḍa* I, 29) Because of this enduring relationship between words and their meanings, we are in a position to construct sentences to communicate.

2. Grammar and meaning: The learned scholars, it is said, would use the words that have popular usage and are supported by grammatical tradition. (*Kāṇḍa* I, 27) Popular

and traditional usage of words are of immense importance. Even if the usage is illogical, it has to be respected from the point of view of social behaviour. (*Kāṇḍa* I, 30)

3. Tradition and logic: The linguistic tradition has unmeasurable hold on language. Social behaviour cannot be countered by any logic. (*Kāṇḍa* I, 31) And those who follow the *āgama*, i.e., popular tradition need not be baffled by logical arguments against them. (*Kāṇḍa* I, 41-42) The vision that the sages have cannot be countered by logic and sense perception. (*Kāṇḍa* I, 38) Grammarians study *śāstras* to understand the unimposing natural behaviour of words. (*Kāṇḍa* I, 43) Correctness or otherwise of words are determined by the Grammarians with reference to tradition. (*Kāṇḍa* I, 142) Since science of grammar is considered to be the supreme and wonderful means of knowledge (*Kāṇḍa* I, 29, 43, 143), the knowledge acquired by tradition cannot be questioned by logic.

4. Use and usage: There are several passages that emphasise the usage part of a word. The meaning of a word is whatever we understand when that word is uttered. (*Kāṇḍa* II, 328) If we use a word in a deviant manner for substantially long duration, which would become natural to that word. (*Kāṇḍa* II, 255) For instance, *jalaja* is conventionally used to refer to lotus, though its literal meaning would be something that is born in water. It is also said that when we assign new meaning to a word, its previous meaning is hindered. (*Kāṇḍa* I, 33) For instance, the word 'mouse' has acquired new meaning in the computer age by interfering with the conventional use of this word. There is also a suggestion that normal criteria of meaning should not be frustrated. (*Kāṇḍa* I, 34) Popular usage, social behaviour and tradition ought to be respected, it is remarked. (*Kāṇḍa* I, 27, 31) Apart from all this, it is clearly stated that a use of a word without definite object or a definite sense is useless or meaningless. (*Kāṇḍa* I, 56)

5. Primary and secondary: We do not speak of primary and secondary meaning in the context of sentences. (*Kāṇḍa* II, 269) But at the level of words, the need to recognise the primary and secondary meanings seems to have arisen because of the following reasons:

   (a) A word has primary meaning if it is used in accordance with its usage, if it is used in a deviant manner, then it has secondary meaning. (*Kāṇḍa* II, 263, 265, 281, 285) Frequency of usage determines what is the primary meaning of a word. (*Kāṇḍa* II, 253) Infrequent use of a word is considered to have secondary meaning.

   (b) If the meaning of a word is dependent on the context or some other word, then word has secondary meaning. (*Kāṇḍa* II, 264)

   (c) When a word finds its application through the use of another word requiring special effort to understand it, then it has secondary meaning. (*Kāṇḍa* II, 266, 278)

   (d) When a universal is absent, but it indicates the similar quality in an object, then it has secondary meaning. (*Kāṇḍa* II, 273)

   (e) When a universal is found in another object due to a misapprehension, then the meaning conveyed is secondary. (*Kāṇḍa* II, 274) Any error in perception would have secondary meaning like in the case of water in the mirage. (*Kāṇḍa* II, 287)

   (f) Derived names have secondary meaning. For instance, *agnidatta* has secondary meaning. (*Kāṇḍa* II, 282)

   (g) Extended use of words would have secondary meaning. a mountain in the picture, a river in a mirror, a fort in our imaginary city, an idol of tiger, poison in a dream will have secondary meaning. (*Kāṇḍa* II, 290-95)

Assuming that the above three theses have been established

with arguments we may now turn to some of the difficulties that we see in accepting them all.

Some unresolved problems

If we take the **use** as the basis of meaning as is largely argued in the West following Wittgenstein, then the distinction between primary and secondary meaning cannot be sustained. For instance, when a deviant use becomes normal to a term, that use would have as much acceptability as any other normal use and hence, the meaning expressed by such terms would be normal to them. Thus, primary meaning of *jalaja* would be lotus and not 'water born' because of the long usage. However, this does not seem to be acceptable to *Vākyapadīya* as 'lotus' is derived meaning from 'water born' and primary meaning is logically prior to the derived meaning. And therefore, on this consideration *jalaja* cannot have lotus as the primary meaning even after long usage.

Vākyapadīya seems to embrace referential theory of meaning when it speaks of primary and secondary meaning. For instance, while explaining why water in mirage and the mountain in the picture have secondary meaning, Bharatṛhari explains them in terms of the properties of the objects denoted by these terms. The water in the mirage cannot be used for bathing and the mountain that is so huge in reality cannot fit into a small frame. Meaning of any term cannot have physical dimension unless the object referred to is taken to be the meaning of the term. Referential theory has the difficulty of explaining the meaningfulness of the negative sentences such as 'There is no water in the well'. We cannot even say 'Mr. N.N. is dead' meaningfully if referential theory of meaning is true points out Wittgenstein.[1]

If use is the source of meaning, then how can word be ambiguous? Ambiguity is possible only if there is a possibility of distinguishing one use from another. And this distinction can be

---

1. Ludwig Wittgenstein, *Philosophical Investigations*, tr. G.E.M. Anscombe, Basil Blackwell, Oxford, 1953, Section-40.

there on some ontological foundation. For instance, it is intelligible within the referential theory of meaning to speak of two different uses of the word 'bat', for, the ontological status of a cricket bat is different from the ontological status of the mammal bat. By pointing out the ontological difference, one can speak of the difference in meaning.

However, if we assume that the use of any word implicitly assumes this ontological categorisation, then by pointing out the contexts that are ontologically of two types, one can speak of different uses of terms. What is noteworthy in this analysis is that two uses could be distinguished only by referring to two types of objects or contexts in which we use the term. That is to say, we are giving backdoor entry to the referential theory of meaning in enriching the model of **use theory** of meaning.

It is quite difficult to understand how one can distinguish between primary meaning and secondary meaning without treating meaning as an entity. In our understanding, the use theory of meaning was proposed in the West to do away with precisely this notion of meaning as entity.

Meaning of words is said to be both eternal as well as changing. In *Kāṇḍa* I of *Vākyapadīya*, it is forcefully argued how the meaning of a word is eternally related to its meaning. In explaining tradition and change in tradition, it is shown how interpretation is possible and new uses of words are made possible. This has been repeated in *Kāṇḍa* II as well. Of course, unless there is reasonable stability to the use of words, language would be impossible. Reasonable stability is one thing and eternal relation is another. Stability in use of words is the marker of the maturity of a civilization, but change in the use of words is the indicator of a progressive society. Either the thesis of eternal relation is over statement or dynamism in language is not properly acknowledged in *Vākyapadīya*.

Interpretation of the meaning is inevitable due to the possibility of perceptual error, varied linguistic competence due to training or lack of it, the failure of understanding of the intention of the speaker is due to the varied traditions. Sometimes, unintended meaning accompanies the intended meaning. (*Kāṇḍa* II, 299-301) Unintended meaning cannot be separated from intended meaning and hence communication failure cannot be avoided.

We seem to contradict ourselves at least mildly when we say both: we can make grammatical corrections to sentences and the meaning of the sentence is grasped as a whole. If we are able to understand the sentence without the grammatical corrections, then the sentence communicates what it ought to even if corrections are not made; and if we are not able to understand the sentence without the grammatical correction and we make the sentence intelligible by making the appropriate corrections, then the question of authenticity of meaning would arise. We cannot ensure whether we made the right grammatical correction unless we are the authors of the sentence.

If there is no partial meaning, when we have long sentences with Clauses, the understanding can be hampered totally even if a single word is not familiar to us. This seems to be far from our experience. In a complex sentence, we understand some individual segment perfectly if all the words are familiar to us even if we fail to understand one segment due to lack of familiarity of a word or two. If we say that partial understanding is not complete and correct understanding, that goes without saying. But if partial understanding is no understanding, that would be a different issue. If it is felt that in the sentence 'Touch me not' if someone does not know the significance of the last word 'not', then the understanding is quite faulty and one may do just the opposite of what is being said.

It is said that any understanding of the world is only through language (*Kāṇḍa* I, 123-28) and still it seems that we have erroneous understanding of reality at times and also possible to correct them. It is like saying that the things look blue because we are wearing blue glasses and we can still know the real colour of blue through blue glasses. In other words how language is embedded in understanding of each reality and how at the same time through language we can correct our erroneous understanding of the world is not clear. At least there is circularity of a certain type, if not an unresolvable one.

The term 'context' itself is full of controversies. Even an ostensive context can be vague depending on several factors. It may be vague because the manner in which something is pointed out was not clear. Instead of looking at the thing pointed out, a child may look at the finger against other fingers. And even when one looks at the object pointed out, one may not understand what to look for: the colour, the shape, the craftsmanship, the substratum and so on.[2] The context might include institutional factors which themselves need to be interpreted further. If someone tells you to buy the shares when the market is down, the term 'down' would be relative, and relative to a certain parameters. Moreover, there may be several ways of buying, either through agents or directly by becoming an agent oneself, etc.

Sometimes the intangible thing like the purpose may be part of the context. For instance, who is a customer in a marketplace? One who wants to buy a product or wants to hire service, is a customer. Without the knowledge of the intention of the individual, we cannot consider someone as a customer.

Another difficulty is about the word versus sentences as unit of meaning. We seem to be able to artificially divide a sentence into its words for convenience according to *Vākyapadīya*. What is the basis of such a remark is not clear. Is it natural to us to think that the sentence is the unit of meaning? If so, arguments are not needed and the fact would be obvious. If it is not the case, then we need to give arguments why one should consider sentence as primary as opposed to words. *Vākyapadīya* advances some arguments that we have listed earlier, but those arguments are self-defeating since elsewhere in the same text we find elaborate discussion on word-meaning as if it is natural to words to have meaning. It is so difficult to appreciate the discussion on word-meaning in *Vākyapadīya* if word-meaning is not natural and real. Taking a sentence as the primary unit of meaning must have some philosophical advantages. The advantages of holding the view that sentences are the unit of meaning seem to be

2. Ludwig Wittgenstein, *Philosophical Investigations*, tr. G.E.M. Anscombe, Basil Blackwell, Oxford, 1953, Section-35.

following: Communication can be more precise and pointed in the case of sentences, whereas words can have primary and secondary meaning or can have general meaning and hence imprecise. Another one seems to be action that is related to sentences. Cognisance itself is considered to be a mental act, and in that sense, understanding any sentence would involve act. Similarly, large number of sentences that we utter in our daily activities are linked to acts. Commands, praises, condemnation are all linked to acts directly. (*Kāṇḍa* II, 445-57)

The purpose of uttering a sentence may not be to communicate always. *Vākyapadīya* suggests that if the contrary to the normal use of words is found, then we could consider the contextual parameters including the purpose of the speaker to resolve the issue. The normal assumption is that the speakers want to communicate something. This is the assumption underlying even when we make grammatical corrections to the sentences. *Vākyapadīya* also notes that a *mantra* may have different significance for *ātman*, god and rituals. (*Kāṇḍa* III, 254) Individuals use sentences for varied purposes, some of them could be for self-expressions, some of them may be to cut jokes, some of them may be wishes and so on. Overemphasis on communicative aspect of language by *Vākyapadīya* seems to limit the scope of language unduly.

Vākyapadīya admits that there are intended meanings and there are unintended meanings of sentences. (*Kāṇḍa* II, 299-301) Unintended meanings accompany the intended meaning the way smoke accompanies the fire. That is to say, to the extent unintended meaning accompanies the intended meaning, partial miscommunication is inevitable. If this is theoretical position of *Vākyapadīya*, how are we sure that we know the intention of the other person even if he explicitly states his intention?

When there is the doubt about the intention of the speaker, it is said that the context would resolve the issue of interpretation. It might happen that the issue is resolved for the time being, but it might surface again later. The same sentence can be interpreted and re-interpreted depending on what is considered to be the intention of the speaker. It may also happen that the context includes the intention of other individuals. In an advertising situation, an agent of an insurance company may explain the benefits of holding a policy. On the surface of it, it may seem that the agent is explaining the advantages of holding a policy. On reflection, one may understand the act as serving the interest of the insurance company and not its customers. Without the intention of promoting the interest of the insurance company, an agent would not be a proper agent at all.

We notice at times the realist tendencies in *Vākyapadīya* where it appears as though words and their meanings are real and they have mutual eternal relationship with one another. We notice phenomenological tendencies when we notice that there is no possibility of understanding anything without the use of language, thus modifying our understanding of the reality by language all the time. (*Kāṇḍa* I, 123-28) We also notice, the hermeneutic tendencies strongly stepping in when language itself creates problems of uncertainty, ambiguity. The intentional component on the one hand, and the contextual component on the other, allows the users to have free hand in interpreting the sentences keeping in mind the linguistic tradition. Therefore, it is apt to conclude that *Vākyapadīya* lacks a coherent view even though it is full of insights about meaning and language.

Bibliography

Iyer, K.A. Subramania, *The Vākyapadīya of Bhartṛhari*, Kāṇḍa II, Motilal Banarsidass, 1977.

Varma, Satyakam, *Vākyapadīyam (Brahmakāṇḍa)*, Kāṇḍa I, Munshiram Manoharlal, New Delhi, 1970.

6

Intention and Linguistic Communication

The Bhartṛharian Perspective

Tandra Patnaik

> We cannot discover new truths in philosophy, but we can do something novel by presenting old truths propounded by ancients in modern terminology.
>
> — *Nyāya Mañjarī, Āhnika* 1.8

ALL that is a part of antiquity need not be obsolete. Rather, the present is always enriched by the wisdom of the past. In case of the philosophy of language the venture to delve into the past is more challenging, for the obsession with *śabda* or *vāk* (language) is as old as Indian civilization itself whereas the philosophy of language is of much later origin in the West. Here I take up for discussion the views of one of the oldest philosophers of language, viz., Bhartṛhari. This fifth-century philosopher of language and grammar has long been disregarded as a mere Grammarian. His *magnum opus Vākyapadīya*, as the title indicates, is about sentences and words. Unlike other grammarians, in this work he talks less of the grammar of sentences and words and more of their philosophical dimensions. His major concern is to unfold the semantics and pragmatics of natural language to establish ultimately the metaphysics of Linguistic Monism (*Śabdādvaitavāda*). In this paper, I shall concentrate on his views on the communicative intention aspect of language. My choice of the topic is guided by the fact that it can allow me to take a comparative stock of the ancient and modern ways of handling this debatable issue. In the first part, I shall present Bhartṛhari's views on intention in brief. The second part would be devoted to the development of the notion of intention and speech-act theory by some modern Western philosophers. In the third part I would give an estimate of Bhartṛhari's views on some of the issues raised by the modern theories, and the last part will focus on the relevance of Bhartṛhari's theory of *sphoṭa* as a plausible solution to all the problems associated with the communicative intention theory.

I

Bhartṛhari analyses language from three angles —

(I) *Śabda* (broadly translated it means 'language') as a *tattva* or the metaphysical principle.

(II) *Śabda* as a matter of *loka-vyavahāra*, i.e., as it is used.

(III) *Śabda* as a matter of *śāstra-vyavahāra*, as an object of analytical and grammatical study.

Here, my focus would be on the second dimension, i.e., *loka-vyavahāra*. He uses the term *vyavahāra* very often to mean 'the use of words to communicate one's thought, verbal usage or exchange of ideas'.[1] Thus, it is obvious that, for Bhartṛhari, language is primarily communicative in nature. It is not only an act itself, but also the source of all activities in the world.[2] As an act, it involves the speaker's expression of his intention through the utterance act and the hearer's ability to grasp what is being expressed along with the intention of the speaker.

One of the interesting features of Bhartṛhari's account of

1. K.A.S., Iyer, *The Vākyapadīya of Bhartṛhari*, ch.I., Deccan College, Poona, 1965, *Vṛtti* on I.1; Iyer's notes. Here, he draws support from Helarāja's commentary.

2. Bhartṛhari, *The Vākyapadīya of Bhartṛhari*, Kāṇḍa II, tr. K.A. Subramania Iyer, Motilal Banarsidass, Delhi, 1977, II.399-400. For Language as the source of all human activities, see I.127.

language is his detailed analysis of the elements involved, from the speaker's angle. This approach is somehow different from the general trend of doing philosophy of language in the classical Indian tradition. Language, as a mode of communication can be explicated from two angles — the speaker's and the hearer's. Some of the important schools like Nyāya and Mīmāṁsā prefer the hearer's stand point. But Bhartṛhari prefers the other angle. By this, I do not mean that he was totally oblivious of the hearer's standpoint. He pays attention to this aspect too.

The utterance act, according to Bhartṛhari, involves a network of constitutive factors. From his writings it is clear that he identifies four such factors — (1) sound pattern (*dhvani/nāda*), which is primarily phonetic in nature, (2) form of the words (*vācaka*), which refers to the syntactic pattern of utterance, (3) then meaning (*vācya*), which is the semantic element, and (4) intention of the speaker (*vivakṣā*), the pragmatic element.

1. *Dhvani/nāda* — *Dhvani* occurs due to the presence of our vocal organ. The phonetic element is characterised by accent, pitch, intonation that vary from speaker to speaker.

2. *Vācaka* — It consists of the phonemes and words presented in a particular order. It is that to which the hearer pays attention when the speaker intends to communicate something. Thus, it is the conveyer of meaning. Its role is crucial, as Bhartṛhari points out, 'both the speaker and the hearer have to think of words first before thinking of the meaning'. (1.53)

3. *Vācya* — It is the content of the speech — the meaning. *Vācya* is that which is conveyed and manifested through the *vācaka*. The relationship between the *vācya* and *vācaka* is very intimate, because words have a natural fitness (*yogyatā*) to express the meaning.

4. Intention of the speaker is the fourth constitutive factor. As Bhartṛhari points out 'the uttered level of speech is possible

because the speaker intends to communicate'. (III.1) The relationship between speech and intention is described as *kārya-kāraṇabhāva*, a relationship of cause and effect. Bhartṛhari explains that it is the intention of the speaker which necessitates the use of particular forms of words, so it is the relationship of *kārya* (cause). 'When the speaker seeks to superimpose linguistic forms on to his intended meaning, the language appears to change its nature into something else (meaning) and projects it as sounds from the vocal organ.' (I. 47-48) Thus, when the speaker intends to communicate he uses the expressive word or words (*vācaka*) that are appropriate to the intentions. The intention of the speaker is the cause of the utterance; on the other hand, it is the utterance which arouses in the hearer the need to understand what the speaker intends to say. So there is a relation of cause and effect between the intention of the speaker and the language used for the communication of meaning. Bhartṛhari, while elaborating the principle of the use of meaning (*artha-pravṛtti*), very emphatically expresses the importance of the intention of the speaker. He points out, 'the basis for the expression of a meaning is that, what the speaker intends to communicate, not whether the object-meant has external existence as object or not'. (*vṛtti* on I.13)

It should be noted in this context that Bhartṛhari is the only Indian thinker who systematically explains the role of intention in linguistic communication. Nyāya, Mīmāṁsā and others admit the importance of intention. But it is in connection with the hearers understanding of the import of what the speakers utter. Thus, they talk of *tātparya* as one of the conditions of sentence-meaning which is needed in connection with disambiguation of a certain words. Many interpreters translate *tātparya* as the intention but in the true sense of the term, it means the import of a sentence that has to be deciphered by the hearer based on contextual factors. But, on the other hand, Bhartṛhari uses the term *vivakṣā* to refer to the intention of the speaker. Etymologically, *vivakṣā* means the desire to speak on the part of the speaker, i.e., *vaktur ichhā*. However, it is not just the desire to speak, it also implies the desire to express a particular intention through the act of utterance. It is evident from the following explanatory notes on I.13 — 'Desire to communicate depends upon the existence of suitable words which the desire to communicate brings into the mind of the speaker. It is like applying the right sense-organ when one wants to cognise anything directly'. Thus, it is clear that *vivakṣā* implies the intention of the speaker. Sometimes, he also uses the word *abhisandhi* to mean the speaker's intention.

Once the intention of the speaker is accepted as an integral part of the communicative — act, certain corollaries have to be assumed. Bhartṛhari's interpretation of utterance in terms of *vivakṣā*, thus, leads to the following corollaries:

(a) What the speaker communicates is the 'sense', not the meaning. It is not a case that here is the word, there is the meaning. The sense can only be conveyed by a sentence. Thus, it is the sentence, not the words that should be the primary unit of meaning. We notice that Bhartṛhari propounds a strict form of sentence-holism known as *akhaṇḍa-pakṣa* as opposed to the *khaṇḍa-pakṣa* theory of Mīmāṁsā, which insist on the primacy of word-meaning. For Mīmāṁsā, the meanings of the component words determine the sentence-meaning, whereas for Bhartṛhari word-meaning have no independence, it is always the sense conveyed by the sentence. What the hearer ultimately grasps is the sense of what is being conveyed.

(b) Bhartṛhari's insistence on the primacy of 'sense' expressed through a sentence allows him to explicate variations in the 'force', for the same sentence can be used with different 'force'. The scope for varied interpretation of the sense conveyed becomes possible because of his acknowledgement of the role of the speaker's intention. He clearly states, 'Meaning of words seem to be created by the intention of the speaker'. (III, 4.570)

(c) Not only does the speaker express his intention but he also has a desire to 'secure an uptake'. Sometimes he can do this with metaphorical use, sometimes by maintaining a gap between 'what is said' and 'what is meant'.

Thus the ultimate thesis regarding the workings of natural language, according to Bhartṛhari can be summed up as follows: Speaking language is indulging in a communicative act by which the speaker not only expresses what he intends to say, but also secures an uptake from the hearer through the hearer's recognition of what the speaker intends to communicate.

II

In the backdrop of this ancient theory of communication-intention, let us have cursory look at the modern theories expounded by Grice, Austin, Searle and Kent Bach.

How the structure of language represents the world has been the major concern of the philosophers of language for quite a long time. The major thrust of such theories are the discovery of the structural rules of language in terms of which any significant utterance could be judged as true or false. In their case, thus, statements are regarded as the paradigmatic use of language. We all know how the scenario changed with later Wittgenstein's dictum, 'Don't ask for the meaning, ask for the use.' But it is Grice, who in his small paper entitled 'Meaning'[3] brings to our notice the depth of the communicative role of meaning. Meaning by an utterance, according

3. H.P., Grice, 'Meaning', *Philosophical Review*, LXVI, 1957.

to him, is as good as somebody intending to produce an effect on the hearer. Moreover, for him, there cannot be a language *simple citer*, there must be a speaker claiming to utter it. On the other hand, Austin[4] successfully drew our attention to the fact that language is not only meant for communication, it also is a network of acts — locutionary, illocutionary and perlocutionary. However, unlike Wittgenstein, he does not conflate meaning to use. Rather, he very carefully maintains a distinction between the 'meaning' and 'force', which largely determines how the utterance is used. Suppose, for example, a person of a locality says to a stranger 'This is not a good place' — here the speaker is not only making statement about the place (locutionary act/meaning), but also warning one about the dangers involved (illocutionary act/force), and he wants to 'secure an uptake' from the hearer, i.e., he should leave the place (perlocutionary act). However, the problem with Austin is, he not only segregates 'meaning' from 'force' but explicates 'force' in terms of institutionalised conventions. 'Force' is not exactly the 'intention' as we understand the term today. Strawson[5] very rightly points out this weakness in Austin's theory. He argues that in most cases illocutionary acts succeed not by conformity to conventions, but by recognition of the intention. Intention plays a very important role in the three levels of speech-act. In saying 'This is not a good place' the utterer intends to warn the stranger and also wishes that the hearer recognises his intention that the speaker wants him to leave the place. In this case, the utterer does not have to say 'I warn that this is not a good place'. What is being conveyed is more than what is being said. Understanding of an utterrance is not just decoding it, nor is meaningful utterance is a matter of encoding by the speaker. The other weakness in Grice's as well as in Austin's theory is a total neglect of the hearer's role. No theory of communication-intention can be successful without the explication of how the hearer understands not only what is being said, but also what the hearer

4. J.L., Austin, *How to Do Things with Words*, Oxford University Press, London, 1962.

5. P.F., Strawson, 'Intention and convention in Speech-acts', *Philosophical Review*, LXXIII, 1964, pp. 439-66.

intends. Searle's[6] account of speech-acts is more explicit about the hearer's role. But like Austin he, too, proposes to express illocutionary acts in terms of the constitutive rules (conventions) for using 'force-indicating' devices, such as performative verbs and sentential moods. However, the same sorts of illocutionary acts can be performed without such devices. One need not use to the performative, as in 'I demand, you be quiet' or the imperative mood 'Be quiet'. Kent Bach rightly observes that a theory, which relies on rules for using such devices, is not equipped to explain illocutionary forces of utterances, lacking such devices. No such difficulty arises for a theory according to which most illocutionary acts are performed not with an intention to conform to convention but with a communicative intention.

Kent Bach[7] while developing the theory of communicative intention in speech-acts brings to our notice some of the peculiarities associated with natural language like the presence of ambiguous words and context sensitive expressions like indexicals. But important are the following peculiarities

(I) indirect speech-act, wherein we perform speech-acts by way of performing another;

(II) non-literal speech-act, where the sense communicated largely depends on the type of words used;

(III) implicit speech-act wherein it is not spelt out what is meant.

In case of indirection, single utterance is the performance of one illocutionary act by way of performing another illocutionary act. For example, 'I am thirsty', although it has the force of a statement, may actually be a form of request to give a glass of water. In case of non-literal speech-acts we do not mean what the words state. In such cases, illocutionary forces cannot be predicated just from the meaning of words. Here, he mostly refers to the figurative use of language.

6. J., Searle, *Speech-Acts: An Essay in Philosophy of Language*, Cambridge University Press, Cambridge, 1969.

7. Kent Bach, 'Conversational Implicature', *Mind and Language*, 1994, 9: 124-62.

Sometimes it can be both indirect and non-literal, like 'I love the sound of your voice'. Here the speaker tells non-literally that she cannot stand the sound of his voice but thereby also implies that he should stop singing. Implicit speech-acts are those where the words used do not express the full meaning. But are either in need of expansion or in need of completion. For example, if one's spouse says 'I will be home later' it actually means she will be home late that night. Here the sentence needs expansion by way of adding the word 'tonight'. In other cases, such as 'Jack is ready and Jill is late', the sentence does not express a complete proposition; for it does not express completely what is that for which Jack is claimed to be ready and Jill is late. In such cases what one means is the completion of what one says.

According Bach

> Non-literality and indirection are two main ways in which the semantic content of a sentence can fail to determine the full force and content of the illocutionary act being performed in using the sentence.[8]

The problem of indirection has been covered by Grice[9] in connection with what he called 'conversational implicature'.

However, there can be cases of implicit speech-acts, which can be explained only in terms of completion and expansion. Bach calls them 'Impliciture'. In such cases, a part of what is meant is communicated not explicitly but implicitly.

Both, in case of the 'implicature' as well as the 'impliciture' there is a tendency to go beyond what is explicitly stated, but this is done in two different ways:

> An implicature is completely separate from what is said and inferred from it (more precisely, from saying if it). What is said is one proposition and what is communicated in

---

8. Kent Bach, 'Speech-Acts' *Routledge Encyclopedia of Philosophy.*

9. H.P., Grice, *Studies in the Way of Words*, Harvard University Press, Cambridge, Mass., 1989.

> addition to that is a conceptually independent proposition, a proposition with perhaps no constituents in common with what is said. In contrast, implicitures are built up from the explicit content of the utterance by conceptual strengthening . . . which yields what would have been made fully explicit if the appropriate lexical material had been included in the utterance.[10]

Implicatures are *implied* by what is being said; whereas implicitures are *implicit* in what is said.

III

Let us now make an assessment of how Bhartṛhari would have handled such cases of communication acts where there is a gap between, what is 'said', and what is 'communicated'. It seems obvious from the detailed study of his *Vākyapadīya* that he was aware of the possibilities of, both, the 'implied meaning' and the 'implicit meaning'. He very clearly states, 'sometimes what is said is not what is meant' (I.136). Supposing, for example, when a fellow traveller says to his companion, 'we must go and look at the sun', the meaning conveyed by the speaker is not that of looking at the sun, but the hearer must realise how late it is in the day. (II.327) In the above example, the implied meaning is 'it is getting late, we must hurry up'. Thus, the implied meaning is conceptually independent of what is said by the speaker. He also exemplifies the cases where the speech-act is both indirect and non-literal. He points out,

> From a sentence, the chief meaning of which are praise or blame, a different meaning is to be understood than the one obtained from the individual words. (II.247)

These are the cases of ironic statements, where what is meant is a condemnation; and what is said is of the nature of a praise. Thus, Bhartṛhari is very much aware of what Bach and Grice call 'implicature'.

---

10. Kent Bach, 'Conversational Implicature', *Mind and Language*, 1994.

Now coming to the problem of 'impliciture' we notice that Bach includes two categories of semantically under-determinate expressions under this class. One of them refers to the syntactic incompleteness and the other to the semantic incompleteness. The former needs 'completion' and the latter needs semantic 'enrichment'. Again, we notice that Bhartṛhari is very much aware of such peculiarities of the natural language and they find a place in his discussion. However, I would like to take up the question of semantic completeness first. The other issue, that of syntactic completeness, is a matter of serious debate in Indian philosophy of language. Therefore, it needs a little more deliberation. Let us look at the following example. A boy is told 'save the butter from the crows'. Here the word 'crow' needs expansion; thus the word 'crows' includes any destructive agent in general, who may spoil the butter. So, Bhartṛhari elaborates,

> when a boy is told: 'save the butter from the crows'; he does not refrain from protecting it from dogs, etc., knowing that the order refers to the destructive agents in general. (II. 312)

It is a case where the intended meaning is not independent of what is stated but is implicitly present. An averagely intelligent hearer is supposed to grasp the implicit meaning.

Coming to the question of syntactic incompleteness we must notice that the issue gets considerable attention in Indian Philosophy of Language. The Indian version of this phenomenon is known as *ākāṅkṣā*. Very broadly, the term can be translated as 'mutual expectancy' or 'mutual interdependence' of the constituents of a sentence. Mīmāṁsā and Nyāya uphold the *khaṇḍa-pakṣa* theory as opposed to Bhartṛhari's *akhaṇḍa-pakṣa* (sentence-holism) theory. According to the former, word-meanings are autonomous; thus a concatenation of word-meanings ultimately build up the sentence-meaning. So according to Nyāya and Mīmāṁsā, the constituent word-meanings must be mutually interdependent. In other words, the syntactic completeness is a condition of the sentence-meaning. This in fact is ingrained in the very definition of a sentence. Jaimini, in his *Mīmāṁsā Sūtra*, defines a sentence (*vākya*) in the following way: 'a group of words serving a single purpose forms a sentence when on analysis words are found to have mutually expectancy'. (II.1.46) This definition, actually, contains two conditions — (I) it must serve a single purpose; and (II) on analysis the constituent words are found to be in need of one another. The second condition is known as *ākāṅkṣā*. Both Mīmāṁsā and Nyāya insist on the fulfilment of the condition of *ākāṅkṣā* in any case of sentence-meaning. *ākāṅkṣā*, implies the need for syntactic completeness. The hearer, in order to grasp the meaning conveyed to him, expects the sentence to be syntactically complete. But Bhartṛhari would beg to differ with Mīmāṁsā and Nyāya on this count. For him, what is important in the conveyance of meaning through a sentence is the singleness of purpose. Bhartṛhari follows Patañjali's definition of a sentence. According to him unity of purpose of meaning (*ekārthībhāva*) and mutual interconnectedness (*vyāpekṣa*) are mutually exclusive. Acceptance of mutual interconnectedness of words would mean that words are supposed to retain their individual meanings in a sentence. This may lead to certain problems. Therefore, the unity of the purpose should be the only criterion of sentence-meaning. Bhartṛhari's *akhaṇḍa-pakṣa* theory is a logical development of Patañjali's notion of *ekārthībhāva*. So Bhartṛhari insists on the completeness of the 'sense' conveyed, not the syntactic completeness. Thus, even a single word like, 'door' can be said to communicate a complete sense to the hearer. If it is winter, the intended meaning is 'close the door', and if it is summer the intended meaning is 'open the door'. (II. 430) For him though syntax is very important in linguistic communication we do not always strictly stick to the rules of syntax. So, it is the speaker who decides how to present the facts.

> With whatever use a meaning/object-meant is sought to be conveyed by the speaker, the meaning is established like that (in that context), because meaning has several capacities. (II. 314)

Again, Bhartṛhari says,

> where there is a bare statement of fact and its implications are understood from its expressive power (*śruteḥ*) without the use of words to express them, then also the sentence is complete. (II. 446)

Bhartṛhari's position seems to be one-sided. Is he not over-emphasising the role of the speaker at the cost of the hearer? After all, linguistic communication is a matter of co-ordination between the speaker and the hearer. Without some such conditions of deciphering what actually is intended by the speaker, language cannot serve as an adequate means of communication. But, Bhartṛhari spells out in detail the contextual factors which help the hearer to understand the implicit as well as the implied meaning. He says, 'the meaning of words are determined according to sentence, situation, purpose, propriety, place and time, and not according to mere external forms'. Śaṅkuka in his *Bṛhaddevatā*, originally gave this list of contextual conditions. Bhartṛhari, however, gives another extended list of twelve conditions which covers a wide range of contexts. It should be noted here, that, it is Bhartṛhari who is quoted by others while explaining the importance of contextual factors in understanding the import of a sentence.

But the question that can be raised is, even if contextual factors play a role, what exactly is the process through which the hearer understands the implicit meaning (especially, syntactically incomplete sentences)? Bach suggests,

> completion and expansion are both the processes whereby the hearer supplies the missing portions of what is otherwise being expressed explicitly. With completion a propositional radical is filled in, and with expansion a complete but a skeletal proposition is fleshed out.[11]

Here the process is nothing more than the process of inference, whereby the hearer mentally computes the missing semantical and syntactical elements. Mīmāṁsā also holds a similar position. This

11. Kent Bach,'Conversational Implicature', *Mind and Language*, 1994.

process of inference is called *śrutārthapatti*. But Bhartṛhari rejects this proposal by arguing,

> whatever meaning is understood, whenever certain word is uttered, that meaning belongs to that word (and to that word only). There is not more correct definition of meaning than this. (II. 333)

In other words, Bhartṛhari insists on hearer's understanding of the meaning, only on the basis of what is being said. Kent Bach, also realises that mental computation of missing lexical constituents is not the solution to the problem of 'implicatures'. Therefore, he admits that 'what is said' forms the basis of what is understood by the hearer. It is, 'what is said', that provides a default value for the hearer's understanding. However, Bhartṛhari's solution is different. He would say that there is no question of inference. The hearer always 'grasps' the meaning instantaneously. However, how does the hearer know, how and when a word is used, with what meaning? Bhartṛhari's answer would be —

> Human reasoning is the power of words. . . . It is the word which is the instructor. Speakers follow the power of words and act when urged by a desire to speak based on the availability of the right word. When the hearer follows the fixed power of words to understand a meaning through reasoning, based on meaning, context, indication, interconnection, etc., people look upon the capacity of words as the reasoning of the hearer. (I.137)

The above lines are very crucial, as they expose the crux of Bhartṛhari's philosophy of language. To understand the full implications of this remark we have to keep in mind the basic tenets of his philosophy of language.

(i) For Bhartṛhari the nature of linguistic communicability cannot be adequately explained if we just confine ourselves to the level of utterance only. It will be too simplistic to say that the meaning is conveyed because the speaker utters syntactically a perfect string of words; because the hearer follows the same rule of syntax, he will understand the meaning just by listening to the utterances. For Bhartṛhari, utterance level is just a part of the *linguistic expressibility*. It points to a deeper level, i.e., the level of thought.

(ii) The level of thought, according to Bhartṛhari, is word-determined. No thought, no consciousness, no cognition is possible without being intertwined with the word. In other words, man is a 'languaging being'. As a conscious being, he is endowed with the linguistic potency (*śabda-bhāvanā*). In case of the speaker, it is this potency, which urges him to express his thought by means of the utterances, in case of the hearer, it is this linguistic potency that allows him to understand the sense expressed intuitively. The hearer's ability to intuit the meaning, i.e., *pratibhā* is, in a sense, another name for the *śabdha-bhāvanā*. (I.122)

(iii) Bhartṛhari, while analysing the semantics and pragmatics of natural language has made it absolutely clear that it can be very flexible. There is always a possibility of a gap between what is 'said' and what is 'meant'. Thus the problem of explaining how does the speaker transfer the meaning to the hearer is very crucial. Definitely transference of meaning is not like loading the contents of a car into another. Nor is the process clearly determined by the rules of syntax. For Bhartṛhari, it is always the 'sense', which is communicated, not the isolated meanings of the constituent words that the speaker uses. So there has to be a common ground for the transmission of the sense. Bhartṛhari locates it in the concept of *śabda* or *sphoṭa*. Of course, *sphoṭa* has been seen by many philosophers as a mysterious entity. However, a dispassionate analysis can help us to realise that there is nothing mysterious about it. *Sphoṭa*, etymologically speaking, is derived from the word *sphuṭ*, which means bursting forth. Following Nāgeśa Bhaṭṭa, we can interpret it as that, from which meaning bursts forth or the principle which is

> expressible through utterances. It is the indivisible unit of meaning which is connected with the verbal dispositional ability of the speaker, as well as the hearer. It is indivisible, because before the utterances are made, all the distinction between the form of words and meaning remain in unmanifested and in indivisible form. In case of the hearer, it is this unit of meaning which is referred to when the utterances are heard as distinguished from the meaning. Besides, the utterances are uttered and also heard sequentially, syllable by syllable. Once a syllable is uttered, it is replaced by another. (This is another peculiarity of linguistic communication, to which Western Philosophers, virtually, pay no attention.) The hearer does not compute the series of syllables and infer the meaning. Thus, for the communication of a unitary 'sense' an undifferentiated, sequenceless principle is assumed. This is *sphoṭa* or *śabda*. So for Bhartṛhari linguistic communicability is to be understood in terms of *sphoṭa/śabda* (i.e., the non-differentiated language-principle) and *śabda-bhāvanā* (the linguistic potency). These two principles help him to sort out the problem of the communication of the implied, implicit, as well as, the explicit meaning. So, when Bhartṛhari says, 'it is the **word** which is the instructor' — the term **word** should be understood as *śabda* or *sphoṭa*. This is the very basis of the human power of using language for communication.

One may find Bhartṛhari's notions of *sphoṭa, śabda* or *śabda-bhāvanā* unacceptable. But the problem, how communication succeeds, continues to remain unsolved. Kent Bach waives off the problem by saying, that 'to describe the general character of communication is not to explain how it succeeds'. But can we close our eyes to this issue? The speech-act theorists, and very broadly speaking the communication — intention theorists, in their process of highlighting on the speech-acts (also speaker's intention), pay scanty attention to the hearer's role. When it comes to the hearer's understanding, they work with the basic idea that

> communication essentially involves an audience — directed reflexive intention, so that whether or not the utterance can plausibly be taken at face-value, the hearer must rely on the presupposition that the speaker intends what he is communicating to be recognised (partly on the basis of that intention).[12]

Thus, communication is a kind of 'co-ordination-game'. But can such a game be played without locating a basic co-ordinating principle? This remains unexplored as far as speech act/communication-intention theorists are concerned.

12. Kent Bach, 'Conversational Implicature', *Mind and Language*, 1994.

7

Śābdabodha and the Epistemic Primacy of Sense

An Exercise in Comparative Philosophy of Language

Amitabha Dasgupta

The idea of a comparative framework

THE concept of sense or *sinn* is a Western concept introduced by Frege. Its importance in the analytic tradition of philosophy of language is undeniable. However, the conceptual significance of sense is neither confined only to Western philosophical tradition nor can it be said to be intrinsic to Frege's philosophy of language only. The thematic content that is represented by the expression and the theoretical significance that is associated with it is universal in its scope. The same idea of sense may be found in other systems of philosophy of language. It does not matter in what form or in mode it exists. The important fact is the thesis that it signifies, namely, the knowledge of sense constitutes the knowledge of reference. The universal applicability of this thesis is not thus restricted either to any single author or to a tradition.

Considering the universal applicability of sense, the main objective of the present paper is to explore the primary role that the expression 'sense' plays in the Nyāya philosophy of language. In this respect, it is important to spell out here the approach adopted in this paper.

First, the conceptual background. Certainly, Frege's notion of 'sense' forms the starting point of our discussion since it provides the general perspective on sense. It is through the discussion on Frege's stand on sense that we have tried to establish the importance of sense in the study of meaning. But this Fregean perspective emphasising on the primacy of sense in semantics has been seriously challenged in the contemporary time. The post-Fregean critique of sense replaces the primacy of sense by the primacy of reference. The Fregean doctrine of sense and the critique of it thus together form the conceptual background of this paper.

In the light of this conceptual background, the Nyāya doctrine of sense has been approached. The Nyāya doctrine of *śābdabodha* offers a different framework of understanding in terms of which the primacy of sense can be established. In this respect, our main thrust lies on the epistemic priority of sense. Accordingly, the main focus of the paper is to show how the concept of sense is posited in Nyāya as the part of its epistemological concern. The significance of sense derives its entire justification from its epistemic counterpart. This constitutes the epistemological foundation of sense.

The primary thrust of Frege's notion of 'sense' is also epistemic. But, Frege did not provide an adequate epistemological foundation to sense. It is due to this lack of proper foundation, Frege's doctrine of sense becomes more like a heuristic device designed to pick-out the referent correctly. This approach thus deviates from its original epistemological thrust which is meant to give an account of what constitutes the understanding of the meaning of a sentence. As a result, the emphasis of the theory is solely directed to the idea of reference-fixing. The post-Fregean critique of sense was developed along with this line and thus its major focus of attack was to point out the failure of sense in determining the reference. All of Kripke's and Putnam's counter examples are construed with a view to show how Frege's model of sense failed in capturing the correct reference.

The post-Fregean critique of sense is, indeed, based on a lop-sided interpretation of Frege's thought. Of course, for this, Frege himself should be partially blamed. His formulation that sense determines reference becomes a principal source for equating sense with reference-fixing. A distinction must be made between the knowledge of sense and reference-fixing. Frege is primarily concerned with the knowledge of sense and not with reference-fixing. The latter is one of the characteristics of sense and is certainly not the principal one. Sense has a multi-faceted nature. As Michel Dummett[1] pointed out, Frege's 'sense' is a composite notion with having many characteristics of its own. These characteristics are: First, it is the mode of presentation, second, it is one which is grasped in thought, third, it determines reference where reference is taken to be the function of sense, fourth, it fixes reference, *ala* Kripke, fifth, it is the object of oblique discourse. From this, it is evident that reference-fixing cannot be made to be the primary function of sense nor can it be made equal to sense. As pointed out earlier, Frege's failure was that he could not provide a strong epistemological foundation for sense that could prevent it from such deviant interpretation.

In view of this uncertainty over the primacy of sense, when we look at the doctrine of *śābdabodha* of Nyāya, we find the presence of a rigorously worked out epistemological model defending the primacy of sense. It is a model which clearly articulates the relationship existing between the meaning of a word and the object meant.

In this connection a question may be most pertinently raised regarding whether there is a separate place kept for sense in Nyāya theory of meaning. The point that is raised is that the Nyāya theory of meaning is purely referential where words directly refer to objects and a sentence refers to a complex relational object. Accordingly, understanding a sentence is nothing other than knowing the object. This theory thus allows the possibility of reference without the mediation of sense. This is how the notion of sense is ruled out in the theory of meaning proposed in Nyāya. In view of this, how do we respond to this objection? The present paper offers a different interpretation which allows a distinction between sense and

1. M. Dummett, *Frege: Philosophy of Language*, Duckworth, London, 1973.

reference in Nyāya theory of meaning. A separate place for sense may be thus construed within its semantic formulation. In this respect, the present paper mostly depends on the interpretation offered by Bimal Krishna Matilal,[2] J.L.Shaw,[3] Sibajiban Bhattacharya[4] and others. For the following reasons the model of *śābdabodha* may be said to be keeping a separate place for sense. First, it can be asserted that the notion of meaning conceived in Nyāya may be identified as being identical with the content of *śābdabodha*. The content of *śābdabodha* qualifies to be what may be called the 'sense' of a linguistic expression because it is the one which is grasped in thought. Second, the element that strongly suggests the presence of sense in the model of *śābdabodha* is the notion of *avacchedaka* or limitor. It is the property that constitutes the reason for the application of the expression. To put it in the Fregean terminology, it picks out the object for the hearer. Third, the mode of presentation, which is one of the chief characteristics of Frege's theory of sense, can be equally found in the Nyāya theory of proper name. On these three basic grounds it may be argued that there is a distinct concept of sense found in the semantic tradition of Nyāya. However, it should be kept in mind that this interpretation may not be acceptable

2. B. K. Matilal, *Epistemology, Logic and Grammar in Indian Philosophical Analysis*, Mouton Co, The Hague, 1971; 'Awareness and Meaning in Navya-Nyāya' in B.K. Matilal and J.L. Shaw (ed.), *Analytical Philosophy in Contemporary Perspective*, D. Reidel Publishing Co, Holland, 1986; 'The Context Principle and Some Indian Controversies over Meaning' (with P.K. Sen), *Mind*, January, 1988; *The Word and the World*, Oxford University Press, New Delhi, 1990.

3. J.L. Shaw, 'The Nyāya on Existence, Knowability and Nameability', *Journal of Indian Philosophy*, 1978; 'The Nyāya on Cognition and Negation', *Journal of Indian Philosophy*, 1980; 'Proper Names: Contemporary Philosophy and the Nyāya', in *Analytical Philosophy in Contemporary Perspective*; 'Professor Mohanty on Meaning and Transformation in Indian Philosophy', in Daya Krishna and K.L. Sharma (ed.), *The Philosophy of J.N.Mohanty*, ICPR Series, Munshiram Manoharlal Publishers, New Delhi, 1991.

4. S. Bhattacharya, *Gadādhara's Theory of Objectivity* in two volumes Indian Council of Philosophical Research in association with Motilal Banarsidass, Delhi, 1990.

to all. J.N. Mohanty, for example, argues that in Nyāya no distinction is made between sense and reference since it upholds only theory of reference. Mohanty[5] is particularly critical of the interpretation offered by Matilal and Shaw. However, in spite of his critical attitude towards constructing a theory of sense in Nyāya he accepts the possibility of alternative interpretation of *śābdabodha*. Beside this liberal attitude expressed by Mohanty, there is also a difference between his perspective and that of the present paper. Mohanty's main concern is to find out whether there is a place for Fregean sense in Indian theories of semantics. We, on the other hand, do not share the same concern with him. Our inquiry starts by accepting that there is a place for sense in Nyāya theory of meaning. On the basis of this, we argue for the following theses. First, to interpret *śābdabodha* in such a way that the notion of 'sense' can be shown to be constitutive of it. Second, to argue that the Nyāya concept of sense must be understood within the epistemological model of Nyāya, and third, to give an account of how according to Nyāya reference-failure occurs. It is evident from this that the thrust of this paper is not to search for whether there is a presence of Fregean sense in Nyāya or not. In the context of this paper, the discussion on Frege's theory of sense and the critique of it must be seen as serving a methodological purpose. The purpose that it serves is that it provides the conceptual background of the inquiry.

There is one more point to be clarified. Our presentation of the Nyāya standpoint assumes that there is uniformity in terms of its approach to meaning. But as we know, that there are differences found within the Nyāya standpoint. We may particularly mention here Raghunāth Śiromaṇi's view on *avacchedaka* and proper name. His view on proper name may be viewed in the same line as that of the view propounded by Kripke. This implies going against the primacy of sense. Raghunāth's view has its limitation. However, the present paper is not interested to go into all these controversies.

5. J. Mohanty, 'Indian Theories of Truth: Thoughts on their Common Framework'; 'Language and meaning' in *Reason and Tradition in Indian thought*, Clrendon Press, Oxford, 1992. 'Recollections and Response', in *The Philosophy of J.N. Mohanty.*

Its major concern is to show how the primacy of sense can be more effectively defended through the model of *śābdabodha.*

In the above, I have described the idea of a comparative framework as used in this inquiry. It is obvious that this study is not interested to make a comparison between Frege and Nyāya. On the other hand, it is in the light of the analytic philosophers' perspective on sense the model of *śābdabodha* has been construed with a purpose to show that it offers an alternative account of sense based on certain primary epistemological consideration. In view of this stated objective, the paper will have three sections. The first section will present the Fregean standpoint of sense and the contemporary critique of it. This will form the conceptual background of the paper. Accordingly, the second section will be devoted in explaining the Nyāya doctrine of sense with an explicit aim to establish the epistemic primacy of sense. The third section will give a brief account of how reference failure is explained in Nyāya.

I

Forming the background issues: Frege's doctrine of sense

This discussion will mainly address to the three following questions: what is sense? What is its significance in the context of understanding a language? And finally, How is it justified? The sense of a sentence is understood by a competent speaker-hearer without knowing who said the sentence — where, when and why — which amounts to saying that language to a large extent speaks for itself. Due to this conception of sense, Frege believes that an adequate semantic theory must address itself to this fact. Accordingly, for Frege, the purpose of language does not consist in merely sending message from one person to another, but, on the other hand, to explain how these messages are understood without taking into account of contextual clues like where, when and how these messages are sent. This clearly points out that, for Frege, language essentially expresses thought and thus it cannot be conceived as merely a matter of communication. Of course, he did not deny the communicative role of language but he considered it as only secondary.

Further, while characterising the nature of sense, Frege carefully distinguishes, sense both from ideas like mental images and physical objects. Sense may be characterised as objective on the ground that the same sense can be shared by many people. It is thus objective due to its property of shareability in contrast to ideas or images which lack this property. But at the same time it cannot be situated in space and time because it does not have the character of a physical object. However, it is not a fictitious entity because it has an ontological status. It can be grasped by human beings by competent speakers who use language to express thoughts.

Our next question is: How does Frege justify sense? What are the linguistic compulsions due to which acceptance of sense becomes necessary? On this, Frege has given number of arguments which can be classified broadly under four heads.

The first argument that prominently comes in this respect is Frege's argument explaining how to correctly analyse certain identity statements which contain cognitive value, i.e., which are informative in nature. To give Frege's well-known example, the difference between the two statements, such as, $a = a$ and $a = b$ (where $a = b$ is true) cannot be explained unless we admit that a and b have different sense. Though both are identity statements the second statement conveys a kind of information which the first one doesn't. They differ in cognitive status because the first statement is uninformative whereas the second statement may contain information regarding important empirical discovery, such as, 'the morning star is the evening star'. According to Frege, the only way to analyse the statement $a = b$ will be to take into account of the role that the sign a and b play. It will be wrong if we take that the sign a differs from the sign b only as an object. This may be called objectual self-identity statement in which the cognitive significance of $a = a$ and $a = b$ will be same. The correct way to approach this statement will be to see them as linguistic signs and the way (or the manner as Frege says) in which they designate objects. This approach reveals that there is a fundamental difference between these two types of identity statements where $a = a$ is an analytic statement and $a = b$ is a synthetic statement which may not be necessarily justified in an *a priori* manner. The basis of the synthetic nature of the statement lies on the crucial fact that though in the statement $a = b$, the sign a and the sign b have the same referent they nevertheless differ in terms of their sense.

Through the analysis of identity statement, Frege introduced his celebrated distinction between sense and reference. The knowledge or sense tells us how to apply the term to an object. This is known as the condition of applicability. Sense gives us the condition of applicability. In other words, what Frege says: Sense determines reference. In Frege's theory, between the two, thus, sense becomes primary and reference is made subservient to it. The reason is that reference does not form a part of meaning. It is only the consequence of meaning. On the basis of this consideration, Frege claims that the same sense/reference distinction holds with other aspects of language like proper names, complex expressions, sentences, indirect speech act, etc. Hence, some of the important Fregean arguments regarding the primacy of sense can be seen in the light of his analysis of some of these above-mentioned items

We now thus come to the analysis of proper name which constitutes Frege's second most important argument for the primacy of sense. According to Frege, proper name has both sense and reference. But why to accept that proper name has a sense? Frege's answer is that in order to identify the referent of a proper name we need to accept the sense of a proper name. Take Frege's example of the term 'Aristotle'. This is a context where the referent of the term cannot be presented to us. The only way we can refer to him is with the help of certain identifying descriptions, such as, 'the teacher of Alexander the Great'. It is always possible that there may be parallel descriptions used by different people to identify Aristotle. In this way, as Frege observes, the criterion of identity may vary depending on the description to be used by different people. But, suppose if the referent of a proper name is present before us, do we still require an identifying description? Frege's response to this question is affirmative. He insists on identifying descriptions because without them we cannot distinguish referents of different proper names.

Recall, Frege's earlier example of identity statement $a = b$. The only way that we can distinguish the referents of a and b will be on the basis of identifying descriptions. They may be viewed as criteria for identity. The sense of a proper name as expressed through the definite description constitutes the criterion of a proper name. The Fregean formulation thus holds that to know the sense of a proper name implies acquiring the ability to identify the referent of it.

Frege's third argument on the primacy of sense is based on the consideration that the meaning of a proper name cannot be identified with its referent. His aim is to show the independent nature of sense. Based on this he tries to establish the sentences having meaning even though they do not have reference. In this respect, the two examples that Frege gave may be specially mentioned. Consider the two following expressions: 'The heavenly body which has the greatest distance from earth' and 'The series with the least convergence'. In the first example, it is not clear whether there is any fixed referent, whereas, in the second example, the expression does not have any referent. Frege argues that though these expressions do not refer to any object. We understand them as meaningful. That means, we have to grant that these expressions have senses and by virtue of it they become meaningful. Failure to do it will imply that they are meaningless. On the basis of this, Frege concludes that the meaning of a proper name must be distinguished from its referent so that the former will not be equated with the latter.

The fourth argument for the primacy of sense that Frege offers is based on his analysis of indirect discourse. According to Frege, the context of indirect discourse is a situation involving what is described by him as signs of signs. It means that in indirect speech one talks about the sense of another person's remark. It is due to this words do not have their customary reference and instead designate what is usually their sense. This shows that in indirect speech words have indirect reference. The Fregean explanation of indirect discourse is same as that of the earlier one. In the earlier context, Frege argues that the meaning of an expression which does not have reference cannot be explained unless we grant that the expression has sense.

On the same consideration, here too, Frege argues that the meaning of an indirect discourse in which a proper name occurs cannot be explained unless we grant that it has a sense which constitutes the referent in this context. Frege's attempt is to show how sentences occurring in oblique context can be regarded as meaningful in the light of his analysis. Then, consider his sentence: 'Copernicus believes that the heavenly body which has the greatest distance from the earth is round'. In Frege's analysis, the subordinate clause in the sentence has a referent which is a sense and not a truth-value.

Finally, all these arguments for the primacy of sense lead to the suggestion that there is a separate place for the knowledge of sense which constitutes the part of speakers' knowledge of language. Frege's thesis on the knowledge of sense makes it evident that it is central to the understanding of language. Frege asks: How could a speaker be able to associate a word with its referent? He argues that it cannot be based on mere association. There must be, on the other hand, some mechanism working due to which such an association is possible. In Frege's submission, the knowledge of this mechanism constitutes the speaker's grasp of the sense of the word. In Frege's formulation, understanding of language thus consists in having knowledge of sense. Accordingly, understanding of reference becomes a consequence of the speaker's understanding of sense. This is how the knowledge of sense becomes the pre-condition for understanding a language.

As a corollary to this it must be pointed out the special nature of this knowledge. It is a knowledge which is mentally represented. For a speaker to have a knowledge of the sense of a term implies having a mental representation of the necessary and sufficient conditions for its application. This, in other words, is to give a mentalistic account of the knowledge of sense as possessed by the competent speaker of a language. With this discussion, we now come to the post-Fregean critique of sense — a critique that has been developed in the contemporary time emphasising the primary role that reference plays in language.

The post-Fregean critique of sense: towards the primacy of reference

The post-Fregean critique of sense has been developed by the contemporary philosophers notably among them are Putnam and Kripke. It is an approach which seeks to show that the picture that Frege has offered about language in terms of sense-reference distinction is too simplistic, inadequate and even erroneous in certain vital aspects. His account is questionable regarding referential mechanism operative in natural language. The post-Fregean critique's attempt is two fold. First, as a, critique, it tries to show that Frege's idea of the primacy of sense is untenable. His basic thesis that the sense of a term includes its condition of applicability has a limited significance. In most cases, we refer to objects without the help of Fregean sense. This has been established on the basis of counter examples refuting the claim that sense determines reference. The second is the constructive thesis which leads to the development of a new theory of reference. The post-Fregean critique thus offers an alternative model arguing for the primacy of reference instead of sense. In the context of the present paper which seeks to argue for the primacy of sense the discussion on the post-Fregean critique of sense has undeniable significance. It is through this discussion we can see that the Fregean doctrine on the primacy of sense does not seem to have a strong foundation. Our presentation of the post-Fregean critique will be brief. We will do it essentially in terms of the two sets of counter examples to Frege's thesis that Putnam and Kripke offered respectively.

Putnam's counter example: the twin earth argument

In the context of this enquiry the significance of the 'Twin Earth' argument[6] is to show that sense does not determine reference. The two speakers may have the same knowledge of sense but its reference may differ. Suppose there is a planet which is exactly like Earth

6. H. Putnam, 'The Meaning of Meaning' in *Mind, Language and Reality*, Philosophical papers, vol. 2, Cambridge University Press, Cambridge, 1981.

except it differs in some minor respect. Putnam calls this planet 'Twin Earth'. Earth and Twin Earth are not only physically alike but they are also alike in terms of their inhabitants. Thus, a speaker in Earth has a counterpart whose mental structure is same as that of the speaker in Twin Earth. On the basis of this supposition, Putnam then describes a situation through which he shows what is wrong with Frege's approach to sense. To put it in nutshell, in Twin Earth, there is a liquid substance which though has the same phenomenological features as that of water differs from water in respect of its chemical structure described as *XYZ* given the phenomenological similarity, as speaker from Earth at first instance will find that the meaning of water is same both in Earth and in Twin Earth. But later, when he comes to know that water in Earth and water in Twin Earth are different due to their having different chemical structure, he revised his opinion. Thus, for him, 'water' now means *XYZ*. Putnam then asks us to imagine a situation when valency theory in Chemistry was not developed. People were unaware of different chemical structures associated with elements. But even at that time, as Putnam states, the term 'Water' on Earth, meant H_2O and on Twin Earth it was meant *XYZ*. Now, recall Putnam's earlier assumption that people on Earth have their counterparts on Twin Earth — with having same mental structure. From this it follows that when people use the term 'water' both on Earth and on Twin Earth they must be in the same mental state. The reason is that they understand (in the sense of grasping) water in the same way (on the basis of phenomenological feature) and thus they are in the same mental state. But the fact remains that when speakers on Earth use 'Water' they mean H_2O, and when speakers on Twin Earth use 'Water' they mean *XYZ*. This shows that reference of the term 'water' on Earth and Twin Earth are different though the corresponding mental states of the users are same. The outcome of it is that sense does not determine its reference. There is nothing in Frege's theory which can prevent the possibility of the term 'water' being attached to H_2O and *XYZ* simultanecusly.

Kripke's counter example

Kripke's critique[7] of the doctrine of sense is based on his seminal work on proper name. In this respect, his target of attack is not just Frege. His critique takes into account of the works of all those important philosophers, such as, Russell, Wittgenstein, Searle, Strawson, etc., who tried to argue for the primacy of sense in their respective theories of proper name. Kripke's critique may be said to have two-fold objectives. First is critical. It seeks to show that description theories of name fail to identify the object referred to in the description uniquely. We identify the object not any description. Second is constructive. It seeks to show how we identify objects by placing them in a causal chain. This led Kripke to develop a new theory of reference. In fact, Putnam and Kripke share the same theory of reference. These two together establish that it is not sense but reference which is primary. In our presentation, we will concentrate on the first objective and will state Kripke's arguments against the primacy of sense on the basis of the counter examples that he constructed to the description or sense theory of names.

THE STATEMENT OF THE DESCRIPTION THEORY

For every name X, there is a cluster of properties Ø associated, and the speaker A thus believes that X can be designated by the properties Ø which may be symbolically expressed as ØX.

Given this statement of the theory, Kripke says that there are three claims that form the description theory:

Claim 1

In view of the existence of ØX the speaker *A* believes that one of the properties belonging to the set ØX will enable him/her to pick out some individual uniquely.

7. S. Kripke, 'Naming and Necessity' in D. Davidson and G. Harman (ed.), *Semantics of Natural Language*, D. Reidel, Dordrecht, 1972.

Claim 2

If it is found that most of the properties of the set ØX are satisfied by the object Y uniquely, then Y must be regarded as the referent of X.

Claim 3

Corresponding to a set of descriptions associated with a name if there is no object satisfying it then a name does not refer to anything.[8]

Kripke now offers counter examples to all these three claims made by the description theory.

COUNTER EXAMPLE 1

The claim 1 is false. The reason is in the example 'Faynman is a famous physicist' the description involved does not refer to someone uniquely. But this is not true of the name 'Faynman'. As Kripke argues the name 'Faynman' still refers to Faynman even in the absence of any definite description associated with the name. This counter example questions Frege's thesis that in our use of proper name we refer to an object via its sense, i.e., description. A distinction must be thus made between the name and its description.

COUNTER EXAMPLE 2

In Kripke's analysis, the claim made in 2 is false. According to him, we can very well imagine a situation where most of the properties (i.e., Ø's) expressed by the definite descriptions are satisfied by the object Y uniquely and yet Y may not be the referent of the name X. To site Kripke's example, the definite description 'the man who proved the incompleteness theorem' is always associated with the name 'Godel'. But, suppose, it was found that it was not Godel but someone called 'Schmidt' who discovered the incompleteness theorem. This implies that whenever we talk about 'Godel', we in fact refer to Schmidt unknowingly. But the description or sense theory of name

8. S. Kripke, 'Naming and Necessity' in D. Davidson and G. Harman (ed.), *Semantics of Natural Language*, D. Reidel, Dordrecht, 1972. p. 285.

does not allow this. This counter example of Kripke shows that there is no strict conceptual connection existing between descriptions and the object referred to by the name.

COUNTER EXAMPLE 3

Kripke's refutation of the claim 3 of the description theory of the name is as follows. The claim 3 of the theory says that if there is no object which satisfies the descriptions associated with the name (X), then X does not refer to anything. To this Kripke's reply is that the name X still refers even though there may not be any object corresponding to it. To prove his point, Kripke sites the Biblical name 'Jonah'. As Kripke argues, for Biblical scholars, Jonah really existed. They are convinced about it not because they think that there is someone who satisfies the conditions such as, 'the one who was swallowed by a big fish or went to Nineveh to preach'. It is quite possible that these conditions may not be satisfied by anyone 'and yet the name "Jonah" really has a referent'.

This discussion on the post-Fregean critique of sense as figured in the works of Putnam and Kripke convincingly shows that there is no rigid connection existing between sense and reference. The connection between the two is loose and even in some case non-existing. The counter examples of both Putnam and Kripke show that when we refer we do not refer through our knowledge of sense. Hence, sense does not determine reference nor its knowledge is mentally represented. It is thus through their critique they argue against the primacy of sense and, instead, argue for the primacy of reference. But how do we refer?

This brings us to the constructive thesis which tells us how do we refer without the help of sense. The gist of the thesis may be presented in terms of the following propositions. Reference of a term has a history and thus how a term gets its reference must be located within that particular frame of history. First, reference of a term is fixed by an initial introductory event. Kripke calls it naming ceremony where for the first time the term is dubbed on to the object. This is how the connection is established between the name and the object.

The next is the second stage. After the initial dubbing ceremony is over, reference fixed for the term continues in the same way for the future use. This establishes a causal chain connecting the future use of the term with the initial dubbing ceremony. This is a new theory of reference which is often characterised in the literature as the causal theory of reference. The sameness of reference is thus preserved on the basis of the causal chain which actually explains the mechanism that accounts for the referring function of language. In this account of language, sense does not play any role for making reference. It does not constitute the condition of applicability. The condition of applicability, on the other hand, is provided by the initial dubbing ceremony which forms the causal chain that legitimises the subsequent application of the term. This is how it is argued that reference assumes its primacy.

Our brief discussion on the post-Fregean critique of sense shows that Frege's arguments for the primacy of sense do not stand on a firm ground. But in view of this critique, can we dismiss the notion of sense altogether? Frege's arguments may not be strong enough to prevent the lacunas raised by Putnam or Kripke. In fact, our discussion testifies this. However, this fact should not blind us. It should not lead us to think that the notion of sense does not have any significance or it is redundant as the Putnam-Kripke approach says. Far from being redundant, the notion of sense enjoys a unique privilege. It is the one which accounts for what constitutes the understanding of a sentence. Its purpose is not to tell us how to fix the referent of a term. These are two different functions and the former should not be confused with the latter. The former performs the epistemic function and thus sense may be characterised fundamentally as epistemic in nature. Whereas, reference fixing is mostly concerned with a person's practical linguistic ability and thus involves inquiry into the social and historical roots of language and meaning. The thesis on the primacy of sense derives its strength and significance from the epistemic thrust of sense.

Frege had the correct insight when he considered sense in epistemic term. But what went wrong was that he could not safeguard his theory adequately. His formulation was primarily logical which allowed him to make sense/reference distinction with a claim that the sense of a term provided the condition of its applicability. Later on, the condition of applicability aspect became more important than the epistemic aspect of sense. The counter examples were construed with a view to refute Frege's doctrine of sense entirely.

Coming back to what was wrong with Frege's doctrine of sense, Frege did not put the epistemic claim of sense on a firm ground. To do this, Frege needs to bring the notion of sense under an epistemological model. The knowledge of sense constitutes a part of knowledge in general. In every respect, it shares the characteristics of the other parts of knowledge. Hence, sense has an epistemological structure the details of which needs to be spelt out. The second is about the passage establishing the linkage between sense and reference. Frege while elaborating this subscribes to a deterministic thesis which may be characterised as sense-determinism due to which he is forced to accept that sense determines reference. This deterministic position of Frege is ultimately responsible for its own destruction giving rise to the view that reference is primary. But accepting the primacy of sense does not necessarily mean accepting the rigid thesis that sense determines reference. Thus, along with the epistemological, reconstruction of sense, the second important task will be to explain how is reference possible without falling into the deterministic thesis of Frege. For this, one needs to reconstruct the entire connection between sense and reference. As stated, in the introductory remarks, the Nyāya model of sense in this direction can be highly significant. With this brief discussion on what is wrong with Frege's doctrine of sense, we now come to the Nyāya doctrine of sense that seeks to establish the primacy of sense.

II

Śābdabodha: an alternative model of sense

With regard to meaning, we find in the Nyāya philosophy of language there are three interrelated stages of account. The first is about the nature of a sentence. The second is about the meaning of a sentence and the third is about understanding the meaning of a sentence. Our account will be mostly concerned with understanding the meaning of a sentence. Hence, the discussion will include the three following questions:

1. How is understanding the meaning of a sentence possible?
2. What are the structural components of this understanding?, and,
3. How is reference possible?

Our discussion on *śābdabodha* will mainly follow the line of thought as specified in the above three questions. Keeping in view of the guidelines suggested above while pointing out what is wrong with Frege's model of sense, the conception of *śābdabodha* may be thus claimed to be offering a model alternative to that of Frege arguing for the primacy of sense.

We will now start with the first question: How is understanding the meaning of a sentence possible? We have seen that Frege answers to this question by employing the notion of sense. Nyāya too will have a similar response to this question because both share the same epistemological concern. However, as stated earlier, Frege could not provide adequate epistemological foundation to sense whereas in the Nyāya tradition the inquiry into sense is taken to be the part of its general epistemological inquiry. The notion of sense has an epistemological underpinning and one needs to make it explicit in order to explain how is understanding the meaning of a sentence possible?

The qualifier -qualificand structure of cognition

We start with what according to Nyāya are the general principles of knowledge. The most important clarification to be made at the beginning is that in Nyāya what we normally call knowledge is defined as awareness. The reason is the word *jñāna* in the Nyāya tradition cannot be translated as knowledge. Thus, keeping its conceptual viewpoint in the mind, the correct translation of *jñāna* must be awareness. But why should *jñāna* be viewed as awareness and not as knowledge? The reason is that in Nyāya *jñāna* is never interpreted as an abstract entity like proposition. It is on the other hand, defined with reference to a mental state that is associated whenever we experience a perceptual or conceptual awareness. Considering this awareness is a piece of knowledge. It is also an event — an episode that takes place in a subject. Thus, spelling out the principles of knowledge in Nyāya is strictly meant to be spelling out the epistemic principles of awareness. On the basis of the initial clarification of the term 'knowledge' understood as awareness we can now go into the structural composition of awareness. In this respect, our main concern is to spell out what constitutes the awareness of an object. That is, what is it that I am aware of when I am aware of an object? Following Matilal's analysis,[9] it may be pointed out that there are two principal aspects involved when I say that I am aware of an object X. These two may be thus characterised as to use Matilal's phrase, awareness of the object as qualified and awareness of the qualifier.

To say the object is qualified — the very characterisation implies that I am aware of the object as something. It never figures in my awareness as bare object but necessarily as qualified something. That means, I am aware of X as F and can thus express it in the verbalisable form: X is F. Hence, F is the distinguishing element — the mode under which the object is figured in my awareness and due to which it is distinguished in a particular way. This constitutes the qualificative awareness which cannot be obtained unless a precondition is satisfied. The precondition to be satisfied will be to having the prior awareness of the qualifier — the distinguishing element (*viśeṣaṇa*) due to which we have distinguishing awareness. This reveals that when I am aware of the object as something there are two things involved. One is the qualifier and the other is the object itself — the qualificand. This forms the qualifer-qualificand structure of awareness. Accordingly, the content of any piece of

9. B.K. Matilal, 'Awareness and Meaning in Navya-Nyāya', in *Analytical Philosophy in Contemporary Perspective*, pp.373-80.

knowledge will conform to this structure. The only exception admitted in Nyāya is the non-constructive (*nirvikalpa*) awareness where the object is presented as bare without any qualification. However, an awareness of this kind is never considered as knowledge in Nyāya.

It is evident that in this view all cases of seeing is seeing-as because seeing is necessarily associated with a qualifier due to which seeing becomes seeing-as. The notion of pure seeing hardly has any place in this view since it does not involve any qualificative awareness responsible for knowledge.

The qualifier-qualificand structure embodied in knowledge tells us that a rigid distinction cannot be made between propositional knowledge and knowledge of things. The reason is that the analysis of knowledge of things will show that it implicitly involves in its content a propositional structure which, following Matilal, may be expressed as $F(a)$. This formulation shows that a is qualified or distinguished by F-ness. Thus, the knowledge of F means to know what is F which in turn, means the property called F-ness that distinguishes F from the rest. Now when I verbalise this knowledge it cannot be dissociated from the property F-ness (say cowness or elephanthood) that qualifies a — the qualificand. It may be noted that this epistemic principle has a direct bearing on how linguistic utterances get their meaning. For particular object being denoted by a word implies, that the utterance of the word generates in the hearer's mind the awareness of the object that is necessarily qualified by a purported property. We will come back to this discussion little later. However, the important point to be noted in this connection is that the meaning of a word is never decided in isolation from the distinguishing property of the object. This semantic consideration is based on the basic epistemological stand of Nyāya which argues that my knowledge of the object cannot be separated from the way the object is presented in my awareness. This, in fact, provides the epistemological foundation of the Nyāya doctrine of sense. Like Frege, for Naiyāyikas too the primary thrust of sense is epistemic. But, unlike Frege, they did not stop it at this point. Their attempt on the other hand, was how to situate the notion of sense within their epistemological model particularly with the help of the qualifier-qualificand structure which they proposed while formulating the epistemic principles of awareness. With these remarks, we will now go to the next phase of our discussion dealing with the notion of *śābdabodha* that explains how the meaning of an expression is generated through a meaning-complex.

Śābdabodha and its semantic complex

As well known, the expression, *śabda* implies human speech and it may be thus understood as linguistic utterances. Utterances are made by a speaker who is regarded as the one who is a member in a linguistic community. Now the question is: How does a linguistic utterance generate awareness or knowledge of an object in a hearer's mind? In other words: How is *śābdabodha* attained? This leads us to the mechanism or the process involved in *śābdabodha*. The mechanism involved assumes the following steps.[10] First, the speaker makes a linguistic utterance with a view to communicate some knowledge or information to a hearer. Second, the hearer belongs to the same linguistic community as that of the speaker and thus both share the same linguistic competence. Third, the utterance is normally expressed through the form of a sentence composed of words. It is sometimes even expressed through a word only. Fourth, the hearer correctly recognises each word of the sentence. Fifth, the hearer as a consequence could establish the meanings or objects associated with each word. This leads to the culminating point — the end product of the whole process where we find the hearer is having knowledge of the connected meaning of the utterance made by the speaker and, thereby, he comes to know what is being communicated to him by the utterance.

In the above, I have described the process that leads to *śābdabodha*. The conditions involved in this process are mostly empirical. But there are certain formal semantic conditions of *śābdabodha*. In this sense, they are the conditions of *śābdabodha* itself. Thus, in order to

10. B.K. Matilal, *The Word and the World*, p. 49.

obtain the final knowledge, the following semantic conditions are to be fulfilled. First, syntactic expectancy (*ākāṅkṣā*), words must be syntactically related to form a linguistic sentence. This satisfies the grammatical acceptability of the sentence uttered by the speaker. Second, semantic fitness (*yogyatā*), the meaning of words must be semantically compatible with each other so that the hearer will not have problem in knowing the meaning of the sentence. Take the sentence 'He is sprinkling with fire'. If the hearer knows that the meaning of the word 'sprinkle' and the meaning of the word 'fire' are not semantically compatible he will not have *śābdabodha* from the utterance. Third, proximity between the different words of a sentence (*āsatti*), for a sentence to be intelligible its constituent words meant be continuous with one another in time or space. Fourth, intention (*tātparya*) of the speaker, if the sentence is ambiguous, the hearer should find out the exact meaning of the sentence from the intention of the speaker who is using it in a certain context.

We shall now argue, how language generated awareness (*śābdabodha*) and the knowledge of the meaning of the sentence (*vākyārtha-bodha*) became indistinguishable and thus form an identity. When we talk about the *śābdabodha* of a sentence-utterance we do it by giving a description of the knowledge that is produced in the hearer by the utterance. In exact term, this consists of giving a description of the message communicated through the utterance. This involves explication of the meaning intended by the speaker in the original sentence. *Śābdabodha* of a sentence thus becomes identical with its *vākyārtha-bodha*.

An important feature of Indian philosophy of language is its emphasis on the hearer's concept of meaning.[11] This is where we find that there is a crucial difference between Indian philosophy of language and Western philosophy of language since the latter always upholds the speaker's notion of meaning. The notion of 'hearer' in Indian philosophy of language is always projected as ideal hearer who has the same linguistic competence like any other

11. K. Bhattacharya, 'Some Problems concerning Meaning', in B.K. Matilal and J.L. Shaw (ed.), *Analytical Philosophy in Contemporary Perspective*.

members of his linguistic community. This is essentially to argue that the knowledge which is generated in the ideal hearer's mind is inter-subjectively available. It is inter-subjectively available because of the inter-subjective nature of meaning as expressed through the sentence. The ideal hearer's knowledge of the object-complex is thus articulated on the basis of the articulation of the meaning of the sentence. The meaning here is the object-complex which the hearer comes to know while he hears the sentence uttered. This point conforms the thesis how *śābdabodha* becomes indistinguishable with *vākyārtha-bodha*.

The epistemological analysis of the hearer's awareness will reveal that it has the same qualifier-qualificand structure where the hearer is aware of the object *X* as *F*. *F* is the qualifier or the distinguisher which distinguishes the object. Thus, for example, when the utterance of a proper name, such as, 'Socrates' generates awareness in the hearer's mind, the hearer is aware of the object Socrates under a mode of presentation. It is the mode of presentation which acts as a distinguisher qualifying who and what is Socrates. As we can see, the role of distinguisher becomes very important because it is with the help of the distinguisher (or *F*) that we pick out the relevant object. Following this line of presentation, it becomes evident that the main thrust of *śābdabodha* is directed on words focussing particularly on the question: What do the words signify for the hearer? In actual term, this will be going into the inquiry of the meaning-complex associated with a word. We shall now, following the works of Matilal and Shaw, give an account of the formation of the meaning-complex and the structural pattern found in it.

The denotative power of the word

First is the process involved through which the hearer gets knowledge. We find in this respect that there are two stages of knowledge involved. The first is the knowledge of words that leads to the second stage consisting of the knowledge of meaning. These two cannot be conceived separately or in isolation since one leads to the other. The utterance of words generates in the hearer's mind the knowledge of those words. To have knowledge of these words imply having awareness of the objects meant by these words. This process leads to the final stage of knowledge giving rise to the knowledge of meaning.

The next issue that arises in this connection is the denoting power or *śakti* of the word. Matilal[12] calls this the meaning-linkage that is existing between the word and its meaning by virtue of which the hearer knows what the object is meant. Thus meaning or what the object is meant is possible primarily due to the denoting power of the word. However, it is also accepted in Nyāya that there are occasions where a word may not have the denoting power in the same way in which other words have. In such an occasion, it is assumed that a word has a different power by virtue of it a word gets its meaning, i.e., the object meant. This power of word is called *lakṣaṇā* which may be roughly translated as metaphor in English. It is the power through which the hearer comes to know the denotative range of the word which is not apparent in the word or in the sentence itself. The knowledge of the denotative range of the word enables the hearer to pickup the right object in accordance with the context or the intention of the speaker. To give the standard example often cited in the text will help to explain the point. Take the word 'river' and the sentence 'the house is on the river'. An utterance of the word 'river' will generate in the hearer's mind the awareness of the object being qualified by the property of riverhood. Here there is no confusion over the denotative power of the word. But when we come to the sentence, 'the house is on the river', the word 'river' loses its earlier denotative power. What is denoted in this use is not the river but the bank of the river. This is a metaphorical use and the hearer understands it and accordingly, he takes 'bank of the river' as secondary referent being connected with the primary referent river.

From the notion of the denoting power of the word we now come to the discussion of how does a word get its denotative power?

---

12. B.K. Matilal, 'Awareness and Meaning in Navya-Nyāya', in *Analytical Philosophy in Contemporary Perspective*, p. 381.

According to Nyāya, there are two ways by which a word can get its denotative power. It is either by the will of God or by modern stipulation. The will of God does not imply any special significance. On the other hand, as the recent commentators have pointed out, it only implies the conventions whose origins are not known to us. The important point to be noted here is that both are conventions. The one is called ancient convention, *śakti* and the other is called modern convention or *paribhāṣā*. To give examples of these two conventions, the word 'cow' and its referent is an example of *śakti* because we do not know when this convention was first introduced, whereas, for proper names or technical terms, the relation between an expression and its referent is an example of *paribhāṣā*.

The structure of the meaning-complex

On the basis of this general understanding, we can now try to explicate the notion of meaning complex and the structural pattern of it. Regarding the structure or composition of the meaning complex, there are different views in Nyāya. In this respect the controversy between the old school of Nyāya and Navya-Nyāya over whether or not the configuration of the particulars or *ākṛti* to be included as the member of the complex is to be specially noted. However, whatever importance these controversies may have we will not enter into it in the present discussion.

In line with its qualifier-qualificand structure, the meaning complex was accordingly conceived and formed in Nyāya (notably in Navya-Nyāya). Thus, the utterance of the word 'cow' generates the awareness of an object *X* in the hearer's mind which is qualified by cowness. Cowness is the property and the object *X* is, hence, distinguished or determined by this property. Cowness, so conceived, is characterised in Nyāya as the delimitor or distinguisher of the object meant by the word 'cow'. This is, in short, the idea behind Nyāya concept of *avacchedaka* which being a delimitor determines the referent uniquely. We may note here the change — the change from epistemology to semantics. The concept of qualifier in Nyāya theory of epistemology is now changed into the concept of *avacchedaka* which is essentially a semantic concept. However, this change does not suggest an absolute departure from one to the other. The concept of *avacchedaka* though semantic in nature has its foundation in epistemology. It has an epistemic root.

The formation of the meaning-complex of the word 'cow' will thus includes as its members the following three, namely, individual cows, the property of cowness and the relation of inherence. The last notion is postulated with a specific purpose, i.e., for relating the property of cowness to individual cows. Following Shaw, the same may be thus represented as:

> The word 'cow' means (individual cow, inherence relation and cowness).

The above representation constitutes the formation of the meaning-complex of the word 'cow'. In this, the first member is called the *śakya* which is the referent (i.e., the object) of the expression and the third member is called *śakyatāvacchedaka* that signifies the limitor of the property constituting the referent of the expression. The second member of this complex is the relation of inherence. Its function is to relate cowness to individual cows. Accordingly, individual cow or cow-individual is placed in the first term (*anuyogin*) and cowness is placed in the second term (*pratiyogin*) of the relation of inherence.

It is evident that the notion of *śakyatāvacchedaka* plays a crucial role in determining the referential mechanism operative in natural language. It provides the reason or the ground for the application of a term to the object to which it applies. It is thus closer to Frege's notion of sense which in the same way provides the condition of applicability of a term. This idea is also expressed in Nyāya by the term *pravṛtti-nimitta*. In the later development of Nyāya this idea of referential mechanism conceived through the limitor being placed in the meaning-complex of the word assumes a great deal of importance.

To unpack the notion of *śakyatāvacchedaka* or *pravṛtti-nimitta*[13] will reveal its internal diversity. Depending on the nature of the term, the associated *pravṛtti-nimitta* of the term will differ. Thus, for example, the *pravṛtti-nimitta* of a term need not be always expressing a universal property or a class-character. In the context of the word 'cow' since it is a class-expression, the *pravṛtti-nimitta* of the term is also universal. It is cowness that forms the reason or the ground for application of the term. But the same is not true of the *pravṛtti-nimitta* of a term, say, 'animal' which expresses a complex property like having a tail or a hairy body, etc. They are not universals like cowness expressing *jāti*. Similarly, for a definite description like: 'The father of Rāma' the *pravṛtti-nimitta* of it will be a complex property — the property that constitutes the father of Rāma. Finally the proper name, such as, Rāma, the *pravṛtti-nimitta* of it expresses the property that constitutes the uniqueness of Rāma.

In the above, we have stated only how *pravṛtti-nimitta* of a term differs in accordance with the nature of the term. But we have not so far said anything about the nature of *pravṛtti-nimitta* itself. As to its nature, there is no view uniformly held in Nyāya. Following Shaw's account,[14] there may be three major views found in this connection.

First is the view of Vardhamāna Upādhyāya offering a definition of *pravṛtti-nimitta* constructed in terms of three conditions. Thus, *X* will be called *pravṛtti-nimitta* of the term *Y* if it satisfies the three following conditions:

1. *X* must be the part of the meaning-complex of the term *Y*.

2. *X* must qualify the referent of the term *Y*.

3. *X* acts as a qualifier when we remember the referent of *Y*.

Shaw rightly points out the comprehensive nature of this definition which takes into account of both the epistemic and the

13. J.L. Shaw, 'Proper Names: Contemporary Philosophy and the Nyāya', in *Analytical Philosophy in Contemporary Perspective*, p. 350.

14. J.L. Shaw, 'Professor Mohanty on Meaning and Transformation in Indian Philosophy', in *The Philosophy of J.N. Mohanty*, pp. 147-48.

semantic aspects of *pravṛtti-nimitta*. At the semantic level, its function is to qualify the referent, whereas, at the level of thought, it performs the epistemic function of being the qualifier of a qualificand.

The second definition is suggested by Gadādhara which is not substantially different from the definition suggested by Vardhamāna. According to this definition, *pravṛtti-nimitta* of a term is a constituent of the meaning-complex and since it qualifies the referent, it belongs to the referent of the word, which again is one of the constituents of the same complex. In his definition, Gadādhara does not include the epistemic condition which is figured as the third condition of Vardhamāna's definition.

The third definition offered by Raghunātha Śiromaṇi is a crucial one because it signifies a standpoint which is totally different from that of Vardhamāna. According to him *pravṛtti-nimitta* of a term does not constitute the part of the meaning complex of the term. Its function, on the other hand, is to indicate the referent of the term. It is thus regarded as the indicator or *upalakṣaṇā* of the object to which the term is applied. Raghunātha is not giving up the notion of *pravṛtti-nimitta*, but he is changing its constitutive role. Cowness which is a *pravṛtti-nimitta* of the term 'cow' does no longer form the part of the meaning-complex of the term 'cow'. The role of cowness is only to indicate the referent or the object to which the term 'cow' applies. It is thus a device (and not a part of the meaning/sense) by which the referent of a term, such as, 'cow' is fixed.

The two definitions offered by Vardhamāna and Raghunātha indicate two extreme standpoints within Nyāya. In Vardhamāna's definition, *pravṛtti-nimitta* is like Frege's mode of presentation constituting the condition of applicability of the term. It determines the referent. Whereas, in the approach of Raghunātha, it acts as a method of fixing the referent of a name. This is done with the help of referential descriptions. Raghunātha's approach may be thus seen as parallel to Kripke's approach.

Meaning of proper name

Regarding the meaning of proper name there is a major difficulty arises. Here, the issue to be decided is whether the qualifier or *pravṛtti-nimitta* — the mode of presentation be included as the part of the meaning of a proper name or not. On this problem, there are standpoints found in the Nyāya tradition which are radically different from each other.[15] The older Naiyāyikas like Jayanta represents the standpoint according to which the meaning of a proper name is the object itself. The main argument for this view lies on the distinction between a proper name and a general name. Unlike a general name where a universal (e.g., cowness) is included in the associated meaning-complex of the word a proper name does not keep any place for such universal or class-character. The reason is that a proper name like Devadatta or Socrates is applicable to only one object and thus it cannot include universals. Further, the individual object is understood here as bare object without having its properties and relations. The notion of a proper name so conceived suggested that its meaning does not include anything other than the object itself. To put it in concrete terms, the name Devadatta means individual Devadatta.

It follows from this standpoint that the Fregean idea of conceiving the meaning of a proper name in terms of a set of definite descriptions can no longer be tenable on a logical ground. Apart from the general argument regarding the distinction between proper names and general terms, the philosophers of Nyāya offered a very persuasive arguments to show that a proper name and its associated definite description which forms an identity statement does not generate any cognition. To state the argument briefly: Frege's proposal is that, the meaning of the name, such as, 'Aristotle' consists in being the teacher of Alexander the Great. The proposal thus equates the meaning of the name 'Aristotle' with the meaning of the expression 'the teacher of Alexander the Great'. As a result, the

---

15. J.L. Shaw, 'Proper Names: Contemporary Philosophy and the Nyāya', in *Analytical Philosophy in Contemporary Perspective*, pp. 356-62.

sentence 'Aristotle is the teacher of Alexander the Great' becomes an identity sentence. The Nyāya explanation for it is that in this sentence the limitor of the subject becomes same as the limitor of the predicate. As Matilal puts it, the qualifying property of the subject-entity becomes identical with the qualifier expressing the predicate-property. In view of this consideration, one can bring out the strange consequence according to which the sentence, 'Aristotle is the teacher of Alexander the Great' is no way different from the sentence, 'The teacher of Alexander the Great is the teacher of Alexander the Great'. But this violates the basic principle of Nyāya's thesis on language-generated awareness according to which the knowledge that is generated must be informative. In view of this no identity statement can be said to have knowledge-claims because they are not informative. The meaning of a proper name cannot be thus identified with its definite description. The only option that is left for us is to admit that the meaning of a proper name is the object itself.

A radically different from Jayanta's view is the view proposed by Jagadīśa on proper name. Unlike the other view, Jagadīśa holds that there is no fundamental difference between proper name and general term. The conceptual/semantic organisation of terms belonging to both these categories are same. The argument given for this standpoint is as follows. We all know that a general word, such as, 'cow' refers to all individual cows due to the class-character called cowness. The same consideration may be applied to a proper name like Devadatta. First, as 'cow' refers to all individual cows the name 'Devadatta' refers to different phases of the individual Devadatta, such as, boyhood, adulthood, etc. In this way, Devadatta — the individual may be conceived as a series consisting of different phases of Devadatta. As Shaw suggests, they may be characterised as Devadatta — individuals in the same way as we characterise cow-individuals. Hence, we use the same name 'Devadatta' since all Devadatta-individuals share the property of being Devadatta. Given this perspective, it can be further shown that the meaning-complex which is constructed for a general term like 'cow' be also constructed in the same way for a proper name like 'Devadatta'. The meaning-complex of a proper name will have the same structure as that of the meaning-complex of a general term. Thus, similar to the meaning-complex of the word 'cow' which is consisting of three elements, namely, the referents of the word 'cow', the cowness and the relation of inherence, the meaning-complex of Devadatta, accordingly, consists of the referents (i.e., different Devadatta-individuals), Devadattahood (i.e., the essential property shared by all the individuals referred to by the name 'Devadatta') and the relation of inherence that relates the two.

This view on proper name was criticised on a number of grounds. The most important among them is the criticism that this view does not accept the distinction between a general term and proper name. This led to the failure of understanding the relationship that holds among the referents of a general term 'cow' and the relationship that holds among the referents (Devadatta-individuals) of a proper name Devadatta. In the former case there are different individual cows are involved where one is not dependent on the other except that all of them possess the property called cowness. But in the latter case the different phases/stages of the individual Devadatta cannot be conceived as independent individuals. The reason is that one is dependent on the other and thus they together form a sequence. But the same sequence cannot be thought of in the context of individual cows. This distinction was completely overlooked because of ignoring the distinction between general term and proper name.

The third view of proper name is the view of Raghunātha Śiromaṇi. It has been already mentioned that Raghunātha does not include *pravṛtti-nimitta* as the part of the meaning-complex of the word. In this view, the meaning of a proper name is thus turned out to be referent itself and the associated definite descriptions are taken to be mere *upalakṣaṇā* indicating the referent. This view though influential was not acceptable to all. In fact, it was criticised by large number of philosophers belonging to Navya-Nyāya school. The main thrust of their criticism is that the acceptance of Raghunātha's view implies a consequence which is fatal to Nyāya ontology. To explain the point briefly, Raghunātha's view tells us that we cannot identify the property of being Devadatta with the individual Devadatta. To hold this will be to hold that the property of being Devadatta assumes the status of a separate irreducible entity and it, thereby, allows Nyāya ontology to be unnecessarily overpopulated by such entities. This is how Raghunātha's view comes in sharp conflict with the fundamental principle of Nyāya, viz., the law parsimony. We thus come to an unresolvable situation involving the two mutually standpoints on proper name.

III

Can there be reference-failure in śābdabodha?

Our last questions is: Can there be a reference failure? In the context of *śābdabodha*, the question that may be posed is: Can there be a false *śābdabodha*? The notion of a false *śābdabodha* is ruled out in Nyāya. Such a notion is a contradiction in terms because all *śābdabodha* is *pramā*, i.e., true by definition. A false sentence, such as, 'He is sprinkling with fire' is ruled out from generating *śābdabodha* because it does not satisfy the formal semantic condition of compatibility or fitness. But, take the sentence, 'The cat is on the mat' uttered in the occasion when the cat referred to is not on the mat, or, consider the sentence, 'Socrates is wise' where the person referred to by the name 'Socrate' is not wise. Apparently, they satisfy the conditions of *śābdabodha*. But they are false sentences and as false sentences there cannot be any *śābdabodha* corresponding to them. How do we explain it? Should we consider them *ala* Kripke as counter examples? They are not treated in Nyāya as counter examples. The fact of reference failure is explained in Nyāya on a purely linguistic ground. The central to reference failure is the notion of false belief. False beliefs are transmitted due to some defect in linguistic mechanism itself. The Nyāya standpoint on this issue may be elaborated in the following way.

We start with the distinction between linguistic understanding and linguistic knowledge. In Western philosophy, it is commonly held that linguistic understanding is prior to linguistic knowledge. The reason is that no matter whether the sentence heard is true or false there will be linguistic understanding. I can understand the meaning of a sentence without committing to its actual truth or falsity. It is in this sense non-commital and is prior to knowledge or believing. The Indian standpoint, on the other hand, upholds the priority of linguistic knowledge over understanding. If all the conditions (i.e., formal conditions of *śābdabodha*) are met then the sentence uttered cannot be other than being true. The logical outcome of this state will be that the hearer will have knowledge of what is said. On this basic consideration it is thus argued that we cannot be said to know when the sentence heard is false. There cannot be *śābdabodha* for a false sentence. But the crucial question that remains to be answered is: How is false cognition possible?, How is it transmitted through words? The answer to these questions will enable us to explain the problem of reference failure.

Coming to false cognition, we start with the qualifer-qualificand structure of knowledge. To recall what has been said earlier, the speaker's utterance, 'Socrates is wise' is viewed by the hearer as the one where Socrates — the person or the object is identified with something that is qualified by wisdom. This description follows from the generalised structure of cognition where qualificandhood and qualifierhood are viewed as co-relative features and thus as a result one is conditioned by the other. Since, this is generalised structure of cognition, false belief too assumes the same structural pattern. So in a false cognition, i.e., false belief, there is qualifer and qualificand but what goes wrong is that the qualifier does not qualify the qualificand. This results in false cognition. False cognition is thus a case of misconnection.[16] It is a misconnection between two elements. But the utterance, on the contrary, gives the impression that they are connected and this led to the cognition of disconnected items as connected. This is the cause of false cognition or belief due to which failure in reference occurs.

As a corollary to this, there is one more point to be mentioned in this connection. The knowledge derived from *śābdabodha* is always accompanied with an element called trust. A particular linguistic

16. B.K. Matilal, *The Word and the World*, pp. 62-68.

utterance along with trust (i.e., the hearer has a trust on what the speaker is saying) can alone generate knowledge. Thus, a teacher when he says that Einstein discovered the theory of relativity students accept it on trust. The knowledge derived from *śābdabodha* thus in an important sense rests on the notion of trust. By using the same argument we can further point out that false cognition may occur due to absence of required trust. In fact, the hearer will not accept the statement coming from an untrustworthy person. Thus, many of Kripke's counter examples can be shown to be ineffective if we consider the trust element being implicit in knowledge. In the standpoint of *śābdabodha*, the possibility of occurring such cases will be ruled out. The genuine cases of reference failure are those which occur due to false cognition caused by misconnection of elements.

Concluding remark: can sense be totally eliminated?

As a concluding remark we would like to argue that the idea of sense could not be shown to be redundant. Its presence and its role is unavoidable. In this respect, one may particularly mention the crucial role that sense plays in learning a language. Learning of common nouns, for example, is one area which cannot be explained without postulating the mechanism of sense being operative while we learn language. In the context of learning mass and count terms, Naiyāyikas argue that learning of these terms will not be possible unless we refer to the 'quality' (*guṇa*) or 'class property' (*jāti*) associated with these terms. It is only with the help of these characteristics that we can avoid committing promiscuity (*vyabhicāra*). For this, the explanation they offer is simple. It is assumed that when a term is used to pickout many individuals a prior connection must have been already established between the two. In the absence of it the application of the term may turn out to be promiscuous in its use. Reference to class characteristic associated with common nouns thus becomes a necessary part of the meaning of general terms. These characteristics may be described as sense characteristics and by virtue of it a prior connection is established between the term and the individuals falling under its application. Kalidas Bhattacharya[17] very eloquently brings out the significance of this aspect of linguistic reference through a simple example. A child when she perceives an elephant in the second time (after being introduced with the term 'elephant' and the application of it) immediately cries out 'An elephant!' As Bhattacharya points out, she has no time to compare the two instances for abstract out the common features. Yet, she makes no mistake to say that it is elephant. In Bhattacharya's account, this is possible because the child perceived 'the Universal Elephant' in the very first presentation of the elephant. It is due to this knowledge she could unmistakably recognise something as elephant when it is presented to her. This, in other words, shows having knowledge of the sense characteristics associated with the term. This is how the role of sense becomes crucially important for learning language.

Our next argument[18] regarding why the notion of sense cannot be disassociated from the semantic structure of language is based on the controversy concerning the use of natural kind terms in belief contexts. This is a controversy originated in contemporary analytic philosophy of language. Its main focus of attention is: Do natural kind terms have sense or are they purely connotationless referring expressions? It was a controversy which did not lead to any definite conclusion. But by using the argument from Nyāya we can arrive at a definite conclusion showing that the use of natural kind terms presupposes sense or the primacy of sense.

To put the controversy briefly, imagine a belief context where we have the two following belief sentences: 'John believes that water is tasty' and 'John believes that H_2O is tasty'. It is possible that these two sentences differ in truth-value. That is a claim may be simultaneously made that while the first sentence is true, the second sentence is false. Now, the question that is raised is: How can we explain this difference in two sentences despite the fact that water is identical with H_2O? The proponents of sense theory will argue that

17. K. Bhattacharya, 'Some Problems Concerning Meaning', in *Analytical Philosophy in Contemporary Perspective*, pp. 179-80.

18. B.K. Matilal, *Analytical Philosophy in Contemporary Perspective*, p. 22.

the difference we see between the two sentences is basically due to the semantic differences found between 'water' and H_2O. The two expressions are having two different senses. In this respect, they argue against the view which says that there is no difference between 'water' and H_2O since they are connotationless rigid designators of the same substance. As against this, the sense theorists' reply is that given this position that 'Water' and H_2O are rigid designators of the same substance it should be possible, in principle, to substitute one expression for the other and vice versa. But, the fact remains that such substitution is not possible. This substitution failure shows that there must be significant semantic difference between the two terms which can be explained only on the basis of difference in sense associated with these two different terms.

As against this perspective, Kripke argues that this objection against substitution failure is not based on any genuine ground. In fact, it is due to certain inconsistent assumptions in the theory that we find that there is substitution failure. What is fundamentally lacking here is the availability of certain crucial metalinguistic information stating that 'water' and H_2O refer to the same substance. If we do not take this into account then we will land up in holding premises which are mutually inconsistent, that is, 'water is tasty' and 'H_2O is not tasty'. This is a situation which is similar to when we translate foreign language. Translation becomes possible only on the basis of relevant metalinguistic information. In the absence of this information a speaker who does not know the alien language will hold inconsistent premises with regard to an alien expression. Thus the sense theorist appeal to the notion of sense to explain the semantic difference between 'water' and 'H_2O' is ruled out. This implies that there is no semantic difference existing between the two expressions. What will be sense theorists reply to this? Matilal suggests that in Nyāya we find that there is an alternative explanation defending the thesis that 'Water' and 'H_2O' have significant semantic difference.

In the Nyāya standpoint the response to this situation may be articulated on the basis of their idea of *avacchedaka*. Corresponding to these two words 'Water' and 'H_2O' there is the notion of *avacchedaka* determining the application of these two words. True that these two words have the same referent but the power to designate something is different. The difference lies on their respective delimitors due to which interchangeability between two expressions is not possible. The difference that we find here is with respect to body of knowledge that we associate with 'water' and 'H_2O' respectively. These are two different sets of knowledge and thus they cannot be taken to be identical. However, there is a possibility that in some cases they may overlap. Further, Kripke's solution is more of an interpretation rather than a translation between the two terms. As Matilal points out, a proper translation is possible only on the basis of sense and not on reference alone. In fact, the distinction between translation and interpretation will collapse if we disassociate sense from expressions. All these arguments from Nyāya lead to the final conclusion that sense cannot be replaced by reference. This, in other words, implies assuming primacy of sense.

8

A Nyāya Interpretation of Proper Names

Brinda Sen

THIS paper tries to deal mainly with three queries — (1) What is a proper name from the Nyāya point of view? (2) How does a proper name refer to an object? (3) Are the proper names, as understood by the Nyāya philosophers, loaded with sense?

Let us start with the first question. Roughly speaking, a proper name is that which uniquely refers to a particular single object. For example, the proper name 'Rabindra Nath Tagore' uniquely refers to a particular person. If the characteristic feature of a proper name is to uniquely designate a single thing then the so-called definite descriptions should also be treated as proper names, e.g., 'the Indian poet who composed *Gītāñjalī*', etc. The Nyāya philosophers treat these two types of expressions at par.

What is a Nyāya counterpart of proper name? In order to understand this we have to understand the classification of words as made by the Nyāya philosophers. It has been stated in *Śabdaśaktiprakāśikā* of Jagadīśa Tarkālaṁkāra that a sentence proper is constituted of the words that are *sārthaka*. What is a *sārthaka* word?

Śabdāntaram apekṣyaiva sārthakaḥ svārthabodhakṛt.[1] When a word,

---

1. Jagadīśa Tarkālaṁkāra, *Śabdaśaktiprakāśikā*, ed. with footnotes by Pandit Dhundhiraj Sastri, The Chowkhamba Sanskrit Series Office, Varanasi, 1973, p. 29.

in order to signify its own meaning requires another word, it is said to be *sārthaka*. In the sentence *ghaṭamānaya*, the word *ghaṭa* in order to signify the referent *ghaṭa* requires at least the case ending *am*, which is used as a suffix of *ghaṭa*. These *sārthaka* words are of three kinds: (i) *prakṛti*, (ii) *pratyaya*, and (iii) *nipāta*.

prakṛtiḥ pratyayaścaiva nipātaśceti sa tridhā?[2].

Under the head *nipāta* fall words like preposition and particle, e.g., *na* (no), *tu* (but), *ca* (and), etc. Under the head *pratyaya* fall words like case-endings — nominal suffixes and verbal suffixes. In addition, under the head *prakṛti* fall root words. In Sanskrit, there are two sorts of root words: (i) *nāma* or *pratipādika*, i.e., root words that are not verbs, e.g., *ghaṭa*, and (ii) *dhātu* or verbs, e.g., the verb *kṛ* (to do). This *nāma* can be of four kinds — *rūḍha*, *yogarūḍha*, *lakṣaka* and *yaugika*. A *rūḍha* word is a word whose significatory capacity is the capacity of the word in its entirety, e.g., the word *ghaṭa* or 'pot'. A *yogarūḍha* word is a word whose significatory capacity is partly derived from the constituents, e.g., the word *paṅkaja*. It usually means a lotus. But in its etymological meaning, it is that which is born in mud. In that sense, the word can also be applied to such thing as water lily. But conventionally it applies to lotus. A *lakṣaka* word is a word whose meaning is signified by an indirect significatory capacity (*lakṣaṇā*). For example, if we consider the sentence 'The Ganges is on fire' to be meaningful, then we have to take some word as having indirect significatory capacity. In this case we may take 'Ganges' to mean a boat on the Ganges instead of the river Ganges. The boat is related with Ganges though it is not directly signified by the word 'Ganges'. Therefore here 'Ganges' is the *lakṣaka* word. The fourth kind of *pratipādika* is *yaugika*. A word whose significatory capacity is wholly derived from the meaning of its constituents including grammatical roots, prefixes, suffixes, etc., is termed as a *yaugika* word. For example, the word *pācaka* (i.e., one who cooks) is formed by the root word *pac*, which means to 'to cook' along with the addition of the suffix *ṇvul* in the sense of 'being an agent of some activity'.

2. Jagadīśa Tarkālaṁkāra, *Śabdaśaktiprakāśikā*, p. 29.

Now, we have to take special care of *rūḍha* word, since *vyakti-vācaka pada* or singular term is included in this group. *Rūḍham saṅketavannāma*[3] — A *rūḍha* word is a *nāma*, which has a direct significatory capacity. These *rūḍha* words are of three types: (i) *naimittika*, (ii) *aupādhika*, and (iii) *pāribhāṣika*.

A *rūḍha* word which signifies an object which is qualified by some universal (*jāti*) is called *naimittika*. The word 'cow' (*go*) directly signifies an individual cow having universal cowness (*gotva*). Therefore, this word is a *naimittika* word.

If a *rūḍha* word signifies an object qualified by *upādhi* or a general quality not tantamount to universal, it is called an *aupādhika* word. The word *mūrtta* signifies an object qualified by *mūrttatva*, which is an *upādhi*. Therefore, this word is an *aupādhika* word.

Now we have arrived at the most important group of terms for our paper. This is the third kind of *rūḍha* word, which is called *pāribhāṣika*. It refers to an individual thing having a property not present in two objects. That is, the property is present in that particular, individual thing only. For example, the word *ākāśa* or 'sky' refers to an object which is qualified by *ākāśatva* or skyness which is not present in two objects or we may say which is present in the object sky only.

ubhayāvṛttidharmeṇa saṁjñā syāt pāribhāṣikī.[4]

This is explained by Jagadīśa in the following way. The quality, which qualifies the object signified by the *pāribhāṣika* word, does not reside in both the *anuyogin* and *pratiyogin* of a particular negation. Let us explain it. *Ākāśa* or 'sky' is a *pāribhāṣika* word. Sky is one. Therefore, the word 'sky' signifies a single, individual thing. Skyness is present in sky, which is the *pratiyogin* of the negation of sky. But skyness is not present in any *anuyogin* of the negation of sky, e.g., it is not present in the table, in the book, etc. This skyness qualifies sky

3. Jagadīśa Tarkālaṁkāra, *Śabdaśaktiprakāśikā*, p. 76

4. *Ibid*, p. 117.

and the word 'sky' which signifies the object sky is called a *pāribhāṣika* word or let us say a singular word or a singular term.

Pandit Visvabandhu Bhattacharya considers this *pāribhāṣika* word to be the Naiyāyika counterpart of proper name or singular term.[5]

It is very interesting to note that the terms which we ordinarily call proper names, e.g., 'Rabindra Nath Tagore', 'Mahatma Gandhi', 'Rāma', etc., do not satisfy the definition of a *pāribhāṣika* word according to the conception of the Naiyāyikas. The Naiyāyikas would say that the proper name, for instance, 'Rāma' does not refer to a single individual. They think that a proper name refers to Rāma's body and as his body changes from childhood to youth and from youth to old age. Rāma has different bodies, because if the constituents of a whole change, the whole does not remain the same. Therefore, the proper name 'Rāma' refers to different bodies and not to a particular individual body. We, however, consider proper name to be signifying a single individual thing. Hence, words like 'Rāma', etc., are not proper names. From this it follows that perhaps from the Nyāya point of view demonstratives like 'this', etc., are to be regarded as proper names and the ordinary proper names are not to be treated as proper names. This claim seems to be very strong. So let us return to the former position that we designate the body of Rāma at a particular period by some name and that name is a singular term. If that be so, then can we say that 'Child Rāma' (*śisu* Rāma), 'Young Rāma' (*yuvaka* Rāma), etc., are singular terms and act as proper names? These terms cannot be names, because in each of them, more than one *sārthaka* terms are present. And as such, these words amount to a sentence or *vākya* in Nyāya philosophy. If we refer to different

5. This has been suggested by Pandit Visvabandhu Bhattacharya in his paper entitled *Vyaktivācaka Śabda* presented at a seminar of Jadavpur University, Calcutta in 1979. Page 6 from the cyclostyled copy. For an English translation of this article refer Visvabandhu Bhattacharyya, 'Proper names and individuals' tr. B.K. Matilal in *Knowing from words: Western and Indian Philosophical Analysis of understanding and testimony* ed. by Bimal Krishna Matilal and Arindam Chakrabarti, Kluwer, Academic Publishers, 1994, pp. 325-46.

bodies by 'Rāma$_1$', 'Rāma$_2$', 'Rāma$_3$', etc., then, of course, these are singular terms and proper names. However, terms, which we ordinarily call personal proper names, are not considered to be singular terms by the Nyāya philosophers.

A charge may be raised that the Naiyāyikas do not reflect the intuition of the ordinary people (*lokānubhava*) and our intuition dictates us to accept that a single object is designated by the proper name 'Rāma'. In that case, the Naiyāyikas may reply that because different bodies are similar, we do not understand their difference; —just as we think that there is one single flame of a lamp though the flame changes as its fuel changes.

The Naiyāyikas may defend their position in various ways. But there is no doubt that the view that Rāma is not a proper name deviates much from the common sense point of view. Here we may mention another Nyāya view which opts for another definition of *pāribhāṣika* word. All the Nyāya philosophers hold that words have significatory capacity (*śaktaṁ padam*).[6] Why is it that a particular word signifies a particular object? Naiyāyikas hold that in the case of certain words the significatory capacity is beginningless. For those words God intends that a particular word would signify a particular object and here the direct significatory capacity is nothing but God's will. As God's will (*icchā*) has no beginning, so also is the case with the direct significatory capacity or *śakti*. But for some words instead of God's will, we, the human beings, intend that this word would signify this object, e.g., when a father decides to call his new-born son say 'Rāma', the direct significatory capacity or *śakti* is the father's will and it therefore has a beginning (*sādi*). These words are called *pāribhāṣika* by a group of Nyāya philosophers.[7] Therefore, the

---

6. Annaṁbhaṭṭa, *Tarkasaṁgraha*, tr. in Bengali by Narayan Chandra Goswami, Kalyani Das Gupta, Calcutta-6, p. 440.

7. *idampadamimamarthebodhayatvitiḥ; asmācchabdādyamartho bodhyavya iti veccha; saṁketarūpā vṛttiḥ. tatrādhunikasaṁketaḥ paribhāṣā; tayā carthabodhakaṁpadaṁ pāribhāṣikaṁ . . .*

— Gadādhara Bhaṭṭācārya, *Śaktivādaḥ*, Benaras, 1929, p. 5.

ordinary proper names are also *pāribhāṣika* words. It may be objected that even in the case where a father gives name to his child, the *śakti* is beginningless as here God's will is manifested through the father's will. How does anybody know it? Because we find that it is written in the scripture that a father would give a name to his son on the eleventh day of the child's birth.[8] The scripture expresses God's will. Hence, in fact God's will is active here. It may be argued that though the scripture suggests that the father would give a name, it does not specify any particular name. Therefore, in a sense a father's will is operative in this case. It may be argued that a *pāribhāṣika* word is not used in rites or rituals. But the ordinary proper names are used in these functions and as such these are not to be treated as *pāribhāṣika* words. Even if we do not consider these names to be *pāribhāṣika* words, we cannot avoid calling certain other words as *pāribhāṣika* words, e.g., if a child gives the name *ḍittha* to his toy-elephant, it is definitely a *pāribhāṣika* word and certainly an instance of ordinary proper name.

Therefore, if we maintain that *pāribhāṣika* words of the Naiyāyikas are the so-called proper names, we can hold that at least a section of the ordinary proper names are proper names according to Nyāya philosophy. Even if we consider the *prācīna* Nyāya view that ordinary proper names like 'Rāma', 'Rabindra Nath Tagore' etc., are not singular terms, there is no doubt that *ḍittha* is a singular term and terms like *ḍittha* are proper names.

Next comes the question — how do we refer by a proper name? The Nyāya theory is very simple in this respect. The Nyāya philosophers think that we can refer to an object by a word, be it a proper name or any other word, because the object has certain property. This is the ground for application of a word. This is called *pravṛtti-nimitta*. For example, the word 'cow' refers to the animal cow, because the animal possesses a certain attribute, viz., cowness. Similarly, a

---

8. *ādhunike nāmni śaktirastyeva, ekādasehani pitā nāma kuryyādi-tīśvarecchāyāḥ sattvāt.* — Viśvanātha Nyāyapañcānana, *Bhīṣāpariccheda* with *Muktāvalī*, tr. and annoted by Pañcānana Bhaṭṭācārya — Calcutta, pp. 416-17.

proper name like *ḍittha* can refer to a particular object, here, toy-elephant, because the toy possesses *ḍitthaness*. A question may be raised here as to what constitutes *ḍitthaness*? That is a different issue.

It seems that every word has referential power or can refer to an object because of *pravṛtti-nimitta*. Some Nyāya philosophers, e.g., Vardhamāna hold that certain words do not have *pravṛtti-nimitta*. Still it refers to an object. For instance, *ākāśa*. How is this reference possible? It is possible because *ākāśa* has *ākāśatva*. *Ākāśatva* is not a *pravṛtti-nimitta*. It is an *upalakṣaṇā*. In order to be a *pravṛtti-nimitta* of a word, a property should be the *vācya* (referent) of the said word. Not only that, it should reside in a *vācya* and must feature as a *prakāra* (qualifier) in the memory of the *vācya*.[9] *Ākāśatva* does not satisfy these conditions, because *ākāśatva* is not *vācya* of the word *ākāśa*. For *ākāśa*, the *śakti* or the will of god is somewhat like this — 'Let *ākāśa* be the qualificandum of the verbal knowledge generated from the word *ākāśa*' (*ākāśapadajanyaśābda bodhaviṣayatāvān ākāśaḥ bhavatu*). Here *ākāśa* is *vācya*, as it is the locus of *viṣayatā*. The *viṣayatā* of *śābdabodha* is not qualified by *ākāśatva*. Hence, it is not *vācya*. Consequently, it is not the *pravṛtti-nimitta*. It is the limitor of the qualificandum or *viśeṣyatāvacchedaka*. That which is *viśeṣyatāvacchedaka* but not *vācyatāvacchedaka* is *upalakṣaṇā*. Therefore, *ākāśatva* is *upalakṣaṇā*. *Ākāśatva* is not *vācyatāvacchedaka* (i.e., the limitor of the referent) because it is not a single character. It is sometimes viewed as the character of being the locus of *śabda*, sometimes as only the locus of *ka, kha, ga*, etc., or it may indicate the character of being a substance different from the eight other substances, etc. Therefore *ākāśatva* is not the *vācyatāvacchedaka* and *pravṛtti-nimitta*. It is *uplakṣaṇa*.

Raghunātha however takes *ākāśatva* as *pravṛtti-nimitta*. I shall not go into the details of Raghunātha's view. I shall only mention that Raghunātha thinks that *ākāśatva* can be treated as *pravṛtti-nimitta*. He opines that in order to be a *pravṛtti-nimitta*, a quality or say, character need not be a *vācya*. It can be treated as *pravṛtti-nimitta*

9. . . . . *vācyatve sati vācyavṛttitve sati vācyopasthitiprakāratvam*
— Gadādhara Bhaṭṭācārya, *Śaktivādaḥ*, Banaras, 1929, p. 41.

even if it resides in a *vācya* or becomes *prakāra* in the memory of a *vācya*.[10]

So, we find that *ākāśatva* may be *pravṛtti-nimitta* or it may be an *upalakṣaṇā*. But it is clear that the singular term *ākāśa* refers to the object *ākāśa*, because the object is qualified by *ākāśatva*.

The same kind of explanation holds good for proper names like *ḍittha*. There is a character called *ḍitthatva*, which is associated with *ḍittha*. Because of this character the name, *ḍittha* refers to the object *ḍittha*. So we can give an answer to the second question with which we started — How do the proper names refer? The proper names can refer because the object referred to by the proper name has certain property (it may be called *pravṛtti-nimitta* or may be called *upalakṣaṇa*).

If we accept the above position then we are prone to admit that proper names are loaded with sense. Before proceeding further we should specify what we mean by the sense of a proper name. Whenever we use a proper name some individuating feature of the individual occurs in our mind, and this constitutes the sense. Now the Nyāya philosophers think that in order to refer to an object, a proper name must have a ground for application, which is a property. Hence, we can say that the proper name in Nyāya philosophy is loaded with sense. For example, if we consider the name *ḍittha*, we see that it is associated with *ḍitthatva* and this constitutes its sense. Taking a suggestion from my teacher Pandit Visvabandhu Bhattacharya's paper we can say that this *ḍitthatva* is *tadvyaktitva*, i.e., the property that constitutes the unique individuality of *ḍittha*. It enables us to distinguish *ḍittha* from non-*ḍittha*. [Jagadīśa has said that this *tadvyaktitva* is identical with *tadvyakti* (*tadvyaktitvastu abhedena śaiva vyaktiḥ*). The relation between *tadvyakti* and *tadvyaktitva* is the relation of identity.]

Therefore we can brand the Nyāya philosophers to be sense theorists in regard to their theory of proper names. Here we may

10. For a detailed discussion regarding *ākāśa* see Brinda Sen, 'Is *Ākāśa* a proper name' in *Jadavpur Journal of Philosophy*, vol. 4, no. 1, 1992, pp. 43-57.

refer to the issue of informative and non-informative identity statements. After the exposition of the sense theory of proper names by Frege, one is inclined to believe that the distinction between the informative and the non-informative identity statements like 'The Morning Star is the Morning Star' and 'The Morning Star is the Evening Star' is possible because the proper names have sense. Both the terms 'Morning Star' and 'Evening Star' are coreferential. Reference wise both the sentences tell us the same thing. But we feel that there is a cognitive difference between the two sentences. The first one is a tautology, while the second one is contingent. These are so because the senses of 'Morning Star' and 'Evening Star' differ. Thus, by adhering to the sense theory of proper names Frege could successfully distinguish between the informative and the non-informative identity statements. The Nyāya philosophers — though adhere to the sense theory of proper names discard the non-informative identity statement like 'The Morning Star is the Morning Star'. According to the Nyāya philosophers there are two parts in a categorical sentence — subject (*uddeśya*) and predicate (*vidheya*). For the Naiyāyikas, in the case of a meaningful sentence generating verbal cognition, apart from the factors of *ākāṅkṣā, yogyatā, sannidhi* and *tātparya,* the *uddeśyatāvacchedaka* or the property that limits *uddeśya* and *vidheyatāvacchedaka* or the property that limits *vidheya* must be different. If in a sentence-like-expression these turn out to be identical, then the sentence becomes repetitive; hence serves no purpose. Such expressions are therefore pseudo-sentences. So according to them sentences like 'The Morning Star is the Morning Star' or *ḍittha* is *ḍittha* lacks cognitive value and should be discarded. Thus, with their sense theory of proper names the Nyāya philosophers do not follow the natural alternative of distinction between informative and non-informative identity sentences. They rather opt for the view, which is most logical.

9

In Search of the Seed of Lakṣaṇā

Raghunath Ghosh

I

THE present paper deals with the root of *lakṣaṇā*, i.e., implicative meaning, which is accepted by the Naiyāyikas, and other systems, which accept *śabda* or verbal comprehension as a means of, right cognition. An effort will be made to evaluate critically the theories that the non-realisability of the intention of the speaker (*tātparyā-nupapatti*) is the root of *lakṣaṇā*, the supremacy of *tātparya* in the phenomenon of verbal comprehension, whether *yogyatānupapatti* can be taken as a seed of *lakṣaṇā* or not, etc.

II

Implication or *lakṣaṇā* is a relation to that which is conveyed by the potency (*śakti*) of a word due to the non-comprehensibility of the intention of the speaker (*lakṣaṇā śakyasambandhastāt-paryānupa-pattitaḥ*). The Naiyāyikas have pointed out the philosophical significance of intention (*tātparya*) first in the context of enquiring the seed of implicative meaning (*lakṣaṇā*). To them the non-realisability of intention or *tātparya* (*tātparyānupapatti*) is the seed of *lakṣaṇā*, i.e., implicative meaning. In fact, the implicative meaning of the term *gaṅgā* as found in the sentence *gaṅgāyāṁ ghoṣaḥ* is 'the bank of the Gaṅgā'. The primary meaning of the terms *ghoṣaḥ* and Gaṅgā are *ghoṣapallī* and a particular flow of water (*jalapravāha-viśeṣa*) respectively. The milk-man-colony cannot remain in a particular flow of water and hence there is non-realisability of the relation (*anvayānupapatti*) between them. This can be removed, if the 'bank of the Gaṅgā' is taken as the meaning of the term Gaṅgā through *lakṣaṇā*. In the same way, the implicative meaning of the term *ghoṣaḥ* is also possible. In the former case *lakṣaṇā* in the term Gaṅgā is accepted, but not in the term *ghoṣaḥ*. In another the reverse case is accepted. If *lakṣaṇā* is accepted in either of the terms, there will not be the non-realisability in respect of relation (*anvayānupapatti*). Hence, it is admitted that the non-realisability of intention, but not of relation is the root of *lakṣaṇā*. The importance of the application of *lakṣaṇā* lies in the fact of removing the non-realisability of intention (*tātparyānupapatti*) of the speaker,[1] which is also supported by Nāgeśa.[2]

Now what is to be understood by the term *tātparya*? The desire of the speaker (*vakturicchā*) is *tātparya*.[3] In other words, it has been stated that when a word or a sentence is uttered with a desire to convey something, it is called *tātparya* (*tātpratitīcchāyā uccaritatvam*).[4] When there is the utterance of a particular word with a desire to convey his own idea to others, this particular desire or intention is *tātparya*. The term *uccaritatva* is superfluous here because of the fact that in the written statement of the dumb persons there is *tātparya* in spite of not having utterance of the same.[5] Moreover, there would arise the possibility of the non-attainment of the meaning of the Vedic texts uttered by an individual having no awareness of its meaning (*arthajñānaśūnyena puruṣenoccaritatvādvedārthapratyayābhāvaprasaṅgāt*).[6] Hence, it is better to accept the former definition

1. *tātparyānupapattirlakṣaṇāvījam* — *Tarkasaṁgraha-dīpikā*.
2. *vastutastu tātparyānupapattipratisandhanameva tadvījaṁ* — *Paramalaghumañjūṣā*.
3. *vakturicchā tu tātparyaṁ parikīrtitaṁ* — *Bhāṣāpariccheda*, verse no. 84.
4. *tatpratītīcchāyā uccāritvarūpatātparyajñānam ca vākyārthajñānahetuḥ* — *Tarkasaṁgraha-dīpikā*.
5. *Ibid*.
6. *Vedāntaparibhāṣā, Āgamapariccheda*.

(i.e., the intention of the speaker is *tātparya*) which is also supported by the Grammarians.

If a speaker bears a particular intention to express that the fish resides in the water and utters the same sentence — *gaṅgāyam ghoṣaḥ*, the implicative meaning is to be accepted as on the term *ghoṣaḥ* denoting fish secondarily in order to bring the realisability in *tātparya*. If a speaker, on the other hand, possesses an intention to make others aware that the milkman-colony exists on the bank of the Gaṅgā and utters the same sentence, the implicative meaning has to be accepted in the term Gaṅgā as per the intention of a speaker as well as for the realisability of *tātparya*. As per the intention of the speaker the implicative meaning of the terms Gaṅgā and *ghoṣaḥ* are to be taken as 'the bank of Gaṅgā' and 'fish' respectively. Hence, the realisability of *tātparya* but not relation is the seed of *lakṣaṇā*. Moreover, this point is substantiated when the implicative meaning is accepted in the sentence — *kākebhyo dadhi rakṣyatām* (i.e., protect the curd from crow, etc.) in which there is obviously *tātparyānupapatti*, but not *anvayānupapatti*. The statements like 'We do not smoke here', 'Thanks for not smoking', etc., have no incompatibility in the relation (*anvayānupapatti*), but there is the incomprehensibility of the intention of the speaker which leads to the implicative meaning like 'Please do not smoke'. In order to incorporate all types of *lakṣaṇā* it is better to accept the non-realisability in respect of *tātparya* as *lakṣaṇā* but not otherwise. Had the incomprehensibility of relation or connection (*anvayānupapatti*) been the cause of implication, there would not have any implicative meaning in the sentence — 'Admit the stick' (*yaṣṭhiḥ praveśaya*). Because the phenomenon of admission is not inconceivable with the stick and hence no *anvayānupapatti*. If the non-realisability of intention is taken as the seed of *lakṣaṇā* then the implicative meaning is applicable to such case. As the entrance of a stick in the dining hall for a feast is non-realisable, the 'stickholders' are to be taken by the term 'stick' through implication.[7]

---

7. *parantu yadyanvayānupapattirlakṣaṇāvījam syāt tadā yaṣṭhiḥ pravaśayetyādau lakṣaṇā na syāt. yaṣṭhiṣu praveśānvayasyānupapatterabhāvāt. tena yaṣṭhipraveśe bhojanatātparyānupapattyā* →

Let us see whether the non-realisability of *tātparya*, which is accepted as the seed of *lakṣaṇā*, belongs to word alone or a group of words. Implication does not belong to a word alone, but a group of words. As in the case of the example — 'There is a milkman-colony on the deep river'; the group of two words 'deep' and 'river' refers to the 'bank' through implication.[8]

It may be argued that as a group of words does not have any potency or import (*śakti*), how can it have implication, which is nothing but a form of relation to that which is conveyed by potency? In reply, it can be said that implication is the relation to that what is conveyed by potency related to a word. Just as the meaning of word is conveyed by potency, the meaning of a sentence is also through it. Hence, there is no inconsistency.[9]

III

Let us examine whether the non-realisability of the semantic competency (*yogyatānupapatti*) may be taken as the root of implication or *lakṣaṇā*. The semantic competency (*yogyatā*) is the relation of the meaning of a word with the meaning of another (*padārthe tatra tadvattā yogyatā parikīrtitā*).[10] Such awareness is the precondition of the verbal comprehension. The sentence — 'sprinkling with water' (*jalena siñcati*) gives a verbal comprehension due to having semantic competency. It is known to us that the instrumentality of water is connected with the other meaning of the word — 'sprinkling'.

In the absence of such *yogyatā* verbal comprehension is not at

→ *yaṣṭhidhareṣu lakṣaṇā. evaṁ kākebhyo dadhi rakṣyatāmityādau kākapadaśya dadhyupaghātake lakṣaṇā, sarvato dadhirakṣāyāstatparyaviṣayatvāt* — *Siddāntamuktāvalī* on verse no 82.

8. *lakṣaṇā ca na padamātravṛttiḥ, kintu vākyavṛttirapi. yathā gambhīrāyāṁ nadyāṁ ghoṣah ityatra gambhīrayām nadyām iti padadvayasamudāyaśya tire lakṣaṇā* — *Vedāntaparibhāṣā.*

9. *nanu vākyasyāśaktatayā kathaṁ śakyasambandharūpā lakṣaṇā? ucyate- śaktyā yat padasambandhena jñāpyate tatsambandho lakṣaṇā. śaktijñāpyaśca yathā padārthastathā vākyārtho pīti na kācidanupapattih* — *Ibid.*

10. *Bhāṣāpariccheda*, verse no. 83.

all possible. In the sentence — 'sprinkling with fire' (*vahninā siñcati*) there is no verbal comprehension, because fire cannot be an instrumental to the action of sprinkling.[11]

If there is the non-realisability of the semantic competency (*yogyatānupapatti*), it may give rise to implicative meaning. Though the sentence — 'sprinkling with fire' (*vahninā siñcati*) does not provide any verbal comprehension due to the lack of *yogyatā*, it can give metaphorical or implicative meaning due to having the non-realisability of the semantic competency (*yogyatānupapatti*). We may quote a line from the *Meghnādavadha* by Madhusūdana Datta, which has no semantic competency, and for this there is a scope for implicative meaning. The sentence goes like this — *fuldal diyā katilā ki vidhātā śālmalī tarubare*?, i.e., does God cut the silk-cotton tree called *śālmalī* with the petal of flower? In fact, the petal of flower cannot cut the hard tree like *śālmalī* and hence it lacks the semantic competency. However, it has got a power of referring to an implicative meaning. The sentence implies that the cutting of the said tree through flower-petal is an impossible phenomenon, which is attained through the non-realisability of *yogyatā*. In the same way, the statement — 'I am building castle in the air' refers to an absurd phenomenon through implication arising from *yogyatānupapatti*.

In this connection it should be kept in mind that *yogyatānupapatti* may lead us to attain the implicative meaning in some cases but not in all. Hence, the non-realisability of intention of the speaker (*tātparyānupapatti*) has been taken as a root of all including the place where there is the non-realisability of the semantic competency.

If the intention of the speaker is realised (*tātparyopapatti*) the primary meaning (*śakyārtha*) is known immediately there. The necessity of exploring any implicative meaning becomes inevitable if there is the non-realisability of the intention (*tātparyānupapatti*) alone which may, of course, be caused by the non-realisability either

11. *ekapadārthe parapadārthasambandho yogyatetyārthaḥ, tajjñānābhāvācca vahninā siñcatityādau na śābdabodhaḥ . . . vahninā siñcatītyādau seke vahnikāraṇakatvābhāvarūpayogyatāniścayena prativandhānna śābdabodhaḥ* — *Siddhāntamuktāvalī* on verse no. 83.

of the semantic competency (*yogyatānupapatti*) or expectancy (*ākāṅkṣānupapatti*).

Now, we may see how the non-realisability of expectancy leads us to the attainment of implicative meaning. A word must have an expectation with another word if the former is not found related without the association of another (*yat padena vinā yasyānubhāvakatā bhavet sākāṅksā*).[12] The *kārakas* cannot generate relation without the help of the verb and hence there is an expectancy of *kārakas* with the verb (*kriyāpadaṁ vinā kārakapadaṁ nānvayabodhaṁ janayatīti tena tasyākāṅkṣā*).[13] If it is said — 'The door please' (*dvāraṁ*), it will provide no meaning due to the lack of expectancy with a verb. This non-realisability of expectancy gives rise to the non-realisability of intention (*tātparyānupapatti*). For this reason the verb 'close' or 'open' is brought here through implication considering the context (*prakāraṇa*) under which it is spoken.[14]

As far as *āsattyānupapatti* (non-realisability of contiguity) is concerned, it cannot be taken as a pointer to the non-realisability of intention (*tātparyānupapatti*) separately. If there is any such *anupapatti* here, it is not different from the non-realisability of expectancy (*ākāṅkṣānupapatti*). I think what is accepted as *āsatti* or contiguity is not essentially different from the expectancy (*ākāṅkṣā*). *Āsatti* is defined as the contiguity of the words (*sannidhānaṁ tu padasyāsttirucyate*).[15] In other words, the contiguity of the terms in forms of subjunct and adjunct forming a relation is called *āsatti*

12. *Bhāṣāpariccheda* on verse no. 84.

13. *Siddāntamuktāvalī* on verse 84.

14. *dvāramityatrādhyāhāraṁ vinā pratiyogyalābhāt na svārthānvayānubhāvakatvaṁ — Tattvacintāmaṇi (Śabdakhaṇḍa).*

    dvāraṁitytretiadhyāhāraṁ vineti ānayatītyādipadādhyāhāraṁ vinā na svārtheti na dvārakarmakānayananukūlakṛtimān ityānvayavodhakajanakatvamityārthaḥ-atra hetumāha-pratiyogyalābhāditi-kāraṇībhūtānvayapratiyogyupasthiterabhāvādityarthaḥ — Mādhuri on Tattvacintāmaṇi (Śabdakhaṇḍa).

15. *Bhāṣāpariccheda*, verse no. 82.

(*anvaya-pratiyogī-anuyogī-padayoravyavadhānamāsatti*).[16] If word is uttered in the morning and another word uttered in the noon, they cannot provide any meaning because they cannot be related at all due having a long temporal gap. It is very difficult to apprehend the relation of both due to the non-identification of the subjunctness and adjunctness (*pratiyogitva* and *anuyogitva*) of the terms in a particular relation. When the first word is uttered in the morning, there remains an expectation of the second term which, though uttered in the noon, cannot be related to the first one as there no criterion or scope to relate this. How do we know that the second word is in relation to the first one? The speaker might have uttered many sentences by this time about which we are least interested. Hence, if there is any lack of *āsatti*, it is nothing but the lack of *ākāṅkṣā*.

IV

Though the Naiyāyikas have accepted four means of verbal comprehension — expectancy (*ākāṅkṣā*), semantic competency (*yogyatā*), contiguity (*āsatti*) and intention of the speaker (*tātparya*), I think the fourth factor, i.e., the intention of the speaker (*tātparya*) has to be taken as the sole factor for the same. It is shown earlier that if there is the realisability of the intention (*tātparya-upapatti*), there is the primary meaning (*śakyārtha*). If there is the non-realisability of the intention (*tātparyānupapatti*), the implicative meaning is to be resorted to. Hence, the *tātparya* has got the prime role in understanding the meaning of a sentence, but not the other three. The sentence — 'There is a jar in the house (*gehe ghaṭa*) is capable of generating a cognition of the relation of a jar (but not that of a cloth) in the house. If a sentence does not have expectancy or semantic competency, it is understandable if the *tātparya* or intention of the speaker is realised or unrealised. In the case of unrealisability the implicative meaning is to be explored as said earlier. In fact, the non-realisability of the intention in the given sentence is the seed of the implicative meaning through which the intention of the speaker is realised. In other words, the inconceivability of the intention in the

16. *Siddāntamuktāvali*, verse no. 82.

primary meaning gives rise to explore the implicative meaning which reveals the true intention (*tātparya-upapatti*) of the speaker.[17]

One can deliberately say a sentence, which has no semantic competency (*yogyatā*) with a particular intention (*tātparya*) in mind or will to speak (*vivakṣā*) in mind. An individual can utter, for example, the sentence — 'The lake has fire' (*hrado vahnimān*) initially to prove indirectly that the lake cannot have fire. This type of cognition is called *āhārya-jñāna* which is defined as follows: *virodhijñāna-kālīnecchaprayojya-jñānatvaṁ āhāryajñānatvaṁ* or *vādhakālinec-chājanyaṁ jñānaṁ*.[18] That is, the cognition, which is generated out of one's own desire at the time when there is the contradictory cognition, is called *āhāryajñāna*. In earlier case it is deliberately said that the lake has fire in spite of knowing that the lake cannot have fire. Though there is no direct result of the deliberation of such artificial cognition due to the lack of semantic competency, it plays a great role in pointing out the exact nature of the object indirectly, i.e., through *reductio-ad-absurdum* method (*tarka*), which is the intention of the speaker. The speaker wants to argue — 'If the lake has fire, it would have smoke also' (*yadi hrado vahnimān syāt tarhi dhūmavānapi syāt*). It is known through our experience that the lake has no smoke and hence it is proved that there is no fire. In the same way, it can be said that the usages that are apparently meaningless may bear some intention of the speaker.

---

17. *gehe ghaṭaḥ iti gehe ghaṭasaṁsargāpratītijananayogyaṁ, na tu paṭasaṁsargāpratītijananayogyamiti tadvākyaṁ ghaṭasaṁsargaparaṁ, na tu paṭasaṁsargaparamityucyate* — *Vedāntaparibhāṣā* (*Āgamapariccheda*).

18. *Nyāyakośa* — M.M. Bhimacharya Jhalkikar (ed.), BORI, Pune, 1928, p. 136.

10

Abhihitānvaya, Anvitābhidhāna and Ananvitābhidhāna

Some Basic Problems

Prabal Kumar Sen

I

INDIAN thinkers have evinced keen interest in the nature and function of sentences. The reasons for their getting interested in this problem vary from case to case. Grammarians are, by the very nature of their job, interested in the nature, composition and function of linguistic expressions. Rhetoricians, while dealing with the specific features of poetry, have to come up with some general theories regarding the nature of linguistic expressions. The Pūrva-Mīmāṁsakas, who maintain that *dharma* can be known only from Vedic injunctions, are also compelled to undertake a detailed study of the nature and classification of Vedic sentences. Finally, for the Naiyāyikas, who have devoted almost all of their energy to an enquiry into the means of valid knowledge (*pramāṇas*) consider *śabda* as an independent and irreducible source of knowledge which involves the use of linguistic expressions.

These thinkers are not always unanimous about the nature of sentences, nor are they unanimous about the process through which sentences uttered by one person produce verbal knowledge in another person listening to it. For the Grammarians, sentences are devoid of components, and they alone are bearers of meaning. One speaks of words that constitute sentences, and also of word-meanings that constitute sentence-meaning. But the so-called words and word-meanings are only unreal abstractions, and can at best be treated as heuristic devices that help us in learning language. Thus, according to this view both sentence and sentence-meaning are indivisible (*niravayavau-vākya-vākyārthau*). This view is known as *akhaṇḍa-pakṣa*. As against this view, the Pūrva-Mīmāṁsakas and the Naiyāyikas maintain that sentences are only collections of words that combine to express some meaning (*ekārtho padasamūho vākyam*), and sentence-meaning is also not independent of word-meaning. Thus, both sentence and sentence-meaning consist of components. This view is known as *khaṇḍa-pakṣa*. The adherents of *khaṇḍa-pakṣa* are also not unanimous about the manner in which we come to grasp the meaning of a sentence. Among the Pūrva-Mīmāṁsakas, the Prābhākara-Mīmāṁsakas maintain a theory known as *anvitābhidhānavāda*, while Bhāṭṭa-Mīmāṁsakas subscribe to a rival theory known as *abhihitānvayavāda*. The Naiyāyikas reject both these views, and support a third view that may be called *ananvitābhidhānavāda* or *anvitapratipattivāda*.[1] In this paper, an attempt will be made at making the distinctions between these three views as clearly as possible. Incidentally, some wrong notions about *abhihitānvayavāda* will also be pointed out.

Some reputed authorities have ascribed *abhihitānvayavāda* to both Bhāṭṭa-Mīmāṁsakas and Naiyāyikas, though this is not correct.[2]

---

1. (i) *anvitārthapratipattyanyathānupapattir iti cenna. ananvitābhidhānenāpyupapatteḥ.* — *Nyāyakusumāñjalī*, autocommentary on verse no. 3/15, p. 408.

   (ii) *anvitapratipattistu bāḍham adhyupagamyate* — *Nyāyamañjarī*, vol. II, p.160.

2. (a) Compare, for example, the following remark of Viśvanātha in his *Śahityadarpaṇa*, and the comments of Rāmacaraṇa Tarkavāgīśa and Kṛṣṇamohana Śāstri thereon:

   (i) *abhidhāyā ekaikapadārthabodhanavirāmāt vākyārtharūpasya padārthānvayasya bodhikā tātparyaṁ nāma vṛttiḥ, tadarthaśca tātparyārthaḥ, tadbodhakastu vākyam — iti ABHIHITĀNVAYA — VĀDINĀṀ MATAM, — Śahityadarpaṇa*, autocommentary on verse no. 2/32, p.82. (Capital letters indicate emphasis added by us).

→

We shall try to show that ascriptions of *abhihitānvayavāda* to the Naiyāyikas is due to some misunderstanding about the exact claim of this theory, and we shall also point out instances where eminent

---

→ (ii) *abhidhayā iti lakṣaṇāyā upalakṣaṇam. abhihitānām abhidhayā lakṣaṇaya va padopasthāpitānām anvayabodhavādinām PRĀCĪNANAIYĀYIKĀNĀM iti arthaḥ.* — *Śahityadarpaṇaṭīkā* of Rāmacaraṇa Tarkavāgīśa, p. 82. (Underline indicate *pratīka*s and capital letters indicate emphasis added by us.)

(iii) *abhihitānvayavādinām padair upasthāpitānām arthānām anvaya iti vādinām BHĀṬṬAMĪMĀṀSAKĀNĀM PRĀCĪNA NAIYĀYIKĀNĀÑCA matam.* — *Lakṣmī* commentary of Kṛṣṇamohana Śāstri on *Sāhityadarpaṇa*, p. 67. (Underline indicate *pratīka*s and capital letters indicate emphasis added by us.)

Viśvanātha says here that the supporters of *abhihitānvayavāda* admit *tātparyaśakti* for explaining our awareness of the interrelatedness of the word-meanings when we grasp the meaning of a sentence. This statement is incorrect, because *tātparyaśakti* has been admitted by earlier Naiyāyikas like Jayanta Bhaṭṭa, who reject *abhihitānvayavāda*. Supporters of *abhihitānvayavāda* like Kumārila Bhaṭṭa do not, on the other hand, admit *tātparyaśakti*. Rāmacaraṇa is correct in ascribing the doctrine of *tātparyaśakti* to the earlier Naiyāyikas, but he is wrong in ascribing *abhihitānvayavāda* to them. Kṛṣṇamohana Śāstri holds the incorrect view that both Bhāṭṭa-Mīmāṁsakas and Naiyāyikas are supporters of *abhihitānvayavāda*.

(b) Consider also the following passages from *Kāvyaprakāśa* of Mammaṭa, *Viveka* of Śrīdhara and *Kāvyapradīpa* of Govinda Ṭhakkura thereon, and also *Pradīpaprabhā* of Vaidyanātha on *Kāvyapradīpa*:

(i) *kramena śabdārthayoḥ svarūpam āha —*
syad vācako lākṣaṇikaḥ śabdo'tra vyañjakas tridhā ।
atreti kāvye. eṣāṁ svarūpaṁ vakṣyate.
vācyādayastadarthāḥ syuḥ
vācyalakṣyavyaṅgyāḥ.
tātparyārtho'pi keṣucit ।।

ākāṅkṣāyogyatāsannidhivaśād vakṣyamāṇasvarūpāṇām padārthānām samavaye tātparyārtho viśeṣavapur apadārtho'pi vākyārthaḥ samullasatīty ABHIHITĀNVAYAVĀDINĀM matam. vācya eva vākyārtha iti ANVITĀBHIDHĀNAVĀDINAḤ. — *Kāvyaprakāśa*, Verse no.2/1 with autocommentary. (Underline indicate the portions in verse, while capital letters indicate emphasis added by us.)

(ii) . . . *arthyanta iti arthā vācakādīnām kramena bodhyā iti. nanu cāstu*

→

Naiyāyikas have categorically rejected *abhihitānvayavāda*. Due to space constraint, we will not discuss most of the arguments adduced by the supporters of *khaṇḍa-pakṣa* and *akhaṇḍa-pakṣa* in favour of

→ *gauṇyā lakṣaṇāyam antarbhāvaḥ, tātparyaśaktis tu atiricyate, tat kimiti tām ādāya śabdārthaprakāras caturtho na gaṇyate ityata āha — tātparyārtho'pi iti. keṣucit vādināṁ mateṣu, ato'sārvalaukikatvāt samaśīrṣikayā na gaṇyata ityārthaḥ. eṣā vṛttir abhidhātaḥ kathaṁ bhidyata ityata āha — ākāṅkṣeti . . . etattritayasahakāricakravyāvartitā śabdasyāvagamanaśaktis tātparyam. samabhivyāhṛtapadārtha-saṁsargāccasya pṛthageva viṣayaḥ. śuddho hi svārthaḥ padasaṅketagocaraḥ. ATA EVA VĀKYĀRTHE LAKṢAṆĀ — ITI BHRĀNTAMATAM APĀSTAM.* — *Viveka* commentary on *Kāvyaprakāśa*, verse no. 2/1 with autocommentary, p.19. (Underline indicate the *pratīkas*, while capital letters indicate emphasis added by us.

(iii) *keṣucin nyāyādinayeṣu. na tu mīmāṁṣakādimateṣvapi. lāghavātpadānām padārthamātre śaktiḥ, na tvanvayāṁśe'pi, gauravād anyalabhyatvācca. tadaṁse hi tātparyārtho vācyādyarthavilakṣaṇaśarīra ākāṅkṣāyogyatā-sattivaśād apadārtho'pi pratīyate. na cāpadārthapratī-tāvatiprasaṅgaḥ. svarūpasataḥ śaktyā'nvayasya niyāmakatvāt. ITYABHIHITĀNVAYAVĀDINĀṀ MATAM.* — *Kāvyapradīpa* on *Kāvyaprakāśa* 2/1 with autocommentary, p.17. (Underline indicate *pratīkas*, while capital letters indicate emphasis added by us.)

(iv) *nyāyādīti. ādinā VAIŚEṢIKA-BHĀṬṬA-NAYA-SAṀGRHAḤ. mīmāṁsakā prābhākarāḥ abhimatāḥ.* — *Pradīpaprabhā* on *Kāvyapradīpa* quoted above. (Underline indicate *pratīkas*, while capital letters indicate emphasis added by us.)

From the passages quoted above, it is clear that for Mammaṭa, the adherents of *abhihitānvayavāda* admit *tātparya-śakti*. As a matter of fact, a section of Naiyāyikas like Jayanta Bhaṭṭa admitted *tātparya-śakti*, as can be seen from the following passages of *Nyāyamañjarī*:

(v) *na hi padārthaḥ prameyībhūtadhūmavat punaḥ pramāṇībhavitum arhanti, kintu padānyeva tatpratipādanadvāreṇa vākyārthapratipattau paryavas yanti . . . . avāntaravyāpāro hi na kārakasya pradhāne vyāpāre kārakatāṁ vyāhanti. padānāṁ hi dvayī śaktir abhidhātri tātparyaśaktiśca. tatrābhidhātrī śaktireṣāṁ padārtheṣūpayuktā, tātparyaśaktistu vākyārthe paryavasyatīti.* — *Nyāyamañjarī*, vol. II, p.140.

(vi) *abhidhātrī matā śaktiḥ padānam svārthaniṣṭhatā* ।
teṣāṁ tātparyaśaktistu saṁsargāvagamāvadhiḥ ।।
— *Nyāyamañjarī*, vol. II, p. 160.

Rhetoricians like Abhinavagupta (see his comments like '*vākyārthe tātparyaśaktiḥ parasparānvite*', '*tātparyaśaktyaiva anvayapratipattiḥ*', →

their views, nor shall we attempt at evaluating the arguments adduced in favour or against *abhihitānvayavāda, anvitābhidhānavāda* or *ananvitābhidhānavāda;* because the debate on these issues has gone on for a few centuries, and it is well-nigh impossible to give an adequate picture of this debate within the ambit of a paper.

II

The supporters of *akhaṇḍa-pakṣa* draw our attention to the fact that we use whole sentences, and not isolated words for expressing ourselves. The sentence 'Devadatta! Bring the white cow' (*devadatta gām abhyāja śuklām*) expresses the intention of the speaker in a proper manner. The word 'Devadatta', taken by itself, can express at best an agent, who may perform some action, but unless we use the word expressing a verb, it is not known for certain as to what this agent is supposed to do. Likewise, the word 'bring', taken by itself, cannot indicate who is supposed to bring, or what is to be brought by him or her. Likewise, the word 'the cow', by itself, cannot make us understand what is to be done with it by whom. But the complete sentence expresses something very specific — the word 'bring' indicates that it is the act of bringing that is to be performed by

---

→ '*dvitīyakakṣānivistatātparyaśakti samarpitānvayabādhakottāsānantaram*' and '*tasmād abhidhā-tātparya lakṣaṇā-vyatiriktas-caturtho'sau vyāpāraḥ*' on pp. 16, 17 and 18 of *Dhvanyālokalocana*, Nirnaya Sagar edition) Mammaṭa and Viśvanātha have, while admitting *tātparya-śakti*, only followed this section of Naiyāyikas. But Mammaṭa overlooked the fact that the supporters of *abhihitānvayavāda* need not admit *tātparya-śakti*, because according to them, the interrelation of word-meanings is revealed by *lakṣaṇā*. Śrīdhara adds to this conceptual muddle by stating that once we admit *abhihitānvayavāda*, the wrong view that sentence-meaning is grasped through *lakṣaṇā* stands rejected. Govinda Ṭhakkūra correctly ascribes the admission of *tātparya-śakti* to the Naiyāyikas, but he also commits the mistake of connecting the admission of *tātparya-śakti* with the acceptance of *abhihitānvayavāda*. Vaidyanātha has made matters worse by clubbing together the Naiyāyikas and Vaiśeṣikas with Bhāṭṭa-Mīmāṁsakas, stating in the sequel that all these three schools support *abhihitānvayavāda*. He perhaps overlooked the fact that according to the Vaiśeṣikas, *vākyārthabuddhi* is a case of inferential cognition!

Devadatta and not any other act; the word 'Devadatta' indicates that the act is to be performed by Devadatta, and not by any one else; the word 'cow' indicates that it is a cow that is to be brought by Devadatta, and not other creatures like a horse or a donkey; the word 'white' indicates what sort of a cow is to be brought, and so on. Each of these words, by virtue of the exclusion of something, makes the statement such that something specific can be expressed by it. Isolated words, taken by themselves, are incapable of expressing such specific things, and consequently, they are not employed for communicating anything. Bhartṛhari has used a very apt simile for making this point clear. Our sense-organs can reveal their respective objects only so long as they are situated in our body. Once they are torn asunder from the body, they cease to reveal their respective objects. In like manner, words can express or reveal their objects only when they occur in a sentence — once they are taken out of that sentence, they cease to express or reveal their objects or meanings.[3] Hence, sentences alone can mean something in the proper sense of the term — words are meaningful only in a derivative sense. Hence, it is not proper to ask as to how from word-meanings one proceeds to sentence-meaning — the process is the other way around. Words and word-meanings are at best imaginary constructions.

The adherents of *khaṇḍa-pakṣa* point out that the argument stated above cannot stand critical examination. It is indeed a fact that we use whole sentences for expressing ourselves, and it is also a fact that the function of a sentence cannot be performed by any of its constituent words taken in isolation. But this does not prove that words or word-meanings are unreal or imaginary constructions. A collection cannot be identified with any of its constituents — but that does not prove that the collection is unanalysable, or that its components are unreal. Moreover, in the genuine absence of constituent words, how could one draw a distinction between two

---

3. *pṛthaṅ nirdiṣṭatattvānām pṛthagarthānupātinām* ।
indriyāṇām yathā kāryam ṛte dehānna labhyate ।।
tathā padānāṁ sarveṣāṁ pṛthagarthānupātinām ।
vākyebhyaḥ pravibhaktānām arthavattā na vidyate ।।
— *Vākyapadīya*, verse nos.2/420-21

sentences that are admitted as different by every one? On the other hand, once we admit the existence of constituent words, we can easily account for the difference between two sentences in terms of the difference of their constituent words. In like manner, words are also collection of letters (*varṇa-samūha*) arranged in a certain sequence. Here again, the difference between two words can be explained in terms of their constituent letters. Once we admit the existence of words that are genuine constituents of meaningful sentences, we may as well admit the existence of word-meanings, because how can the assemblage of some meaningless sounds come to have any meaning? It would not do to say that assemblage of meaningful words like 'cow horse man elephant' does not have any meaning, because while all genuine sentences are assemblages of words, all assemblages of words need not be counted as genuine sentences. To start with, the words must be genuine words having some meaning, not pseudo-words like 'brillig' or 'drollig'. Again, any and every assemblage of even meaningful words is not a sentence — they must occur in a certain sequence, and they must also satisfy some other conditions if their collection is to be considered as a sentence. These conditions are contiguity (*āsatti*), compatibility (*yogyatā*), expectancy (*ākāṅkṣā*) and import (*tātparya*). In this manner, a *prima facie* case can be made in favour of admitting words and word-meanings.

III

Once we admit words and word-meanings in addition to sentences and sentence-meanings, we face a new problem. When we listen to a meaningful sentence and understand what it expresses, we have what is known as verbal cognition (*śābdabodha*), where the meanings of the constituent words are cognised as interrelated. Let us, for example, take the sentence 'Rāma is cooking rice' (*rāmaḥ taṇḍulam pacati*). According to the Nyāya school, the verbal cognition generated by this sentence is of the form — 'Rāma is characterised by an effort that is conducive to the cooking that pertains to rice' (*taṇḍula-niṣṭha-pākānūkulakṛtimān rāmaḥ*). According to Grammarians, however, the resultant verbal cognition is of the form 'the activity performed by Rāma is conducive to the cooking that pertains to rice' (*rāmakṛtakaḥ vyāpāraḥ taṇḍulaniṣṭha-pākānukūlaḥ*). According to the first view, the meaning of the nominative of a sentence features as the chief qualificand in the verbal cognition generated by that sentence. This is known as *kartṛmukhya-viśeṣyaka-śābdabodha*. According to the second view, the meaning of the verb occurring in a sentence features as the chief qualificand in the verbal cognition generated by that sentence. This is known as *vyāpāramukhya-viśeṣyaka-śābdabodha*. On whichever of these views we may choose to accept, it becomes clear that this verbal cognition is a cognition where some entity is revealed as being qualified by some other entity. This is known as *viśiṣṭabuddhi* or cognition of the qualified, where something features as qualificand, and something features as qualifier. Two things cannot feature as qualificand and qualifier if there is no relation between them, and even when there is a relation between them, they cannot be cognised as qualificand and qualifier unless the relation between them is also cognised. Thus, in a verbal cognition generated by a sentence, we are aware not only of the meanings of the words that constitute the sentence in question—we are also aware of the relations that obtain between these meanings. In Sanskrit, the terms used for indicating relations in general, are *sambandha* and *saṁsarga*, while the interrelation between word-meaning that is revealed in verbal cognitions is known as *anvaya*. The entities between which such *anvaya* obtains are called *anvita*. We can now frame the central question of our enquiry. The words employed in a sentence, when taken individually, can express only the entities between which this *anvaya* or *saṁsarga* obtains — no word is employed for expressing the *anvaya*. How then can *anvaya* be revealed in a verbal cognition that is generated by a sentence, which is nothing but a certain collection of words? Here, we cannot say that there is no cause whatsoever that is responsible for our awareness of *anvaya*. Our awareness of *anvaya* is an event, and events must have some cause or other. Such being the case, we have to give a satisfactory casual account of the fact that in a cognition generated by a sentence, we are aware of the *anvaya* that obtain between the meanings of the words that constitute this sentence.

One may try to solve the problem by pointing out that the problem raised here is not a genuine one, because it arises out of a wrong notion about the function of words. Those who find the awareness of *anvaya* in verbal cognition to be a problem start with the wrong assumption that when we listen to a word, we are aware of its meaning **alone**, i.e., the meaning of that word as something unrelated. Such unrelated word-meaning (*ananvita padārtha*) is also called 'pure word-meaning' (*śuddha padārtha*). Under such an assumption, it would be indeed difficult to explain how awareness of *anvaya* becomes an essential feature of verbal cognition. If any entity is not expressed by any of the words constituting a particular sentence, then we cannot be aware of that entity in the verbal cognition produced by that sentence. In the parlance of Indian Philosophers, we can say that if a thing is *a-padārtha*, then it cannot be part of any *vākyārtha*. Thus, the verbal cognition produced by the sentence 'this is a table' cannot have a lion or tiger as its object, because a lion or a tiger is not the meaning of any of the words forming this sentence. In like manner, *anvaya*, which is not the meaning of any word constituting a sentence, should not feature as an object in the verbal cognition generated by that sentence. The interesting thing is that even if we add the word 'relation' to a sentence, the problem raised here will not be solved, because the expression 'This is a table relation' would be as odd as the expression 'cow horse man elephant', and it will not produce any verbal cognition at all. Thus, once we start with the assumption that words stand for unrelated or 'pure' entities (*śuddha padārtha*); the problem raised here would be a vexing one indeed. But if we admit the view that words reveal related entities as their meaning (*anvita padārtha*), the problem would not be as intractable as it seems to be. Thus, words have a dual capacity, they can make us aware of their respective word-meanings, and they can also make us aware of the interrelation that obtains between these word-meanings. Unless both *anvaya* and *padārtha* are individually expressed by a word, that word can never express *anvita padārtha*. Hence, *anvaya* is not to be treated as *a-padārtha*. Being itself a *padārtha*, it may very well become part of *vākyārtha*. This view, where it is held that the primary meaning (*abhidheya*) of a word is some related entity is known as *anvitābhidhāna*. However, no single word can perform this task — a collection of words alone can yield the awareness of *anvaya* in verbal cognition, provided the words concerned are characterised by properties like expectancy, contiguity, etc. This solution is known as *anvitābhidhānavāda* and as we have already stated above, this view is upheld by the Prābhākara-Mīmāṁsakas.

The Bhāṭṭa-Mīmāṁsakas, however, do not favour this view. In their opinion, the primary meaning (*abhidheya*) of a word is an unrelated or pure entity (*śuddha padārtha*). The interrelation (*anvaya*) between word-meanings is indeed *a-padārtha*. The fact that *anvaya* nevertheless features as an object in verbal cognition has to be explained in a different manner. According to the Bhāṭṭas, the *anvaya* is presented to us through the word-meaning, and not through the words. In their vocabulary, *anvaya* is *padārthopasthāpya*, and not *padopasthāpya*. This theory is known as *abhihitānvayavāda*. The presentation of *anvaya* by the *padārtha*s is due to the import (*tātparya*) of the sentence concerned. Kumārila Bhaṭṭa maintains that sentence-meaning (*vākyārtha*) is always presented through *lakṣaṇā*. The exact meaning of this claim will be explained in course of this paper.

The Naiyāyikas have not admitted any of these two rival views. In their opinion, the words express 'pure' or unrelated entities as their primary meaning. In this respect, they agree with the supporters of *abhihitānvayavāda*. But unlike the Bhāṭṭa-Mīmāṁsakas, they do not maintain that *anvaya* is presented to us through the function of *padartha*-s, and here, they clearly disagree with the principal claim of *abhihitānvayavāda*. From what we have stated above, it should be clear that for them, *anvaya* is not *padārtha*, i.e., *anvaya* is *a-padārtha*. Here, their disagreement with the basic tenet of *anvitābhidhānavāda* is quite evident. But the Naiyāyikas are not unanimous about the process through which *anvaya* is presented to us in verbal cognition. According to Naiyāyikas like Jayanta Bhaṭṭa, this *anvaya* is conveyed by the words through their capacity known as *tātparya-śakti*. This view has been mentioned in noted works on Rhetoric like *Kāvyaprakāśa* and *Sāhityadarpaṇa*.[4] But the majority of the Naiyāyikas

4. See the passages quoted in Note No. 2.

refuse to admit *tātparya-śakti*. In their opinion, the mutual relations of word-meanings are revealed in verbal cognition as the words of the sentence concerned are characterised by expectancy (*ākāṅkṣā*). The later Naiyāyikas express this in a different language. According to them, the presentation of *anvaya* in verbal cognition is due to *saṁsarga-maryādā*.[5]

IV

Some detailed discussion of these theories is very much in order. But before we can proceed in that direction, discussion of certain other issues is essential. In order to point out the differences between these theories in a precise manner, we must take into account the corresponding rival theories regarding the manner in which a word presents its object to us. The function, property or capacity through which a word presents its object to us is known as *pada-vṛtti*. A brief resume of the different doctrines regarding the nature and types of *pada-vṛtti* will now be undertaken.

According to the Nyāya school, there are two types of *pada-vṛtti* — (a) *śakti* or *saṅketa*, and (b) *lakṣaṇā*. The objects that they present through these *vṛtti*s are known as *śakya* and *lakṣya* respectively. According to the Nyāya school, the word 'cow' presents to us three entities through *śakti*, viz., (i) the individual cow, (ii) the universal cowness, and (iii) the relation of inherence (*samavāya*) through which cowness characterises the individual cow — because once a competent hearer listens to the word 'cow', he is aware of the cow-individual as characterised by cowness, and this is not possible unless all the three elements mentioned above are presented to us by the word 'cow'. (Some of the Naiyāyikas, however, maintain the view that here, the *śakti* or *saṅketa* belongs not to the word 'cow', but to the cognition of the word 'cow'. This view is known as *jñāna-śaktivāda*.) The *śakya* of a word is directly presented to us that word. There are, however, cases where the intention of the speaker is not properly grasped when we take all the words uttered by him are

5. *śābdabodhe caikapadārthe'parapadārthasya saṁsargaḥ saṁsargamaryādāya bhāsate.* — *Vyutpattivāda*, p.1.

taken in their primary sense. In such cases, some of the words uttered by the speaker are to be understood in a secondary sense. However, what is understood here cannot be any arbitrary thing — it must bear some relation or other to the entity that is the *śakya* of that term. The entity understood in this manner is known as the *lakṣya* of the word concerned. The *vṛtti* of the word that presents the entity to us in this manner is known as *lakṣaṇā*, and it is defined as 'relation with the *śakya*' (*śakya-sambandha*). Rhetoricians recognise, along with these two *vṛttis* a third one, which they call *vyañjanā-vṛtti*. The Mīmāṁsakas also admit three kinds of *vṛtti* — (i) *śakti*, (ii) *lakṣaṇā* and (iii) *gauṇī*. Since we will not have to deal with the functions of *vyañjanā-vṛtti* and *gauṇī-vṛtti* in this paper, their nature need not be discussed here. It would perhaps suffice to say here that the Naiyāyikas have tried to include these two under *lakṣaṇā-vṛtti*, while their proponents have tried to show that they are essentially different from *lakṣaṇā-vṛtti*. Some thinkers have also maintained that what is claimed to be known through *vyañjanā-vṛtti* is actually known through inference.

While all the thinkers mentioned above have admitted *lakṣaṇā-vṛtti*, there is considerable difference of opinion regarding its nature. According to the Naiyāyikas, *lakṣaṇā-vṛtti* resides in the word — it is *pada-niṣṭhā*. According to Mīmāṁsakas and Advaita Vedāntins, however, *lakṣaṇā-vṛtti* belongs primarily to *padārtha*, and secondarily to *pada* in an indirect manner. *Lakṣyārtha* is presented by *padārtha*, while *padārtha* is presented by *pada*. Strictly speaking, *lakṣyārtha* cannot be treated as *padārtha*. Accordingly, the Mīmāṁsakas maintain that the *lakṣya* entity is not *padopasthāpya* — it is *padārthopasthāpya*, or, to be more precise, *artha-niṣṭha*.[6] Moreover, according to Naiyāyikas, *lakṣaṇā-vṛtti* belongs to *pada* alone. *Śakti* also can belong to *pada* only. Thus, the Nyāya view that *lakṣya* is *padopasthāpya* is consistent with its claim that *lakṣaṇā* is *śakya-*

---

6. In a way, such a view is also admitted by rhetoricians like Mammaṭa, as will be evident from the passages quoted below:

(i) *mukhyārthabādhe tadyoge rūḍhito'tha prayojanāt* ।
anyo'rtho lakṣyate yat sā lakṣaṇāropitā kriyā ॥

— *Kāvyaprakāśa*, verse no. 2/4. →

sambandha. The Mīmāṁsakas and Advaita Vedāntins maintain that *lakṣaṇā* can belong to sentences also, just as it can belong to words. Sentences do not have any *śakti*, and accordingly, there is nothing that could be the *śakya* of a sentence. Hence, the Mīmāṁsakas and Advaita Vedāntins do not define *lakṣaṇā* as *śakya-sambandha* — instead, they define it as *svajñāpya-sambandha*.

We may note here another difference of opinion regarding *śakti* and *śakya*. We have stated that for the Naiyāyikas, the word 'cow' presents to us through *śakti* the individual cow characterised by cowness. This view is known as *jātiviśiṣṭaśaktivāda*. The Mīmāṁsakas, however, maintain that the *śakya* of the word 'cow' is only the universal cowness. This view is known as *jātiśaktivāda*. According to this view, the word 'cow' makes us aware of the individual cow through *lakṣaṇā*. When a competent hearer listens to the sentence 'Bring the cow', he brings an individual cow characterised by cowness. He understands that the universal cowness cannot be brought, and accordingly, the intention of the speaker is not properly understood unless the word 'cow' is taken to mean the individual cow. Since the individual cow is related to the universal cowness, it can be the *lakṣya* of the word 'cow'.

V

The following are some of the arguments adduced in favour of *anvitābhidhānavāda*:

(a) Verbal cognition is always determinate or qualificative

→ (ii) *nanu pratipādanam cel lakṣaṇā tarhi śabdadharmaḥ. gaṅgādiśabdānāṁ nīrādikam upasthāpya virāme nīrādyarthenaiva sambandhena tīrādyarthapratipādanād ityata āha — <u>āropitā kriyeti</u>. śakyavyavahita-lakṣyārtha-visayatvāt śabde āropita eva sa vyāpārah. VASTUTO-'RTHANIṢṬHA EVETYARTHAḤ* — *Kāvyapradīpa*, p.27. (Underline indicate the *pratikas*, while capital letters indicate emphasis added by us.)

(iii) . . . *śabdasya lakṣyārthaviṣayatvam laksaṇādhīnam ityataḥ śabde lakṣaṇāropa iti bhāvaḥ. evaṁ ca sva-prayojaka-śaktimattvarūpaparamparā-saṁbandhena śabdavṛttitvād āropitatvoktir iti jñeyam.*

— *Pradīpaprabhā*, p. 27

(*savikalpaka/saprakāraka*) in nature. Verbal cognition that is to be treated as a case of veridical cognition (*pramā*) is, therefore, qualificative as a rule. In a qualificative or determinate cognition, we are aware of a qualifier, a qualificand and the relation between them. A cognition that does not have some relation as its object cannot be qualificative in nature. If some linguistic expression produces a verbal cognition that is not determinate or qualificative, then that expression would cease to be an instrument of veridical cognition (*pramāṇa*). This would seriously compromised if we maintain that words can produce the cognition of unrelated entities (*śuddha-padārtha*), whereas sentence produces a cognition in which the entities meant by its constituent words are presented as inter-related; because under such an assumption, only sentence would be regarded as *śabda-pramāṇa*, while words would cease to be *śabda-pramāṇa*. The relation between a sentence and its constituent words is like the relation between a forest and the trees that constitute it — it is not like the relation between a cloth and the threads out of which it is made. A cloth is a separate substance that exists in its constituent threads, but the forest is nothing over and above the trees. To put it in other words, the relation between a sentence and its constituent words is the relation that obtains between a collection and its members (*samūha-samuhī*) and it is not the relation between a whole and parts (*avavaya-avavayī*). Under such circumstances, one should not maintain that *pada* is not *śabda-pramāṇa*, while *vākya* is a case of *śabda-pramāṇa*. *Pada* and *vākya* thus sink or swim together. Hence, if *vākya* is treated as *śabda-pramāṇa*, then the same status must be accorded to *pada*. But in that case, it cannot be said that *pada* makes us aware of only bare, unrelated entities meant by it. Thus, the *śakya* of a *pada* must be an *itarānvita padārtha*, i.e., an entity that is related to some other entities. Once this claim is admitted, one must also admit *anvitābhidhānavāda*.

(b) *Anvaya*, as we have seen, is the relation between two *padārthas*. It is extremely odd to suggest that while both the relata of *anvaya* are *padārthas*, *anvaya* itself is an *a-padārtha*. But if it is admitted that *anvaya* is also a *padārtha*, then the basic claim of *anvitābhidhānavāda* has to be admitted.

(c) An object that is not the meaning of any of the constituent words of a sentence cannot feature as an object of the verbal cognition generated by that sentence. If this rule is not accepted, then we would face the undesirable consequence that an elephant or horse can also be an object in the verbal cognition generated by the sentence 'bring that cow'. If we admit this rule, then we have also to admit the rule that a cognition that reveals some *a-padārtha* cannot be considered to be a case of verbal cognition at all. Under such circumstances if, we admit the claim of *abhihitānvayavāda* that *anvaya* is *a-padārtha*, then we have to say also that the cognition produced by a sentence is not a case of verbal cognition. Could anything be more absurd than such a claim? In order to avoid such absurdities, one has to admit the view that like the *anvita padārthas*, *anvaya*, too, is a *padārtha*.

Thus, *anvitābhidhānavāda* does not treat sentences as unanalysable or non-composite entities. They admit that each of the terms constituting a sentence plays a specific role by itself in producing the verbal cognition; but they also perform some function jointly, and this function continues until the verbal cognition due to the sentence is produced. A bullock-cart has many constituents like the wheels, the axle, the yoke and so on. The individual functions of these components are different, and each of these functions is necessary if the bullock-cart has to move from one place to another place. However, none of the components can, by itself, make the bullock-cart perform its function. The bullock-cart can move only when each of its components can function in a proper manner. The way in which these components combine and act towards producing a common effect is called *saṁhatyakāritva*. This *saṁhatyakāritva* is also the property of the words that constitute a sentence.

From the writings of later writers of the Nyāya school like Gaṅgeśa Upādhyāya,[7] it becomes clear that while Prābhākara-Mīmāṁsakas admitted *anvitābhidhānavāda*, their doctrine in this regard underwent some modifications in course of time. Earlier writers like Prabhākara Miśra, Sālikanātha, Nandīśvara, etc., admitted what is known as *kāryānvitābhidhānavāda*, while the later Prābhākara-Mīmāṁsakas, whose works are now almost lost for ever, admitted *itarānvitābhidhānavāda*. In order to keep the length of this paper within reasonable limits, we will not enter into any detailed discussion regarding these two versions of *anvitābhidhānavāda*.

VI

The supporters of *abhihitānvayavāda* have not been convinced by these arguments. They point out the incontrovertible fact that a person can understand the meaning of a sentence only when he knows the meaning of each of the constituent words of that sentence. Thus, knowledge that a certain word *X* stands for a certain entity *Y* is an essential precondition for grasping the meaning of any sentence that contains the word *X*.

That the meaning of a sentence invariably involves *anvaya* or interrelation between the meanings presented by the words is admitted by all. One would fail to distinguish sentence-meaning from word-meaning if it is maintained that *anvaya* is presented to us by words as well. Hence, it is only reasonable to maintain that words can present to us their individual meanings in an unrelated manner, and there is nothing further that they can do. Once the word-meanings are grasped, they themselves, along with factors like *ākāṅkṣā, āsatti, yogyatā*, etc., lead to the cognition of the interrelation of those word-meanings. This is the theory known as *abhihitānvayavāda*. The *locus classicus* of this theory is Śabarasvāmin's commentary on *Mīmāṁsāsūtra*, 1.1.25, which contains the following passage:

---

7. *Tattvacintāmaṇi, Śabdakhaṇḍa*, pp. 485-548.

> *padāni hi svam svam artham abhidhāya nivṛttavyāpārāṇi. athedānīm padārtha avagatāḥ santo vākyārthaṁ gamayanti.*

This view has been formulated also in *Nyāyamañjarī* of Jayanta Bhaṭṭa in the following manner:

> *anye manyante-śuddhānām eva padārthānam padair abhidhānam, te tu abhihitāḥ santaḥ parasparaṁ ākāṅkṣā-sannidhi-yogyatvaparyālocanayā saṁsargam adhigamayanti-iti.*[8]

The supporters of *abhihitānvayavāda* point out further that the classification of words according to their meanings cannot be maintained unless we admit that words present their respective meanings in an unrelated manner. Patañjali in his *Mahābhāṣya* asserts the existence of four kinds of words. Some of them stand for universals (*jāti*), some stand for qualities (*guṇa*), some stand for activities (*kriyā*), and some stand for substances/individuals (*dravya*).[9] A similar division has also been admitted by authorities like Daṇḍin, Mammaṭa, etc. This classification cannot be maintained if one says that a word stands for a substance-related to universals, qualities and actions, because under such an assumption, no limit can be set to the exact meaning of a word. The meaning of each word would be some entity that is related with all other entities that are capable of being related to it (*yogyetara-sarvapadārthānvita*). Jayanta Bhaṭṭa has stated this objection in the following words:

> *padārthapravibhāgācca gamyate — asya padasya jātirartho'sya dravyam asya guṇo'sya kriyeti, sa caivaṁ avakalpate yadi tāvat so'rthaḥ padairabhidhīyate, padāntarārthoparakte tu tasminn*

---

8. *Nyāymañjarī*, vol. II. p. 149.

9. *Mahābhāṣya*, vol. I. p. 90.

abhidhīyamāne tadartheyattaiva nāvadhāryate, kadambākārapratīteḥ.[10]

Another difficulty associated with *anvitābhidhānavāda* has also been pointed out by its opponents. They admit, along with the supporters of *anvitābhidhānavāda* that we use sentences for linguistic communication, and they also admit that we learn a particular language by listening to the conversation of competent speakers; who use sentences, and not isolated words, for that purpose. Nevertheless, if we maintain that linguistic expressions can never mean an unrelated entity, then it would be difficult to explain how we understand the meaning of a sentence that we have not heard before, even though we have listened to the words constituting it on different occasions. The fact that we understand the meaning of such sentences can be explained satisfactorily only if we admit that words express only isolated or unrelated entities as their meaning.

A further difficulty associated with *anvitābhidhānavāda* can now be pointed out. According to this theory, the word 'bring' employed in the sentence 'bring the cow' would stand for bringing as related to cow, and the word 'cow' used in the same sentence would stand for cow as related to bringing. In that case, only the first term of sentence would reveal the meaning of the entire sentence — the utterance of other words would be redundant. Such difficulties do not vitiate the doctrine of *abhihitānvayavāda*.

Anvitābhidhānavāda also runs counter to another well-known dictum — *śabda-buddhi-karmaṇāṁ viramya vyāpārābhāvaḥ*. What this dictum states can be paraphrased as — words, cognitions and movements cannot have any *vyāpāra* or operation, once their operations have ceased. Cognition, after revealing its objects, cannot go on to reveal something else. A movement *M*, characterising a substance *X*, causes the disjunction (*vibhāga*) of *X* from its earlier location (*pūrvadeśa*) *Y*, and also the conjunction (*saṁyoga*) of *X* with its subsequent location (*uttaradeśa*) *Z*; but once these two results have been achieved, the movement *M* cannot produce any other

10. *Nyāyamañjarī*, vol. II, pp. 149-50.

effect. Similarly, a word, having presented some objects through some of its *vṛttis*, cannot function again in order to present any other object. The supporters of *anvitābhidhānavāda* maintain that words initially express their individual meanings in an unrelated manner, and then go on to express the inter-relations between these meanings. This is clear from the following verses from *Prakaraṇa-pañcikā* of Sālikanātha, a noted exponent of Prābhākara-Mīmāṁsā:

> *śrūyamāṇaṁ padaṁ sarvam*
> *smāritānanvitārthakam* ।
> *nyāyasampāditavyakti-*
> *paścādvākyārthabodhakam* ॥
> *smṛtisannihitairevam*
> *arthair anvitamātmanaḥ* ।
> *artham āha padaṁ sarvam*
> *iti nānyonyasaṁśrayaḥ* ॥[11]

The *Śabdanirṇaya* of Prakāśātma Yati also states the Prābhākara view as follows:

> *krameṇāvagatān arthān*
> *yugapat samhatān atha* ।
> *pramimīran padānīti*
> *nānyonyāśrayadoṣatā* ॥[12]

This evidently goes against the dictum stated above, the denial of which would lead to infinite regress.

VII

We have noted some of the arguments that have been employed by the supporters of *abhihitānvayavāda* for rejecting *anvitābhidhānavāda*. We shall now note how the supporters of *abhihitānvayavāda* give a positive account of the manner in which *anvaya* can be presented as an object of *śābdabodha*. A neat account of this process has been

11. Quoted in *Nayanaprasādinī*, p. 385.

12. *Ibid.*

given by Sarvajñātimamuni in his *Saṁkṣepaśārīraka* in the following verse:

> *yat kecidahur abhidhāya nijān padārthān*
> *etavatoparatavanti padāni tebhyaḥ* ।
> *paścād viśeṣyaviśeṣaṇatayāpi teṣāṁ*
> *saṁsargabuddhiraparāvatariṣyatīti* ।।[13]

In this verse, it has been stated that when we listen to a sentence, the words constituting that sentence present to us their respective meanings in an unrelated manner, and with this, the function of the words come to an end. Subsequently, the word-meanings get related as qualificand and qualifier, and go on to produce another cognition in which the interrelation between these word-meanings features as an object. This second cognition is known as *anvaya-buddhi, saṁsarga-buddhi* or *vākyārtha-buddhi.*

Here, those who oppose *abhihitānvayavāda* may raise a pertinent question. How can unrelated word-meanings produce the cognition of something related? In answer to this question, Kumārila Bhaṭṭa has shown the possibility of such a cognition in the following verse of his *Ślokavārttika*:

> *paśyataḥ śvetimārūpaṁ*
> *hresāśabdaṁ ca śṛṇvataḥ* ।
> *kṣuranikṣepaśabdañca*
> *śveto'śvo dhāvatīti dhīḥ* ।।[14]

Here, Kumārila Bhaṭṭa mentions a case where a person sees from distance some white colour in an indistinct manner, listens to the neighing sound and also the sound of hooves on hard ground and then comes to have a cognition like 'a white horse is running'. Here the entities like white colour, sounds of different kinds, etc., that have been known in an unrelated manner have produced a qualified cognition of the form 'a white horse is running'. The relations

13. *Saṁkṣepaśārīraka*, verse no. 1/370.

14. Quoted in *Pratyaktattvapradīpikā*, p. 387.

between the entities like white colour, etc., have not been presented to us through any other source. Thus, we have to conclude that the entities (*padārthas*) themselves produce the cognition of something qualified. When we listen to a sentence and understand its meaning, something similar happens. Our cognition of the constituent words results in the cognitions of the respective word meanings (*padārthas*) in an unrelated manner, and subsequently, the word-meanings produce the cognition of sentence-meaning, which is a qualified cognition.

Almost all accounts of *abhihitānvayavāda* contain as quotation a verse of Kumārila Bhaṭṭa, which runs as follows:

na vimuñcati sāmarthyam
vākyeṣvapi padāni naḥ ।
vākyārtho lakṣyamāṇo hi
sarvatraiveti ca sthitiḥ ॥[15]

Here, Kumārila has claimed that sentence-meaning is presented to us through *lakṣaṇā*. This has been explained in a thorough manner by Madhusūdana Sarasvatī in his *Vedāntakalpalatikā, Siddhāntabindu* and *Advaitasiddhi*. Brahmānanda Sarasvatī, in his commentaries on the last two of these works, has embarked on a subtle analysis of the issues that can be raised here. The sum and substance of these discussions on this point is that just as in the case of *lakṣaṇā* pertaining to a word, the word produces a cognition of its meaning, and this word-meaning, in its turn, produces the cognition of the *lakṣyārtha*; similarly, in the case of sentence-meaning, the words constituting the sentence make us aware of their individual meanings, and subsequently, these word-meanings produce the cognition of sentence-meaning. Thus, both *lakṣyārtha* and *vākyārtha* can be said to be *padārthopasthāpya*, and due to this similarity, *vākyārtha* is said to be obtained through *lakṣaṇā*. There is, however, a significant difference to be noted here. A word produces only a memory or reproductive cognition (*smṛti*) of its *lakṣyārtha*, whereas

15. Quoted in *Pratyaktattvapradīpikā*, p. 402.

word-meanings produce a non-reproductive cognition (*anubhava*) of *vākyārtha*.[16]

Having thus stated the basic tenets of *abhihitānvayavāda*, we now proceed to point out a few cases where an erroneous account of this view has been given. Two prominent examples may be cited here. Mammaṭa in his *Kāvyaprakāśa*, while explaining this doctrine, has maintained that *lakṣyārtha* **is directly presented by words** (*sākṣāt-padapratipādya*),[17] and most of the commentators of this famous work have repeated this view. Pratyaksvarūpa, the author of the *Nayanaprasādinī* commentary on Citsukha's *Pratyaktattvapradīpikā*, has likewise stated that words convey the sentence-meaning through *lakṣaṇā* (*padārthānvayapratipattiḥ padaiḥ lakṣaṇayā siddhyati*).[18] Both these statements are wrong; because for the supporters of *abhihitānvayavāda*, *lakṣyārtha* is always *padārthopasthāpya* — it is never *padopasthāpya*. *Mīmāṁsāsūtra*, 1.1.25 runs as — *tadbhūtānām kriyārthena samāmnāyaḥ arthasya tannimittatvāt*; and here, the doctrine of *abhihitānvayavāda* has been stated quite clearly. The portion *arthasya tannimittatvāt* makes it quite evident that according to Jaiminī, our cognition of *vākyārtha* is due to *padārtha*, and not due to *pada*.

VIII

Some eminent scholars like Govinda Ṭhakkura and Nāgeśa Bhaṭṭa have stated in commentary on *Kāvyaprakāśa* that *abhihitānvayavāda* has been admitted by the Naiyāyikas. We have already given our reasons for not accepting this view.[19] The Nyāya theory of sentence-meaning resembles *abhihitānvayavāda* in one important respect — according to both these theories, words present their meanings in an unrelated manner — in a negative way, it can be said that *anvaya*

---

16. *Laughucandrikā* on *Advaitasiddhi*, pp. 701-2.
17. *Kāvyaprakāśa*, autocommentary on verse no. 2/10, p. 28 of Bhaṭṭāchārya's edition.
18. *Nayanaprasādinī*, p. 379.
19. See the passages in Note no. 2.

is not *padopasthāpya*. However, the Nyāya school does not admit that *anvaya* is *padārthopasthāpya* — nor do they admit any role of *lakṣaṇā* in our cognition of *vākyārtha*. Besides, *abhihitānvayavāda* has been rejected in no uncertain terms in a number of standard Nyāya works. Having discussed *anvitābhidhānavāda* and *abhihitānvayavāda* in a thoroughgoing manner, Jayanta Bhaṭṭa has categorically stated that none of these doctrines is acceptable to the Naiyāyikas:

> *matadvayam apīdantu*
> *nāsmabhyam rocatetarām* ।
> *kutonvitābhidānam vā*
> *kuto vā'bhihitānvayaḥ* ॥[20]

These two doctrines have also been discussed and rejected in *Nyāyabhūṣaṇa* of Bhāsarvajña.[21] *Nyāyakusumāñjali* of Udayana[22] and *Tattvacintāmaṇi* of Gaṅgeśa Upādhyāya.[23] This proves conclusively that *abhihitānvayavāda* cannot be ascribed to the Naiyāyikas in any way whatsoever.

---

20. *Nyāyamañjarī*, vol. II, p. 157.

    It may be noted here that while explaining his own theory about the way in which we grasp the meaning of a sentence, Jayanta Bhaṭṭa has quoted twice with approbation the following verse from *Ślokavārttika* of Kumārila Bhaṭṭa:

    vākyārthamitaye teṣāṁ pravṛttau nāntarīyakam ।
    pāke jvāleva kāṣṭhānām padārthapratipādanam ॥
    — See *Nyāyamañjarī*, vol. II, pp. 140 and 160

    This may have led to the wrong notion that *tātparya-vṛtti* admitted by Jayanta Bhaṭṭa is compatible with *abhihitānvayavāda* that has been propounded forcefully by Kumārila Bhaṭṭa. The verse quoted above merely expresses the view that words, in course of producing the cognition of sentence-meaning, also happen to produce the cognitions of the respective word-meanings, just as firewood accomplishes the act of cooking by producing flames. This verse does not express the basic tenet of *abhihitānvayavāda*, viz., our awareness of *vākyārtha* is produced through *lakṣaṇā* by the *padārthas*.

21. *Nyāyabhūṣaṇa*, pp. 279-80.
22. *Nyāyakusumāñjali*, pp. 404-14.
23. *Tattvacintāmaṇi*, pp. 485-555.

Bibliography

Advaitasiddhi of Madhusūdana Sarasvatī with *Siddhivyākhyā* of Balabhadra, *Laghucandrikā* of Brahmānanda Sarasvatī and *Viṭṭhaleśiya* of Vitthaleśa, ed. by Anantakṛṣṇa Śāstrī, Nirnaya Sagar Press, Bombay, 1937.

Kāvyapradīpa of Govinda Ṭhakkura with *Pradīpaprabhā* of Vaidyanātha, ed. by Durgāprasād and V.L. Pansikar, Chowkhamba Sanskrit Sansthan, Varanasi, 1982 (rpt).

Kāvyaprakāśa of Mammaṭa with *Viveka* commentary of Sāndhivigrāhika Śrīdhara, ed. by Śivaprasāda Bhaṭṭāchārya, vol. I, Sanskrit College, Calcutta, 1959.

Laghuchandrikā — See *Advaitasiddhi.*

Lakṣmi — See *Śahityadarpaṇa.*

Mahābhāṣya of Patañjali with *Pradīpa* of Kaiyaṭa and *Uddyota* of Nāgeśa, vol. I (*Navāhnika*) ed. by Śivadatta Kudala and Raghunātha Kāśīnathe Śāstrī, Nirnaya Sagar Press, Bombay, 1938.

Nayanaprasādinī — See *Pratyaktattvapradīpikā.*

Nyāyabhūṣaṇa of Bhāsarvajña, ed. by Svāmī Yogīndrānanda, Ṣaḍdarśana Prakāśana Pratiṣṭhāna, Varanasi, 1968.

Nyāyakusumāñjalī of Udayana, with *Bodhanī* of Varadarāja, *Prakāśa* of Vardhamāna Upādhyāya, *Prakāśikā* of Megha Ṭhakkura and *Makaranda* of Rucidatta Upādhyāya, ed. by Padamprasāda Upādhyāya and Ḍhunḍirāja Śāstrī, Chowkhamba Sanskrit Series, Varanasi, 1957.

Nyāyamañjarī of Jayanta Bhaṭṭa with *Granthibhaṅga* of Cakradhara, vol. II, ed. by Gaurīnātha Śāstrī, Sampūrṇānanda Sanskrit University, Varanasi, 1983.

Pradīpaprabhā — See *Kāvyapradīpa.*

Pratyaktattvapradīpikā of Citsukha with *Nayanaprasādinī* of Pratyaksvarūpa and Hindi translation — ed. by Hanumāndās Ṣaṭśāstrī, Chowkhamba Sanskrit Samsthana, Varanasi, 1987.

Saṁkṣepaśarīraka of Sarvajñātma Muni, with the commentaries of Puruṣottama and Rāmatīrtha, ed. by Raṅganātha Vaidya, 2 vols. Ananda Ashram Series, Poona, 1918.

Sāhityadarpaṇa of Viśvanātha with *Lakṣmī* commentary of Kṛṣṇa-mohana Śāstrī, Chowkhamba Sanskrit Samsthan, Varanasi, 1985.

Sāhityadarpaṇa of Viśvanātha with *Ṭīkā* of Rāmacaraṇa Tarkavāgīśa and Bengālī translation — ed. by Bimalākānta Mukhopādhyāya, Sanskrit Pustak Bhandar, Calcutta, 1969.

Tattvacintāmaṇi of Gaṅgeśa Upādhyāya, vol. IV (*Śabdakhaṇḍa*) with *Rahasya* of Mathurānātha Tarkavāgīśa on certain portions and *Āloka* of Jayadeva Miśra on other portions, ed. by Kāmākhyānātha Tarkavāgīśa, Asiatic Society, Calcutta.

Vākyapadīya of Bhartṛhari, ed. by K.V. Abhyankar and V.P. Limaye, University of Poona, Poona, 1965.

Viveka — See *Kāvyaprakāśa*.

Vyutpattivāda of Gadādhara Bhaṭṭācārya with *Śāstrārthakathā* commentary of Venimādhava Śāstrī, Chowkhamba Sanskrit Series Office, Varanasi, 1968.

11

Can Action be the Import of all Sentences?

A Dialogue with the Prābhākaras

S. Panneerselvam

THERE are two main approaches to the problem of meaning in Indian context, namely, the *khaṇḍa-pakṣa* and the *akhaṇḍa-pakṣa*. In the *khaṇḍa-pakṣa* or the analytical method, a word is an autonomous unit of thought and sense. A sentence is nothing but a concatenation of words. According to the *akhaṇḍa-pakṣa*, a sentence is 'a single integral symbol' (*eko'navayavaḥ śabdaḥ*) revealed by the individual letters and the words that comprise it. Every meaningful word has a definite meaning. When different words are combined, we have a sentence (*vākyam padasamūhaḥ*). A sentence has a unified meaning. This unified meaning is different from the meaning of the isolated words. It is called *śābdabodha*. This means that while isolated words present only single isolated meanings, a sentence conveys a meaning that presents a synthesis (*anvaya*) of the meanings of more than a word.

For Indian philosophers of language, there is no special name for 'proposition' and a *vākya* is identified with the proposition because of the reason that what is discussed under a proposition is discussed under the *vākya*. A proposition contains a subject (*uddeśya*) and a predicate (*vidheya*). A subject must have three characteristics: (i) the characteristic of being referred to (*uddeśyatva*), (ii) that of being already known (*anuvedyatva*), and (iii) that of being a substantive (*viśeṣyatva*). A predicate must also have three characteristics: (i) the quality of being referred to (*vidheyatva*), (ii) that of being newly acquired or known (*upādeyatva*), and (iii) that of being an adjective (*viśeṣaṇatva*). The Mīmāṁsakas define a sentence as a collection (*saṁghāta*) of words, and each word has a certain meaning of its own. A sentence is the 'sequence' (*krama*) of words, and the sentence-meaning belongs to this sequence. Also, a sentence must have a finite verb and if we understand the verb, we understand the sentence.[1]

A question namely, the relation of words in a sentence is discussed at length in Indian tradition. There are two views available on this: According to Vājapyāyana, the meaning of a sentence is the *saṁsarga* or the mutual association of the word meaning. In the phrase, 'the white cow' (*śukla gauḥ*) the word 'cow' connotes 'cowness' merely; the other word which is syntactically connected with it indicates its association with the quality of whiteness. Whereas Vyādi says that the function of a word in a sentence is to distinguish the thing, it means from all similar things. It is the *bheda* or mutual exclusion. Thus, the word 'cow' means not so much what is characterised by cowness as what is distinguished from a horse. In a sentence, words signify things not as having certain attributes but rather as excluding some. In the phrase, 'white cow', the words 'cow' includes cows of all colours and therefore the word 'white' does not indicate the connection of whiteness with the cow. It is to be explained as negatively qualifying the cow, denying all colours other than whiteness to it. In the same way, the word, 'white' can denote anything that is white, including white cows, white horses and so on and hence the term 'cow' in the phrase means only the exclusion of all white things other than cows.[2] The issue namely, what exactly is the relation between the word and the sentence is asked in the Indian tradition. Similarly, the issue, whether the words of a sentence possess the double function of presenting their

---

1. B.K. Matilal, *The Word and the World*, Oxford University Press, Delhi, 1990, pp. 95-96.
2. K. Kunjunni Raja, *Indian Theories of Meaning*, The Adyar Library and Research Centre, Madras, 1963, pp. 191-93.

individual as well as the construed meaning of the sentence or the words only present their individual meanings and the individual meanings subsequently combine to form a single meaning of the sentence is discussed at length. Thus, we have two theories of sentence-meaning, namely the *anvitābhidhānavāda* supported by the Prābhākaras and the *abhihitānvayavāda* supported by the Naiyāyikas and the Bhāṭṭas.

According to *anvitābhidhānavāda*, individual word-meanings and their mutual relation are conveyed by the words themselves. Words in a sentence not only convey their individual meanings, but also the construed meaning of the sentence. Thc Prābhākaras talk about the natural method by which children learn the meanings of words. It is by watching the usage and activity of elders in our daily life that children come to know the significance of words. When the sentence, 'Bring the cow' (*gām ānaya*) is uttered, the hearer immediately brings the cow. A child who hears the sentence uttered by the speaker and the action that is followed, infers vaguely that the meaning of the sentence is a command to carry out an act of bringing the cow. But at this stage, the child understands only that of the whole of that sentence means the whole of what is referred to. Next time, when the child hears the sentence 'Bring the horse' (*aśvam ānaya*), he observes the hearer bringing the horse. From this he again infers that the meaning of this sentence is a command to carry out the act of brining the horse. By comparing the two sentences, the child understands that the word 'bring' (*ānaya*) common to the two sentences must mean the command to bring, and that the terms 'cow' and 'horse' must refer to the two different animals. Thus by comparing the various sentences uttered by people and by observing the action produced, the child is able, by the mental process of exclusion and inclusion (*āvāpa* and *udvāpa* or *anvaya* and *vyatireka*) to have a general idea about the meaning of the individual words.[3]

In this context, the Prābhākaras argue that only the injunctive sentences produce a visible reaction on the part of hearer, and hence

3. K. Kunjunni Raja, *Indian Theories of Meaning*, pp. 195-96.

it is only from these injunctive sentences that the meanings of words can be understood. Since the Mīmāṁsakas give primary importance to the injunctions of the Vedic texts, they have taken this extreme stand. For them, the meaning of words are known only as they occur in injunctive sentences, which have their import in action. The Veda, which is nothing but a book of commandments, consists of injunctions and prohibitions (*vidhi-niṣedha*) and the assertive sentences found in the Vedas are significant only when they are construed with the appropriate injunctive texts. From this it follows that every word must express its meaning only as related to the other factors of the injunction. This means that a word must always be associated syntactically with a verb. The verb expressing an action is the nucleus of a sentence and around it the agent, the object, the instrumental, etc., cluster and are held together through their relationship with the verb.[4] Further, the Prābhākaras argue that words convey their own senses as well as the construed meaning of a sentence. The sentence-meaning is directly conveyed by the words themselves. Construction is presupposed in the very utterance of the words of a sentence (*anvitānām eva abhidhānam na tu abhīhitānam anvayaḥ*). The sentence, according to the Prābhākaras, has a unitary meaning of its own and the constituent words possess meaning only as they are related to this unitary sentence-meaning. In the sentence, 'Bring the cow' the word 'cow' means not the isolated conception of cowness but 'cow as related to the action of bringing'. Similarly, the word 'bring' means the 'action of brining in relation to the cow'. The words give their own meaning and their syntactic relation to the other words in a sentence, so that the sentence-meaning is directly conveyed by the words themselves.[5]

According to the *abhihitānvayavāda*, the meaning of a sentence is a concatenation of the individual items expressed by the words.[6] Words have meanings of their own independently of the sentence in

---

4. D.M. Datta, *The Six Ways of Knowing*, University of Calcutta, Calcutta, 1972, p. 297.

5. K. Kunjunni Raja, *op.cit.*, p. 200.

6. *Ibid.*, p. 203.

which they are embedded. In a sentence, the individual meanings of words one after the other are known at first and then we put together these meanings according to the conditions like *ākāṅkṣā, yogyatā, āsatti* and then we construe the meaning of the sentence. The Bhāṭṭas argue that the meaning of a sentence is always conveyed by the meanings of words obtained from the words themselves. Each word in a sentence has meaning independently of another word. These individual word-meanings are connected with one another and from them follow the meaning of the sentence. A sentence-meaning is not simply a totality of the separate meanings of its constituent words. On the other hand, a sentence possesses a certain unitary meaning, which is due to the synthesis of these separate meanings in accordance with the syntactical rules. The construed meaning to the sentence is obtained not directly form words themselves, but indirectly through the meaning of the words. Bhāṭṭas say that as fuel cannot do cooking but only through the flames of fire, so words cannot directly convey the sentence meaning but only through the word-meanings.[7] The Bhāṭṭas do not accept the Prābhākaras' contention that all words in a sentence are related to the verb. In the sentence, 'Bring the white cow', the adjective 'white' is connected with the noun 'cow' and not directly with the verb 'bring'.[8] The Bhāṭṭas further argue that the claim made by the Prābhākaras that the first word or any one word in its full sense means the unitary sense of the sentence. If this is correct, then the other words in the sentence become superfluous. Also, the *anvitābhidhāna* theory will lead to the fallacy of interdependence. If one of the words in a sentence is to convey its own meaning as well as its relation to the other words, the full meaning of the word can be comprehended only after understanding the other words. Similarly, the meanings of the other words depend on this word. For instance, in the sentence, 'cook in the pot' (*ukhāyām pacet*), the word 'in the pot' (*ukhāyām*) can convey its meaning and the relation to the other word only after knowing

---

7. *Śloka-vārtika*, Vākyādhikaraṇa, 343. tr. Ganganath Jha, Sri Satguru Publications, Delhi, 1983, p. 547.

8. D.M. Datta, *op.cit.*, p. 298.

the meaning of the word 'cook' (*pacet*); so also the meaning of *pacet* depends on that of *ukhāyām*.[9]

The Advaitins who deal with the above problem of sentence-meaning are divided into two groups. Advaitins like Vācaspati, Citsukha and Madhusūdhana Sarasvatī support the Bhāṭṭas whereas the author of *Vivaraṇa* and of the *Vivaraṇaprameya-saṁgraha* agree that both the theories are valid for them.[10] But what is interesting is that though some of the Advaitins accept both the theories of sentence-meaning, they do not agree with the Prābhākaras in full. For instance, Vidyāraṇya who accepts the *anvitābhidhānavāda* interprets the theory in a manner different from that of the Prābhākaras. According to the author of the *Vivaraṇa,* it is not necessary for every word in a sentence to be related to the verb. Relation may be to an attribute, substance, act, causal-correlate, etc.[11]

The contention of the Mīmāṁsakas that the relation between words and their object they stand for, can be known only when words occur in injunctive sentence, is rejected by the Advaitins on the ground that one can know the meaning of the word even without this. Take the sentence, 'Devadatta cooks food in a pot by firewood'. Let us assume that a person knows the meaning of all the words except the word 'firewood' (*kāṣṭha*) in the sentence. But he knows that *kāṣṭhaiaḥ* is the instrumental cause for *kāṣṭha*. This knowledge helps one to understand that the object, which is the instrument by which food is cooked is the meaning of the word *kāṣṭha*.[12] Thus the contention of the Mīmāṁsakas that the significative potency of words can be known only when they occur in injunctive sentences is unacceptable. Similarly, the Upaniṣadic texts, are meaningful in

9. K. Kunjunni Raja, *op.cit.*, p. 201.

10. T.M.P. Mahadevan, *The Philosophy of Advaita*, Arnold-Heinemann Publishers (India), New Delhi, 1976, pp. 52-53.

11. *Ibid.*, p. 53.

12. *Brahmasiddhi*, part I, p. 25, quoted by R. Balasubrmanian, *Advaita Vedānta*, University of Madras, Madras, 1976, p. 11.

their own right. When it is said in the *Bṛhadāraṇyaka Upaniṣad*[13] that *Brahman* is neither gross nor fine, there is no injunction leading to action. We are aware of the meanings of the words like 'short', 'long', 'fine', etc. Due to our ignorance we think that the *ātman* is short, long, gross, etc. The Upaniṣads teach us that the real nature of *ātman* is neither gross nor fine. The attributes here are negated. The above text explains that there is no injunction leading to action and the text is significant and conveys the knowledge of the ultimate reality.[14]

The Prābhākaras maintain that the imperatives induce one to perform some action directly and the other words in a sentence subserve the ends of this inducement to activity. The knowledge of their meaning is known only as they are construed in relation to what is to be accomplished. This means that all words in a sentence denote only what is to be accomplished by activity. This inducement by words to perform the activity is possible by the conduct of elderly persons. The Prābhākaras further maintain that an activity towards what is to be accomplished is based on the words whose connection has been grasped. Since, in the case of *Brahman* there being no grasp of the words, there cannot be authoritativeness for Vedānta. For them, the authoritativeness of the Vedānta is not with reference to an established reality, but only with reference to what is to be accomplished depending on the actions of the elderly persons.

Can there be understanding of the words denoting established objects without any association with action? The Advaitins answer this as follows: In a sentence like, 'The *madhukara* drinks honey from the lotus that has just blossomed', for a person who does not know the meaning of the word *madhurakra* the word-meaning can be known through the proximity of the word *madhukara*, i.e., bee, with other known words. What is important in a sentence is the meaning or the purport of the sentence. What is conveyed is important rather than that of action. It is not correct to claim that each and every word in a

---

13. *Bṛhadāraṇyaka Upaniṣad*, III, viii, 8. tr. Swāmī Mādhavānanda, Advaita Ashrama, Calcutta, 1988, p. 359.

14. R. Balasubramanian, *op.cit.*, p. 12.

sentence should involve a person to perform some action or other. It is true that some sentences involve action. But this cannot be a pre-condition for a sentence. In the sentence, 'He is to offer oblation with gruel', there is some action, which is to be performed. However, in the sentence, 'A son is born to you', a message is conveyed and there is no action, which is expected thereof. The sentence generates happiness to the hearer. The person, who hears this, is happy which is expressed in his beaming face. The birth of a son brings happiness to the father who is informed by somebody. Here there is no action that is expected. The sentence simply indicates or conveys the happy news. There is no knowledge of action that is involved here.

The Mīmāṁsakas argue that while it might be true that one's experience of happiness is assumed through the beaming face and other bodily expressions, it is difficult to say that the sentence 'A son is born to you' is the ground for denoting the cause of pleasure namely, the birth of a son. The words in the sentence being such a ground cannot be arrived at by the process of elimination because there can be numerous causes for pleasure belonging to the past, present and future. But it is the action, which follows the sentence directly. Hence, it is action, which constitutes the first step in the knowledge of things. An action is always with reference to what is to be accomplished. With regard to scriptural sentences like, 'The Self is to be known', only action is enjoined. Similarly, the sentence like *satyam jñānam anantam brahma*, attain syntactical relation with injunctive texts, setting forth the nature of *Brahman* meditating on whom, or knowing whom, the fruit of release is secured.[15] The Mīmāṁsakas argue that the Vedāntic texts are not authoritative in the matter of the knowledge of *Brahman*. The Advaitins' counter-argument is that the above argument of the Mīmāṁsakas might be true if the original cognition of the power of the words dealing with an established entity, as its content is difficult to obtain. In the example, 'A son is born to you'; the cognition of the power of the word dealing with an established entity is possible to obtain. It can simply be concluded that the cause of happiness here is the birth of

15. Citsukha on *Nyāyamakaranda*, p. 161.

the son. It has been seen in the past that such news had brought happiness to the person and hence the person who brings this message to Devadatta knew that Devadatta would be happy to receive this news. It is the known cause for his happiness. In other words, the known cause for Devadatta's happiness is the news namely, that a son is born to him was brought by a person. When this is clear where is the need for one to search for an unknown cause in the past, present and the future? By the process of elimination and exclusion of the various probable causes for Devadatta's happiness, one can conclude that Devadatta's happiness is caused by the direct evidence. Against this, it may be argued that in the sentence, 'A son is born to you', Devadatta's happiness is not due to the birth of a son to him but because his wife had delivered the child without any difficulty. This would have made him happy rather than the news that a son was born to him. This argument, though appear to be acceptable has some basic flaws. First of all, it must be remembered that the sentence, 'A son is born to you', should be construed only on the basis of relation or the words like 'son' and not with the wife. Secondly, in the sentence the words that occurred should be construed in mutual relation and thereby only meaning relating to the son becomes intelligible, and not when relating to wife. The reference, in the sentence, is the son and not the wife.

In a command, the verb becomes an important part and other parts of a sentence such as noun and adjective are only subsidiaries to this principal verb. The injunctive suffix in the sentence is the principal factor and it denotes the activity or what is to be done.[16] Thus for the Mīmāṁsakas what is to be accomplished is alone the inducer to activity. But the Advaitins are of the view that the inducer to activity is the cognition of the capacity of the activity intended by words as a means to achieve the results. The fact that the cognition is the cause of activity is arrived at by the knowledge of the positive and negative instances where the actions seemed to follow and where they did not, with regard to the actions of one's own self. The

16. T.M.P. Mahadevan (ed. & tr.), *The Saṁbandha-vārtika of Sureśvarācārya*, University of Madras, Madras, 1972, p. xviii.

Mīmāṁsakas who believe that what-is-to-be-accomplished alone is the inducer must accept the fact that the cognition of the state of being the instrument of achieving the fruit is a contributory cause in the production of the cognition of what is to be done which becomes the inducer.

The Advaitins further argue that an object cannot constitute the fruit of an action unless it is desired. If a person does not start acting even though he knows how to achieve the object, then it only means that the person has not developed the desire towards the object. To be an object of action, a thing must be an object of desire also. When there is no such desire, the means of accomplishing that desire also cannot be present. It is not possible, hence that there is no attachment and there is the knowledge as to the means of achieving the object of desire and that the activity follows. Desire and the means of accomplishing the desire must go together. This means it cannot be argued that there is no activity in the absence of attachment even when the means are known. Activity, according to the Mīmāṁsakas is perishable and momentary. The injunction to activity like sacrifice with a view to obtain *svarga* cannot be construed with the person who is given the injunction, as qualified by *svarga*, which is not achieved yet, but which is yet to be achieved.

In a simple sentence like 'This is a cow' there is no activity that is involved. The sentence does not involve any activity on the part of the person in relation to the cow, an activity by which the cow is affected in any way. It is not that the cow is known to be there only to be bound, or brought or unbound. The main problem with the Prābhākaras is that they are not able to distinguish between statements of facts and injunctions. This makes them to conclude that it is in virtue of the function of injunction that words readily combine in a sentence to yield a meaning. The Bhāṭṭas who reject the above argument say that in the statement, 'Bring the white cow' the adjective 'white' is connected with the noun 'cow' and not with the verb 'bring'.

The Mīmāṁsakas argue that the purport of the Vedas lies in action. The sentences of the Veda are classified into two groups —

those which are injunctive (*vidhi-vākyas*) and those which are informative about the existent object (*siddhārthabodhaka-vākyas*). While the sentences of the former group enjoin some action to be performed, those of the latter group convey the knowledge of objects already exist. The Prābhākaras maintain that only injunctive sentences of the Veda have validity and informative sentences which occur in the Veda such as — *satyam jñānam anantam brahma* — which describe the nature of *Brahman* are not valid on their own, since they are not injunctive. But these texts form part of the Veda and hence cannot be ignored either. They have to be accommodated by making them subsidiary to the injunctive texts, which are principal. The *arthavādas* in order to be valid, must be construed as subsidiary to the injunctive texts (*vidhi-śeṣa*). A secular sentence like, 'There are fruits (in the trees) on the river bank' which is existential has to depend on another *pramāṇa* or means of valid knowledge for what it conveys and hence has no validity. If a sentence is injunctive, what it enjoins cannot be within the range of another *pramāṇa*; and hence it will have independent validity. Applying the same principle to the *śruti* texts, which are existential, the Mīmāṁsakas argue that they should be treated as injunctive or construed with injunctive texts for preserving their independent validity. Thus, for the Mīmāṁsakas, all *arthavādas* are not authoritative in themselves and they serve as auxiliaries to injunctive statements (*vidhi-vākyas*). This view is not acceptable to the Advaitins for two reasons: (1) It should be noted that dependence on another *pramāṇa* is not due to a sentence being existential, because there is such dependence even in the injunctive sentence like 'Bring a cow'. The reason for dependence on another *pramāṇa* is elsewhere. A sentence uttered by a human being will have to depend on another *pramāṇa* for what it conveys, of whether it is existential or injunctive. Only sentences of human origin have this dependent nature. In the case of *śruti* texts like, 'That thou art', there is no difficulty since they are *apauruṣeya*.[17] If the Mīmāṁsakas say that the *arthavādas* do not have any independent validity, because according to them they are dependent on another

17. R. Balasubramnaian, (ed. & tr.), *The Naiṣkarmyasiddhi of Sureśvara*, University of Madras, Madras, pp. 269-70.

pramāṇa, and hence should be treated as subsidiary to injunctive texts, then the injunctive texts (*vidhi-vākyas*) can also be rejected on the same basis. (2) Knowledge has intrinsic validity (*svataḥprāmāṇyam*) in respect of its both origin (*utpattu*) and ascertainment (*jñaptau*). First of all, the very conditions under which it arise account for its validity. Secondly, even as it arises, it is believed to be valid without requiring verification by some other knowledge. It means, that all knowledge is presumably valid, whatever be the *pramāṇa* from which it arises.[18] If so, then the Mīmāṁsakas' contention that all informative sentences which occur in the Veda are not valid on their own and hence must be construed as subsidiary to injunctive texts is not correct. All sentences are meaningful and valid by themselves and need not be construed to other sentences. Thus, the Advaitins argue that all the *vedānta-vākyas* are purportful because the identity of *Brahman* and the individual self is realised from them. These sentences are not subsidiaries to any ritualistic actions as conceived by the Mīmāṁsakas. When the identity is realised, then there is no necessity for us to practice the ritualistic actions.

The Mīmāṁsakas view that scriptural passages attain their purport only in relation to the injunctive statement is rejected by the Advaitins in another way also. According the Advaitins, there are three kinds of knowledge, which are possible with regard to *Brahman*. They are verbal, imagination and direct intuition. In a verbal cognition, a person can have the knowledge of *Brahman* by knowing the meaning of words. Thus by knowing the meanings of words that describe the nature of *Brahman*, one can understand *Brahman*. This sort of verbal knowledge does not involve any injunctive aspect. In the case of imagination also, there is no injunctive aspect, which is involved because it is established by the co-presence and co-absence of the intensity of knowledge with the intensity of the practice of meditation. Similarly, the third kind of knowledge, i.e., the direct intuition allows two alternatives; either the nature of *Brahman* itself

18. R. Balasubramnaian (ed. & tr.), *The Naiṣkarmyasiddhi of Sureśvara*, pp. 337-38.

or an evolution of internal organ having *Brahman* as its object. Since *Brahman* is eternal and cannot be anything to be accomplished as an effect, there cannot be any injunction with regard to *Brahman*. Similarly, the direct intuition is not based on the other alternative, i.e., the evolution of the integral organ, for the direct intuition as the evolution of the internal organ is a fruit, and this fruit being of the nature of Bliss is desired naturally by every one. So no injunction is especially necessary for the attainment of this Bliss. This means that sentences like, 'The Self should be known' are not injunctive statements and must be interpreted as 'The Self deserves to be known'.

According to the Mīmāṁsakas the purport of the entire Veda is ritualistic action. Injunction or command (*codanā*) is the main character of the Vedāntic texts. The result that is achieved through the performance of the acts enjoined by the Veda is prosperity here and in a hereafter. Even *mokṣa* is to be gained only though the Vedic rites. For Mīmāṁsakas *karma*, is the sole means to *mokṣa*. *Mokṣa* is what is to be accomplished and it requires action for its accomplishment. If this is so, then how about the non-injunctive texts which are available in the Vedas? For example, a Vedāntic text like *tat-tvam-asi* is non-injunctive. For this, the Mīmāṁsakas say that these texts since do not have independent purport, must be treated as eulogistic or condemnatory passage and interpreted in association with the injunctions. This argument is not acceptable to the Advaitins. The eligibility for the Vedānta study is different from that of the *karma-kāṇḍa*. The result is something different. The eligibility is that the person should renounce all attachments. The fruit of *karma* is prosperity, which is what is to be accomplished, and impermanent, whereas the fruit of Vedānta is *mokṣa* which is not what is accomplished. It is eternal and not impermanent.

Injunction is possible only with regard to action. Moreover, anything, which is caused by action, would perish. Action always would lead to any one of the following results: (i) origination, (ii) attachment, (iii) purification, and (iv) modification.[19] Release, which

19. T.M.P. Mahadevan (ed. & tr.), *The Sambandha-vārtika of Sureśvarācārya*, *op.cit.*, p. 236.

is the fruit of knowledge, is none of these. It cannot be originated, because it is not what is made, and is beginningless. It is not what is attained, because it is not what is made, and is beginningless. It is not what is attained, because it is without any relation, and is of the nature of what is eternally attained. It is not what is purified, because it is devoid of qualities and no speciality can attach itself to it. It cannot be modified because it is not a finite entity and is unchangeable.[20] 'Whatever is accomplished through action perishes. *Mokṣa* is eternal. Therefore, it cannot be the fruit of action', says Sureśvara.[21]

Ignorance can be removed by knowledge and not by action. The Mīmāṁsakas' contention that the Vedāntic texts have no purport of their own and should be treated, as *arthavāda* is not correct. The Vedāntic texts have their fruit, i.e., release, it must be noted that while *svarga* which is the ultimate fruit of ritual is an unseen one (*adṛṣṭa*), the result or goal of Vedānta is a seen (*dṛṣṭa*) in the realisation which can be realised here itself. There is no action that is involved here. The Upaniṣads do not prescribe any action here. In an injunctive sentence, the verb is the principal part. The other parts of speech such as noun and adjective have to be understood only as modifying the verb. In the verb, the injunctive suffix (*lin, loṭ* or *tavya*) is the most important factor. The injunctive suffix signifies *niyoga*, what is-to-be-done, what-is-do-be-accomplished.

The Advaitins, who take this argument, answers that the meaning of words is not learnt always in association with action. Even it is so, it cannot be maintained that subsequently also if the meaning of words is to be understood there must be some reference to action. All words cannot be related to *kārya*. If this were so, then there would be mutual relation among the words. The words that constitute a sentence are in mutual relation; they are not always related to *kārya*. The Mīmāṁsakas argue that the cognition of *niyoga* and not desire is what prompts us to some activity or other. But this

20. T.M.P. Mahadevan (ed. & tr.), *The Sambandha-vārtika of Sureśvarācārya*, *op.cit.*, p. 121.

21. *Ibid.*, p. 38.

cannot be correct because activity can always be traced to some desire. The words of the Veda only help one in understanding what is desirable and what is not. If all the words are the cause of action, it implies that everyone who hears them must act. But this is not so.

A man may be active after hearing certain statements of facts. But the activity is not an effect of those statements; it is promoted by the desire, etc., present in the man.

> Even where activity in the form of leaving or taking is found on hearing statements like, 'This road is infested with robbers', 'This spot contains a treasure-trove', the operation does not belong to the words, for those words make known what is established and this have accomplished their purpose and the activity of the person concerned is from his desire alone.[22]

Positive and negative activities are caused not by prescription and prohibition, but by appetition and aversion[23] and here action is not important. For this, the Mīmāṁsakas might say that when the statement that 'This road is infested with robbers' is uttered does it not intend to imply 'Do not for this way'. The reply would be that the sense of words is settled not from the intention of the speaker but from the capacity of the words. Even if it is admitted that a sentence prompts one to activity, the Prābhākaras cannot explain the syntactical construction of words, which are other than injunctive. In other words, it is impossible for the Prābhākaras to claim that the non-injunctive words of the sentence are to be construed in relation to the verb.

Thus, the issue namely whether action is the import of all sentences is seriously dealt with by the Prābhākaras and the Advaitins. The contention of the Prābhākaras cannot be acceptable for the reasons mentioned above. The understanding of the Advaitins to the above problem seems to be more intelligible and meaningful.

---

22. *Saṁbandha-vārtika*, 590b-92a.

23. *Ibid.*, 592b-93a.

12

Word and Act

Pūrva-Mīmāṁsā's Prescriptions for Heaven

Mohini Mullick

IT is of some interest to note that the school of the Pūrva-Mīmāṁsā is known by two other names : *karma-mīmāṁsā* and *vākya-śāstra*. On the face of it, interest in *karma* (action) and concern for the *vākya* appear to have no obvious point of intersection. Do these two appellations then refer to totally independent (even if equally important) areas that Mīmāṁsā investigates? Alternatively, are they in some way linked together perhaps in some larger context, a more fundamental search?

This paper discusses the unique and inextricable nexus between word and action *śabda* and *karma* in Mīmāṁsā's larger search for *dharma*: *dharmajijñāsa* — a search that starts immediately after the study of the Vedas. Our aim is to underscore the unique and novel (can a theory that is two thousand years old be novel?) philosophy of language that emerges in the course of this search. In addition we will touch, *inter alia* some of the themes such as theories of meaning and the relation between meaning and intentionality in Indian thought.

There exists a wide range of views regarding the nature of language in Western thought. At one end of the spectrum is the view of language as an instrument. Like any other instrument it is designed for a function, in its case that of communication. Language is also viewed as a mirror — the mirror of the structure of human thought. A more extreme view is that of language as the progenitor and delimitor of thought. Finally, in Heidegger's words

> Language is the house of Being: Whatever the perspective, human language has been seen essentially as an evolute of the historical process. Its grammar is deeply embedded in the human brain and when it surfaces as a spoken language, it mainly addresses man's social or at least interactive needs (There are no private languages).

Even of the classical Indian Systems that have paid particular attention to language — and amongst these, I include the school of the Grammarians — it is Mīmāṁsā alone that has found for language a much larger role in human affairs. It is this role that we seek to present not only because of the intrinsic interest it possesses as a theoretical position but because of its very real relevance in the world as it presents itself at the inauguration of the third millennium AD of this more later.

As is well known to scholars of Mīmāṁsā, the three defining features of language are the eternal equality of words *śabda-nityatā*, their essentially non-personal *apauruṣeya* nature and the originary *autpattikaḥ* relation between word and its meaning. The status of language *śabdaḥ* in Mīmāṁsā can now be gauged as that of the highest source of enlightenment, not just knowledge (leave alone information). *Śabda-pramāṇa* unlike other *pramāṇa*s is the infallible source which guides man to a realm that is otherwise of inaccessible. And it is codified in the Vedic texts that remain always above and beyond human intentionality. In such a conception, language is mightier than man: it instructs him, it enjoins him to act in the ways of *dharma*. In fact, it quite decenters man. Mundane human purposes, the *puruṣārtha* no doubt exist — but paramount are the purposes of the act *kṛtvārtha* specifically of the sacrifice *yajñyārtha*. The Vedas hold the entire secret of man's salvation, which in Mīmāṁsā appears in the form of *svarga*.

This briefly, then is the setting in which the Mīmāṁsakas developed their system of thought. When we remind ourselves of the fact that even at the time of Jaiminī ~ second century BCE the

Vedas were already ancient texts, written in a language that had become arcane, hence in places unintelligible, even internally inconsistent, we can appreciate the enormity of the task the Mīmāṁsakas had set themselves: not just that of interpreting the texts but of evolving rules for such interpretation for all generations to come, rules that would help resolve contradictions and quite as important rules that would enable the Mīmāṁsakas to reconcile the clash between Vedic norms and the ongoing customs and practices of living societies.

But the acts enjoined by the texts are no ordinary acts: they must be performed in strict accordance with the injunction *vidhi,* in order to bear fruit. How can this be ensured? Do all actions bear fruit? If not how does one distinguish those that do from the others, the primary from the secondary? Is there a criterion of identity for the single complete act? What is the status of the many Vedic sentences that merely describe the deities and their glorious (and sometimes not so glorious) doings? What of the passages of eulogy and of deprecation? For light on these questions no external source can be approached; the Vedas themselves must yield the answers. The text must be analysed, its language interpreted. The well-known Mīmāṁsā rules of interpretation have been the guiding principles of Hindu law for centuries. We will not dwell on them here. Our concern is with the interplay between the Vedic sentence and the agent *kartā*, man the listener and the actor as described by Śabara, Kumārila Bhaṭṭa and Prabhākara. In striking contract to Śaṅkara's Vedānta that derided the path of worldly action, the Mīmāṁsakas belief that *dharma* is to be realised through *karma,* through right doing, was axiomatic to their thought. Now this right doing can only be the result of a listening, *śravaṇa* that understands and is impelled to act.

Not just meaning all meaningfulness is encapsulated in the injunction of the Veda. At the heart of such injunctions — sentences in the imperative or optative mood — is the verb, the *bhāva-śabda,* more precisely the *karma-śabda* that enjoins action.[1] Nouns appear

1. There is considerable discussion on how to accommodate the verb to be: *as, bhu,* etc., which is not directive of action, into this scheme.

to lie at the margins of Vedic discourse. They denote realised entities; they are self-sufficient; in a terminology now obsolete, they are categorematic. Their 'inactivity' has provoked the extreme view propounded in Yāska's *Nirukta* that all nouns are derived from verbs. In such a perspective as Raju puts it, 'the phenomenal world is adverbial' Śabara in his *Bhāṣya* explains to the *pūrvapakṣin* who insists that the relata of an activity — the subject and object — also signify that activity:

> Inasmuch as the objects denoted by these nouns are not momentary (but lasting) any need for others is far away from them; that is they do not stand in need for anything else in the shape of primary (to which they should be subsidiary) these have not got to be produced because they are accomplished entities at the time of being used and spoken of, i.e. — they are already in existence at the time that they are used.[2]

Indicative sentences also pose a problem. They refer to facts, to what is merely the case. There are long disputatious passages in the Mīmāṁsā texts on how to deal with such passages, the *arthavāda* sentences. What significance can mere descriptions, statements of fact, possess? Yet, such sentences do occur in the Vedas. Are they, could they be, meaningless? Clearly not. Mīmāṁsā solves this problem by arguing that such passages lend persuasive force to the Vedic injunctions by praise of the gods the deities, glorification of the deeds and so on. We see then that the significant world for the Mīmāṁsakas is not what is the case. The world is what must be won. In his definite study on *śabda-pramāṇa,* D'Sa says, 'the Mīmāṁsā view of language was founded not so much on information that it provided as on the transformation it worked'.[3] Verbs are unsaturated: They create expectancy *ākāṅkṣā*, they call for the realisation of a goal,

2. *Śabara-bhāṣya*, tr. Ganganath Jha, Gaekwad Oriental Series, Baroda, 1933, p. 172.

3. Francis X. D'Sa, S.J., *Śabdaprāmāṇyam* in *Śabara and Kumārila*, University of Vienna, Vienna, 1980, p. 31.

of a purpose, *artha*. Note here how two important senses of the term *artha* coalesce to perfection: the sense of **purpose** and that of **meaning.**[4] For the Mīmāṁsaka language is essentially purposive not referential or representational. And it is human actions that answer its call. But how is such answering action ensured? So crucial to Mīmāṁsā is this issue that it has worked out a detailed and highly sophisticated analysis of the word — act sequence, a *tour de force* in philosophical psychology could one even say, psychological linguistics.

The central concept that we must look at is that of *bhāvanā*: bringing into being. Two kinds of *bhāvanā* are described, *śābdi-bhāvanā* and *arthī-bhāvanā*: the first alludes to the power to language: to command, to incite to persuade through the verb of an optative sentence which instructs the listener on what should be done to attain heaven and sundry more mundane goals.... Such a sentence when heard sets into motion the *arthī-bhāvanā*, the stirrings within the agent to make the effort to actualise the desirable goal, the *artha* of the *codanā*. How to achieve this is spelt out by the *vidhi-vākya* that tells of the means for such bringing about. Now the verb consists of two parts; The root and its affix (the mood): e.g., Cook-ing in the indicative mood 'should cook' in the optative and 'must cook' in the imperative mood. There is in the literature (and not just in Mīmāṁsā) much debate on which part of the verb instigates action, the root or the affix. For instance, one dominant view argues that the root denotes the *vidhi*, e.g., cook *pac*, whereas the verb ending in *paceta* (the *lin pratyaya*) expresses *codanā*, the drive the instigation to action.

Now there are subtle differences in the interpretation of the *Jaimini Sūtra*s offered by the masters of Mīmāṁsā thought; Kumārila and Prabhākara. The more pragmatic Kumārila has this to say on *bhāvanā*.

> As soon as the *bhāvanā* has been cognised first of all there arises a desire to know what the object of the *bhāvanā* is; because the object is the most important factor in it.... And

4. Another important meaning of *artha* is 'wealth, goods'.

> in every *bhāvanā* that is endowed with an injunction, the injunctiveness . . . is not accepted until the *bhāvanā* as equipped with all its three factors is perceived as being capable of being put into action.[5]

The three factors are: *kimbhāvayet*, *kenabhāvayet* and *kathaṁ bhāvayet*: **what** is to be brought about, **with what** is to be brought about and **how** is it to be brought about.

For Prabhākara on the other hand action is not a means to the realisation of another *artha* or goal; right action is itself the goal to be brought about by *bhāvanā*: *dharma hi niyogaḥ* claims Prabhākara. Hearing a sentence with the optative verb impels the agent to exert himself to actualise, the *kārya* right action, without regard to its result. Prabhākara's analysis has predictably been compared to Kant's categorical imperative, an issue that cannot detain us here. What is noteworthy is the fact that Indian philosophers of the past were seriously concerned to found their ethical theories on a sound psychological basis that makes the moral imperative feasible in action: in this case it is the psychology of command and compliance.[6]

In the *Bṛhatī* Prabhākara says:

> . . . what the injunction really does is to prompt him (the agent) to exertion, and the particular action denoted by the root is only the object of the exertion. Thus, then, what is denoted by the injunctive sentence is the *niyoga*, decree or

5. Kumārila Bhaṭṭa, *Tantravārttika*, tr. Ganganath Jha, Sri Satguru Publications, Delhi, 1983, p. 488.

6. Paul Ricoer could be invoking the Mīmāṁsā notion of *śābdi-bhāvana* and *arthī-bhāvanā* when he writes "when we speak of word as a positive vital reality, we are suggesting an underlying connection between word and the active core of our existence. Word has the power to change our understanding of ourselves. This power does not originally take the form of an imperative. Before addressing itself to the will as an order that must be obeyed, word addresses itself to what I have called our existence as effort and desire. We are changed by the 'listening that understands". — (In D. Idhe, ed., *The Conflict of Interpretations*, North Western University Press, Evansion, 1974, p. 454.)

> mandate; this mandate urges the man to exertion; and this exertion pertains to some sort of action denoted by the verb.[7]

Do these differences between Kumārila and Prabhākara in their understanding of *bhāvanā* have any bearing on the other matter on which they differ, theory of meaning? I believe they do. Whereas Kumārila accepts the *abhihitānvayavāda* theory, Prabhākara argues for the *anvitābhidhānavāda* hypothesis — they are both critical of the grammarian *sphoṭavādins*, rejecting the notion of a sudden burst of meaning — the *sphoṭa* — as an unnecessary and insupportable construct. Kumārila's emphasis on word-meaning and the radical difference between nouns and verbs leads naturally and even necessarily to the view that a sentence acquires meaning through the connectedness of the words that compose it, each with its own prior meaning and function. He says:

> If the words of a sentence have no separate meanings of their own, then the classification of words into nouns, adjectives, verbs, etc., becomes meaningless.... Moreover if the meaning of a sentence were quite independent of the meaning of its constituent words then any sentence could convey any meaning.

Again,

> also the meaning of a brand new sentence is inexplicable without prior acquaintance with the meanings of its constituent words.[8]

The notion of sequence — both of the syllables of a word and of the words in a sentence is important for Kumārila who focuses on the sentence as it is uttered. This temporarily the *sphoṭa* theory fails to take into account. In Kumārila's words,

---

7. Quoted by Ganganath Jha in *Śābara Bhāṣya, Bhāvārthādhikaraṇa*, p. 177.

8. Quoted in S.C. Chatterjee, *Nyāya Theory of Knowledge*, Calcutta University, Calcutta, 1939, p. 372.

> Though we have no other ground (for the cognition of the meaning of the sentence) yet we perceive that the meanings of the words (composing the sentence) are such grounds inasmuch as the cognition of the meaning of a sentence appears only when there is a cognition of the meanings of the word.[9]

Prabhākara on the other hand, urges that words take on meaning only when they occur in a sentence expressing a complete thought. For Prabhākara it is the relation between the entire sentence and its meaning that is eternal, since the sentence alone can express the *codanā* the drive to right action.

> The verb denoting the command ... is the principal word ... and the remaining words possess a meaning only in relation to the action.[10]

Kunjunni Raja's suggestion that Prabhākara lays stress on the natural process by which children learn their mother tongue is of interest.[11] By observing the use of language and the concomitant activity of his elders the child learns that words are never used in isolation but have meaning only in the context of a sentence. Thus in the sentence 'Bring the cow' the word 'cow' means not the isolated concept 'cowness' but cow as related to the action of brining — the same is true of the word 'bring'. It is only in the presence of a syntactic relation that meaning is born.

Thus three principles in the analysis of meaning are enunciated by the Mīmāṁsakas.The first *ākāṅkṣā* expectancy is the most important; the second is *sannidhi* phonetic contiguity and the third is *yogyatā* fitness or logical consistency. They are all illustrated in the sentence: 'Bring the cow'. The Western world had to wait for a

---

9. Kumārila Bhaṭṭa, *Ślokavārttika, Vākyādhikaraṇam*, pp. 110-11, tr. Ganganath Jha, Sri Satguru Publishers, Delhi, 1983.

10. K. Kunjunni Raja, *Indian Theories of Meaning*, The Adyar Library and Research Centre, Madras, 1963, p. 197.

11. The Grammarians and the Naiyāyikas use almost identical argument.

Piaget in the twentieth century for such an intricate analysis. Language may not be **of** or **by** man, but it is nothing if not **for** man. It is man's road to Heaven.

Thus far we have looked at some of the ways in which Mīmāṁsā has employed linguistic analysis in order to relate the *veda-vākya* with *karma* (action) — the *kriyā-kārika-sambandha*. But what is a *vākya*? Is there a principle for the individuation of a single sentence? (The very question may cause puzzlement until one recalls that the Mīmāṁsakas were dealing with very ancient texts not easily decipherable as explained earlier). Interestingly, the affirmative answer that is offered draws reciprocally from Mīmāṁsā's theory of action. Action is defined in terms of purpose — *artha*; each distinct purpose serves to individuate a sentence by the principle *arthaikatva*. In Jaiminī's words,

> So long as a single purpose is served by a number of words, which on being separated are found to be wanting and incapable of effecting the said purpose they form one syntactic unit one complete *mantra*.[12]

Given this criterion many grammatically independent sentences could be construed as one single sentence. The answer to this objection raised by Bhartṛhari is: yes, these constitute a *mahāvākya*.

A word about the relation between meaning and human intention. By now, it must be abundantly clear that the *veda-vākya* being *apauruṣeya*, there can be no role for human intention in interpreting their import. Yet — and this is important — for affairs of the world and everyday *laukika* communication the Mīmāṁsakas were as practical as they come. All the other *pramāṇas* come into play — perception inference analogy, etc. They give due recognition to the languages of the *mlecchas* and the outsiders: The world as it is

---

12. *arthaikatvādhikaṁ vākyam*
sākāṅkṣā cetvebhāge syāt.

Mīmāṁsā-sūtra, II.i.46, tr. from Ganganath Jha in *Śābara-bhāṣya* Gaekwad Oriental Series, Baroda, 1933, p. 213.

given is real.[13] But *svarga, prīti* is another matter. Here only *śabda* is *pramāṇa*. In a Godless world — and theirs is such a one — there is no refuge but the text, for all meaning, all direction.

If that last sentence has a familiar, recognisable ring to it then let me confess that is wholly intentional. I believe that there are lessons to be learnt today from Mīmāṁsā's two thousand year old philosophy of language — even though in an important sense we must first stand it on its head!

For we also live in a world that seeks not *mokṣa* liberation but *svarga*, extreme happiness, complete fulfilment, in a word bliss. What's more, we live in an age of action, not contemplation, an age which measures man by his performance — or is it performances. What role does language play in our search for bliss? Today's *svarga*s are packaged and handed out to us in carefully, cleverly crafted images — images of success, of beauty, power and even of bliss itself. And today's image-makers, the high priest of the 'good life', invoke and chant the necessary *mantra*s — what if they come online! — culled out of contemporary Vedas. Never before in history have words possessed the sort of *śābdi-bhāvanā* as they do today in the making of heaven and more to the point **in instructing us how to get there.** The charisma of the modern *guru* — not least the second order *guru*s of image-making itself the compelling enticement of the **'Just Do It'** slogans the unsolicited prescriptions for perfection all too successfully instigate the 'right' kind of *arthī-bhāvanā* in us — quite literally *arthī*. They enjoin the sacrifices that are mandatory for today's instant, a-click-away paradise.

---

13. In an interesting and important passage Kumārila says 'As for the comparative strength of the upholders of different usages (viz., the *Mlecchas* and the *Aryas*), the superior authority of the latter has been laid down only in matters relating to *Dharma* directly, as for the ordinary wordly things, such as agriculture and the like, all usages are equally authoritative. Consequently in matter relating to menial service, house-building and the like, we can freely admit the superior authority of the *Mlecchas*'. — *Tantravārtika*, p. 222.

In all this it is *śabdaḥ* emanating from remote invisible oracles possessing the same aura of infallibility that create in the unsuspecting captive consumer the need for ever so many more needs, the insatiable desire to bring about a personalised *svarga*.

Western thought has been so obsessed with reason and sense experience as the mutually exhaustive sources of human knowledge and action. It has failed to give full recognition to the power of language to influence human affairs.[14] Wittgenstein appears to have been on the verge of such an insight when he says

> Not: without language we could not communicate with one another — but for sure: without language we cannot influence other people in such-and-such ways; cannot build roads and machines, etc. And also: without the use of speech and writing people could not communicate.[15]

But this insight has remained largely ignored in the West. However, we ignore the Mīmāṁsā philosophy of language at our own peril.

---

14. To be fair, we note that R.M. Hare, distinguishes the phrastic from the neustic of ethical terms and Austin described the perlocutionary act. The speech-act theory however has another focus.

15. Wittgenstein, Ludwig, *Philosophical Investigations*, Part. I, section 491, tr. G.E.M. Anscome, Basil Blackwell, Oxford, 1976.

13

In Search of a Sound Theory of Semantics in Indian Philosophy

K.S. Prasad

I

THE concept of meaning is a fundamental and indispensable aspect of philosophy of language. Language being a form of human activity, chiefly concerned as an instrument of communication. However, communication is not the only function of language. It has yet another important and more basic function which consists in locating and identifying the objects. To have an experience is one thing but to identify the thing so experienced and give a place in the scheme of reality, language is an indispensable tool. In this sense, the various theories of meaning in Indian philosophy form a complex array and each of them are in tune to their metaphysical commitments. The purpose of this paper will be to exhibit some of the structures of Indian theories of meaning and to say something about which of these theories might be appealing to common sense. I shall approach this through an examination of the debate among Grammarians and the two schools of Mīmāṁsā namely Bhāṭṭa-Mīmāṁsā and Prābhākara-Mīmāṁsā over three major theories of sentence comprehension namely *akhaṇḍa-vākyārthavāda, abhihitānvayavāda* and *anvitābhidhānavāda*. Since the debate is lengthy and complex, I shall not attempt to present a historically accurate depiction of these theories but rather confine myself to what I consider to be the most significant formulations of these theories under consideration and the significant arguments in their favour.

The parties in this debate, the Grammarians, and the two schools of Mīmāṁsā showed considerable interest in their literature in developing a theory of language. As the name suggests the Grammarians were mainly interested in the logic of language, i.e., a formal characterisation of Sanskrit syntax. The Mīmāṁsakas with their emphasis on the performance of Vedic rituals and sacrifices to achieve desired results, developed systematic views on the nature of language to understand the Vedic texts.

The guiding force for the differences among these schools under consideration in connection with the problem of the meaning is largely due to their emphasis on what constitutes the basic unit of meaning. There are two approaches: *vākyavāda* and *padavāda*. They are also referred as *akhaṇḍa-pakṣavāda* and *khaṇḍa-pakṣavāda* respectively. According to *vākyavāda* the sentence is the basic indivisible semantic unit, which cannot be split into parts like words and word-meanings, for these words and word-meanings are unreal abstractions meant for certain grammatical purposes. The independent nature of sentence and its meaning is emphasised here. This theory is known as *akhaṇḍa-vākyārthavāda* maintained by Bhartṛhari and other Grammarians. On the other hand, *padavāda* emphasises word as the basic semantic unit. According to this theory, the sentence is a composite entity composed of the words and these words are meaningful units of language. Both the schools of Pūrva-Mīmāṁsā generally admit this theory. However, there are certain differences among them. The Bhāṭṭa school of Pūrva-Mīmāṁsā maintains that the meaning of a sentence is merely the synthesis of the meanings of the separate words composing it. On this view, the sentence meaning is known by connecting the individual word meanings conveyed by the constituent words of that sentence. This theory is known as *abhihitanvayavāda*. While maintaining the reality of the words, Prābhākara School of Pūrva-Mīmāṁsā argue that the words do not have meanings in isolation but acquire meaning only when used in sentences. The meaning of a word is always a related meaning. On this view, a word can complete its function only when all the relata are brought to the mind of the listener by the other words in a sentence. Thus a sentence has a unitary meaning of its own which cannot be resolved into complex meanings of its words. This theory is known as *anvitābhidhānavāda*. Let me briefly expound the structures of these three theories namely *akhaṇḍa-vākyārthavāda*, *abhihitānvayavāda* and *anvitābhidhānavāda* and examine their acceptability as a viable theory semantics in Indian philosophy.

II

According to *akhaṇḍa-vākyārthavāda*, adopted by the Grammarians in general and Bhartṛhari in particular, the sentence is the basic, indivisible semantic unit. According to this theory, sentence is an indivisible whole[1] and the meaning of sentence is also grasped as a whole.[2] It is true that we use several words in a sentence but these words do not have autonomous existence, for communication in daily life is possible only through sentences. The reality belongs only to sentence and its meaning. They argue that the relation between words and sentence is similar to phonemes and word.[3] A word cannot be understood unless all its constituent phonemes are cognised and thus a phoneme is not a basic semantic unit. Similarly, *akhaṇḍa-vākyārthavādins* argue, we cannot understand a sentence unless all its constituent words are cognised and this suggests that word is not a basic semantic unit.[4] A sentence is complete in itself.[5] It possesses an individuality of its own and is not merely an aggregate of words. The unity of a sentence is like a living body, we, of course, can chop off the head, hands and limbs from the body, but neither the body nor the limbs are any longer living. The words as parts of sentence are thus unreal abstractions of the sentence and the word-meanings, which are the intellectual abstractions of the sentence meaning also unreal. Why then the words are abstracted at all? The

1. Bhartṛhari, *Vākyapadīya*, II.22, tr. K.A. Subramania Iyer, Motilal Banarsidass, Delhi, 1977.
2 *Ibid*, II.27.
3. *Ibid*, II.60.
4. *Ibid*, II.54.
5. *Ibid*. II.9.

simple answer is: to help us in our study of the nature of a sentence.[6] The question still persists. How the unreal abstracted words can help in comprehending the real indivisible nature of sentence? Just as an unreal snake in a rope can generate real fear in the cogniser, so also unreal abstracted words may point to the real, where pointing is nothing but drawing our attention to the true.[7]

Akhaṇḍa-vākyārthavādins argue that sentence and its meaning are partless, for the opposed view that the sentence consists of parts leads to absurd conclusions. If a sentence is considered as having parts then words constitute its parts. Letters constitute the parts of a word. A letter also should consist of parts. These parts should also consist of parts and it goes on *ad infinitum*.[8] If we can stop the process of splitting at the stage of letters, why cannot it be at the stage of sentence itself? Further, whenever a sentence is uttered, the listener understands the unitary sense of the sentence expressed by the speaker. The consciousness of meaning of a sentence is like an integral whole, which admits of no parts. Such an awareness can lead to an assumption that sentence is an indivisible unit. What appears to be a part of a sentence is nothing but an illusion.[9] The meaning of a sentence is also an indivisible whole. The unified whole meaning of a sentence cannot be understood if it is analysed during the comprehension of the sentence and its meaning. The analysis may be done after understanding the complete meaning of the sentence, which is an indivisible, self-sufficient unit.

Further, *akhaṇḍa-vākyārthavādins* argue that the acceptance of

---

6. Bhartṛhari, *Vākyapadīya*, II.343.

7. In the world, one sometimes reaches the real through the unreal. We can understand what kind of animal a cow is by looking at a picture of it. That does not mean that the picture of a cow is a real cow. See critical explanation of the text, *Vākyapadīya*, II.344, *op.cit.* p. 148.

8. *Vākyapadīya*, II.28-29, *op. cit.*, p.14.

9. *Ibid.* II.287. *op.cit.* '. . . mere cognition is not enough for determining the existence of an object. We take a mirage to be water, but there is no water there. pp. 125-26.

the autonomy of words and word-meanings lead to contradiction, for, most often the word meanings do not retain their individuality when used in a sentence.[10] For instance in the sentence, *aśvakarṇa-kusumamasti, aśvakarṇakusumam* means the flower of a particular species of tree namely *aśvakarṇa.* If the individual words are taken, then the word *aśva* means a horse, the word *karṇa* means ear and the word *kusuma* means flower. In such a situation, the expression becomes meaningless. Thus in the sentence under consideration, the individual meanings of the constituent words *aśva, karṇa* and *kusuma* do not contribute to the meaning of the sentence. The meaning comes from the sentence as a whole. The Grammarians with the help of negative sentences further reinforce the indivisibility of sentence and sentence meaning.[11] For instance, the sentence *vṛkṣo nāsti* ('tree there is not') can be analysed into two individual words. The first word 'tree' denotes the tree as something that exists and the second word 'there is not' denies its existence. This leads to contradiction for if the tree exists, its existence cannot be denied and if does not exist, its denial is superfluous. This problem is due to the splitting of the sentence into words and trying to understand the sentence through words. However, if the sentence is considered as a whole, this problem does not arise.

Akhaṇḍa-vākyārthavādins advanced several reasons to prove the unreality of word and word-meaning. As it is beyond the scope of this paper to give a detailed account of these reasons, let me summarise some of the important reasons to prove superfluity of the word and word-meaning.

1. Words in isolation are unreal, for they are unfit for communication. People employ only sentences to communicate with others.

2. There is no fixity in the word-meanings, for one and the same word may denote two or more different objects

10. *Vākyapadīya*, II.36.

11. *Ibid*, II.241.

(*saindhava* means both horse and salt) or one and the same thing may be denoted by several words (*kumbha, kalaśa* and *ghaṭa* mean pot) and it is only on the basis of the context that definiteness in meaning is arrived, which is possible only in a sentential structure.[12]

3. Word-meanings do not constitute the sentence-meaning, because each subsequent word in the sentence conveys its meaning as mixed up with those of preceding words and so the meanings conveyed by the preceding words are abandoned in their original form. Therefore, when the sentence meaning is grasped, it will not be due to the preceding words.[13] Just as one can abandon the raft after reaching the shore, so also the listener abandons the word-meanings after grasping the sentence-meaning. The word-meanings are only a means to an end.[14]

The simple argument against *akhaṇḍa-vākyārthavāda* is based on common sense. It is a common experience that whenever we fail to understand the meaning of a particular word of a sentence, we look for its meaning, even though the other meanings of the words of the sentence are known, so that we can understand the meaning of a sentence. The very fact that we are seeking a clarification for a word suggests that the words are not unreal abstractions of the sentence. For instance, consider the following possibilities.

1. 'Bring a loaf of bread from the super market'.
2. 'Bring a pack of asafoetida from the super market'.
3. 'Bring a loaf of bread and a pack of asafetida from the super market'.

In (1) the listener understands the meaning of the sentence and

---

12. *Vākyapadīya*, II. 314; 317-18.

13. *Ibid*, II.34.

14. *Ibid*, II.55.

execute the request as he cognises the meaning of all words of the sentence. In (2) the listener may not know the meaning of one word, namely, 'asafoetida', and therefore he fails to execute the request even though he knows the other meanings of the words of the sentence. He looks for the meaning of the word, asaefoetida. He can execute the request only after knowing the meaning of the word 'asafoetida'. This fact of seeking clarification for the word asafoetida suggests the reality of word. Here it may be raised that the failure to understand the sentence is not related to the failure to understand the word but the entire sentence. However, consider (3), where the listener grasps the meanings of all the words in the sentence except the word, 'asafoetida'. Though he is unable to understand the meaning of the word 'asafoetida', he still proceeds to bring a loaf of bread from super market. The act of bringing loaf bread whose meaning he knows, though he failed to grasp the meaning of the word 'asafoetida' suggest that the words convey their meanings even though the whole sentence is not grasped. That is, the listener though handicapped in not knowing the meaning of one word still is able to understand a part of the sentence and act accordingly. Thus, the words have their meaning, as not knowing the meaning of one word in a sentence does not amount to not knowing the entire meaning of a sentence. From this it follows that words are not unreal abstractions of the sentence and it is the word-meanings that contribute the sentence-meaning.

Another point from where we can critically look at *akhaṇḍa-vākyārthavāda* is that the question of using a substitute becomes understandable only when the individual words are recognised as parts of a sentence. It is a common practice that in the case of a substance with which a particular act is to be performed and if it is not available; a substitute for the same might be employed. To illustrate, consider the following sentences:

> Cut the branches of the tree with an axe.
> In the absence of an axe, a saw can be used as the substitute.

It may be argued by *akhaṇḍa-vākyārthavādins* that these two sentences are two individual wholes conveying two different meanings. From this it follows that the cutting of the branches of the tree with an axe is different from cutting the branches of the tree with saw. However, such view is untenable, for the question of substitute in the above example is restricted to the instrument that is to be used in performing an action and not the action itself. Since the result remains the same and the means are only different, we can argue that the words like 'axe' and 'saw' do convey their meanings. Thus, the reality of the parts of sentence is to be recognised.

Yet, another point from where we can critically look at *akhaṇḍa-vākyārthavāda* is from the language learning process. Language learning is an activity wherein if we are acquainted with the words and their meanings then we can very well make out the meaning of many sentences by means of insertion and elimination. If by means of insertion and elimination the meaning of a word is not grasped then each sentence being an individual unit the number of sentences being infinite, to know all sentences is an impossible task. To illustrate, consider the following sentences:

Bring the car.
Park the car.

By inserting a proper name such as Kṛṣṇa, Gopāl, Gautam, John and Irfan, each to these two sentences we can generate ten sentences. Further, by inserting an adjective in the form colour, say white, to the car in all the ten sentences cited above, we could generate twenty sentences. If we go by the principle that the sentence is an indivisible unit, the words are unreal abstractions of it, then each of the above sentences become one whole, and in the process we may have to learn all the twenty sentences without simplifying, which is absurd. This can be circumscribed on the assumption that word is the basic semantic unit of language and the sentence-meaning is the function of word-meanings. In the example cited above, if we know the meanings of nine words (Kṛṣṇa, Gopāl, Gautam, John, Irfan, bring, park, white and car),[15] we can very well understand all the twenty

15. The definite article is not used in the Sanskrit language.

sentences. This shows how with a limited number of words, an unlimited number of sentences can be produced. Thus, by the rejecting the autonomy to word and word-meanings the ability to grasp the meanings of infinite number of sentences becomes virtually inexplicable.

III

Having argued for the reality of word and word-meaning, however, the semantic completeness or incompleteness of words needs exploration. That is, do the words have any significant existence independent of a sentence or they acquire significance only as parts of the sentence structure. Between the two schools of Pūrva-Mīmāṁsā, the followers of Kumārila Bhaṭṭa subscribe to *abhihitānvayavāda* according to which words have an independent existence and convey their meanings and the sentence-meaning is the subsequent construction from the individual meanings of the words. However, the followers of Prabhākara subscribe to *anvitābhidhānavāda* according to which a sentence is a whole consisting of words as parts and these words convey their meaning not in isolation, but only in a sentence. Of these theories, *anvitābhidhānavāda* is more convincing and this is discussed in the following. To begin with, let me state briefly the *abhihitānvayavāda* of Kumārila Bhaṭṭa.

As the term, *abhihitānvaya* itself suggests that we have first an understanding of the individual meanings of words (*padārtha-jñāna*) of a sentence one after the other and then these word-meanings are combined according to syntactical rules to convey the sentence-meaning (*vākyārtha-jñāna*). That is, that which is expressed (*abhihita*) is construed through mutual synthesis (*anvaya*) of words. On this view, the words of a sentence are not the immediate cause of sentence-meaning. They are only the mediate cause. Just as in the act of cooking fuel cannot directly do the cooking, but only through the flame of fire[16] so words cannot directly communicate sentence-meaning, but

16. *Ślokavārtika*, *Vākyādhikaraṇam*, 290-91, tr. Ganganath Jha, Sri Satguru Publications, Delhi, 1983, p. 538.

only through the meaning of the words. Thus, the knowledge of the meaning of words is the immediate cause of the meaning of a sentence. It is argued by *abhihitānvayavādins* that comprehension or non-comprehension of the sentence-meaning is associated with the comprehension or non-comprehension of the word-meanings. Kumārila says:

> Though we have no other ground (for the cognition of the meaning of the sentence), yet we perceive that the meanings of the words (composing the sentence) are such grounds,—inasmuch as the cognition of the meaning of a sentence appears **only** when there is cognition of the meaning of the words.[17] (emphasis is added)

What is suggested here is that the sentence-meaning is due to the syntactically interrelated word-meanings. The meaning of a sentence cannot be known on its own, unless its component parts, i.e., the word and the word-meanings are known. The relation between the word-meanings and the sentence-meaning is a causal relation. *Ākāṅkṣā*, *yogyatā* and *āsatti*[18] are the determining factors of this relation by which the constituent parts are related with each other to generate the sentence-meaning. The fact that the sentence-meaning is arrived

---

17. *atrābhidhīyate yady apy asti mūlāntaram na naḥ*
padārthānāṁ tu mūlatvaṁ dṛṣṭaṁ tadbhāvabhāvataḥ
— *Ibid*, 110-11, p. 504

18. It is generally believed by all schools of Indian philosophy that a sentence to be meaningful must confirm to the three conditions of *ākāṅkṣā*, *yogyatā* and *āsatti*. *Ākāṅkṣā* is the syntactic need which one word has for another in a sentence to convey the interrelations of the constituent words. The sentence, 'Cat wall on milk drink' is meaningless for it fails to fulfil the condition of *ākāṅkṣā*. *Yogyatā* consists in the absence of contradiction in the relation of the objects denoted by the words of the sentence. For instance, in the sentence, 'Moisten with fire', there is no *yogyatā*. *Āsatti* pertains to the physical aspect of the linguistic elements, which consists in not having any unnecessary interval or intervention between the words of a sentence. The words of a sentence, 'Bring a loaf of bread' will not make sense if the constituent words are uttered at long intervals or written at different places.

at by summing up the word-meanings does not establish the independent nature of the sentence-meaning. The words in a sentence retain their capacity to reveal their independent meanings. Every word, according to Kumārila, has its own definite meaning. This suggests that the sentence-meaning is not an independent entity over and above the words and word-meanings. To quote:

> And inasmuch as the meaning of a sentence is always comprehended in accordance with the meaning of the words (composing the sentence), — the fact of the sentence having a qualified (particular) signification cannot point to the fact of the sentence being independent (of the words). For us, even in the signification of the sentence, the words (composing it) do not lose their significance (potentiality); and it is only because the direct function of the words ends in the signification of their own individual denotations, that we hold the meaning of the sentence to be deduced from the *meanings of the words* (and not from the words directly).[19]

In this context, it is pertinent to note that the meaning of a sentence cannot be considered, as merely the sum of the word-meanings, for such a view would lead to a stage where the role of word-sequence has no sense. In fact, it is only from the word-meanings that a definite and distinct sentential-meaning (*viśiṣta-vākyārtha*) is known. The words in a sentence retain their capacity to reveal their meanings. The same word-meanings, if their sequence were changed would combine together to generate another sentence-meaning. Every word has its own definite meaning. For Kumārila a word primarily denotes a universal (*jāti*).[20] Although the words primarily mean universals,

19. *padārthānugataścaisa vākyārtho gamyate sadā*
na viśiṣṭārthatā tasmād vākyasvātantryasādhinī
na vimuñcanti sāmarthyam vākyārtheṣu padāninaḥ
tanmātrāvasitesveṣu padārthebhyaḥ sa gamyate.
— *Ślokavārtika, Vākyādhikarana*, 228-29, *op.cit.* pp. 527-28

20. *Ślokavārtika*, Section 13 on *ākṛti. op.cit.* pp. 281-95. Kumārila uses the words *ākṛti, jāti, sāmānya* and *śakti* synonymously. ' . . . there is a →

there is nothing to prevent them from referring to the individuals. While the universal is the primary meaning of a word, the individual is its secondary meaning (*lakṣaṇā*). In a sentence, words that primarily denote universals enter into mutual relationship by determining each other to denote a definite and distinct sentential meaning through the force of secondary meaning (*lakṣaṇā*). To quote:

> The revered (author) of the *Vārttika*s desiring all the sentence-meanings to be obtained by means of implication (*lakṣaṇā*). ... It is our position that the meaning of a sentence is, indeed, implied everywhere (i.e. in all case).[21]

On this view, to start with, all that we comprehend on hearing the words of a sentence are the unrelated entities denoted by the distinct words (universals) and then we proceed to assemble these unrelated entities into a unified relational structure (particular) through the force of secondary meaning (*lakṣaṇā*). From this it follows that *lakṣaṇā* belong to the second level at which the sentential meaning is cognised from the word-meanings. Being universal in nature, the primary meaning of the words cannot convey the sentence-meaning. If the words stop by conveying their primary meaning, i.e., universal, the purpose of employing the words in a sentence to convey a unified definite and distinct sentence-meaning would not be fulfilled. For instance, the word 'white' primarily means 'whiteness' as a universal, but in a sentence 'Bring a white car'; it means by secondary denotation the individual car with the attribute of white colour. Similarly, the word 'bring' primarily denotes the act of bringing in

→ distinct object of the Idea of single commonality; and it is a natural property of the Individuals. And as such, it may be named either *Sāmānya*, or *Ākṛti* or *Jāti* or *Śakti'* — *Ibid*, 13-18, p. 284.

Kumārilabhaṭṭa, *Tantravārttika*, Pada. III. 10, tr. Ganganath Jha, Sri Satguru Publications, Delhi, 1983, pp. 323-72.

21. Śālikanātha, a staunch follower of Prabhākara, while repudiating the position of Kumārila Bhaṭṭa in *Vākyārthamātṛkāvṛtti*, quotes this position of Kumārila Bhaṭṭa, tr. Rajendra Nath Sarma, Sri Satguru Publications, Delhi, 1987, p. 22.

general, but by means of secondary denotation denotes the particular act of bringing. Thus, in a sentence, the word-meanings, which are universals, are related with each other with the help of secondary denotation (*lakṣaṇā*) to convey the sentence-meaning.

The following reasons support this theory:

1. If the sentence and its meaning are considered to be independent entities over and above the constituent words and word-meanings, the speaker and the listener should have previous acquaintance with the sentence and its meaning. If this were the case, the listener cannot grasp the meaning of a new sentence with which he is not acquainted and consequently communication fails. When we understand the meaning of a new sentence, we do so on the basis of our knowledge of the words and their separate meanings.

2. If we learn few words and their meanings, a good number of sentences with different combinations and permutations can be understood.[22]

3. If the autonomy of words and word-meanings are not considered, then the classification of words into nouns, verbs, adjectives, etc., becomes meaningless.

Thus, *abhihitānvayavāda* asserts that the constituent words of sentence denote only their isolated meanings, which are combined according to syntactical rules and then these meanings are brought under a synthetic process, which gives the intended meaning. The words of a sentence are not the immediate cause of verbal cognition. They are only mediate cause. The immediate cause of verbal cognition is the knowledge of the meanings of words. In spite of its simplicity, this theory suffers from certain difficulties.

The basic argument against *abhihitānvayavāda* is that it fails to

---

22. *teṣvevaca padārtheṣu praklptastokaśaktiṣu*
āvāpodvāparacanābhedād vākyesv anantatā
— *Ślokavārtika, Vākyādhikaraṇa,* 121, *op.cit.* p. 506.

explain satisfactorily how we can grasp the meaning of a sentence at times, even when the meaning of a particular word of in a sentence is not known. According to *abhihitānvayavāda,* comprehension or non-comprehension of the sentence meaning is associated with the comprehension or non-comprehension of the word-meanings. From this it follows that failure in understanding the meaning of a particular word in a sentence leads to the failure in understanding the meaning of a sentence. However, one may, indeed, hear a sentence wherein a word with unknown meaning occur, and yet, somehow succeed in understanding the meaning of the sentence. Consider the sentence, 'Heinous crime deserves strict punishment'. Assume that the meaning of the word 'heinous' in this sentence is not known, still one may understand the meaning of the sentence. This suggests that the comprehension of all the meanings of the individual words of the sentence is not a necessary condition for comprehending the meaning of the sentence. A plausible defense in favour of *abhihitānvayavāda* is that even though the hearer, in the beginning may not be able to comprehend the meaning of the whole sentence, he will succeed in understanding it by recollecting the meanings of the known words and then by connecting them with the unknown words basing on the context. Such defense inevitably leads to the theory of *anvitābhidhānavāda.*

Another problem with *abhihitānvayavāda* is the role of *lakṣaṇā* leading to the knowledge of the meaning of the sentence. By *lakṣaṇā* is meant the secondary denotation of the word. As a rule, this secondary denotation is resorted to only when the primary denotation of the word does not fit in with the other words of the sentence or with the intention of the speaker. However, *abhihitānvaya-vādins* make use of the force of *lakṣaṇā* for comprehending the meaning of a sentence though there is not the least suggestion of incompatibility regarding the syntactical combination of primary meanings or with the intention of the speaker. Take for instance the sentence, 'Bring a white car'. The meaning of the sentence is plain and there is no problem with the syntactical combination of the primary meanings of the words of the sentence or with the intention of the speaker. Still *abhihitānvayavādins* would have recourse to *lakṣaṇā* for comprehending the meaning of the sentence, which is absurd. Therefore, the conditions necessary to take recourse to *lakṣaṇā* being absent, the thesis that the sentence-meaning is known through the integration of the individual meanings of the words of the sentence with the help of *lakṣaṇā* is difficult to maintain.

Further, it is a common experience that the words are never used in isolation. They are meaningful only when they are related to other words in a sentence. An isolated word is an abstraction from the sentence, which fails to convey a specific meaning. A word is to be related to other word or words to convey a meaning.

Having identified the weakness of *abhihitānvayavāda* in providing a reasonable explanation of sentence comprehension, let me now turn to *anvitābhidhānavāda* proposed by Prābhākara School of Pūrva-Mīmāṁsā.

IV

According to *anvitābhidhānavāda*, the sentence conveys a single unified meaning. An isolated word, without being related to other words in a sentence is never found as being used to convey a meaning. Individual words convey their meanings only when they are related to other words in a sentence.[23] In other words, the words acquire their meanings only in the context of a sentence. We cannot isolate a word from a sentence and fix a meaning to it without referring to the other words in a sentence. An isolated word is an abstraction from the sentence, which fails to convey a specific meaning. A word can convey a meaning only in so far as it and its meaning are related to other words and their meanings respectively. For instance, when a word 'close' is uttered, it fails to convey any meaning. Only when it is related to another word such as 'door' the meaning is conveyed.

---

23. (In a sentence), the meanings (of words only) as related are included and excluded. Therefore, the (denotative) capacity of the word is understood only in respect of the related (meanings).

    The Vākyārathamātṛkā, of Śālikanātha Miśra with his own Vṛtti tr. Rajendra Nath Sarma, Sri Satguru Publications, Delhi, 1987, p. 8.

The word 'close' alone or 'door' alone will not generate this cognition. The cognition of a word specifying an action promotes the cogniser, to inquire about the object, the performer, the place, the time as the case may be, connected with that action. Thus, a word is always a related word and the meaning is always a related meaning. On this view, the words of the sentence are the immediate cause of sentence-meaning and not the meanings of the words as argued by *abhihitānavayavādins.* In the words of Śālikanātha, a staunch follower of Prabhākara,

> We explain the view of the teacher Prabhākara as that the understanding of a sentence-meaning results (arises out of) from the very words only.[24]

The relation between word and sentence is similar to the relation between the parts and the whole of a machine. Just as the parts cannot perform their function without being related to the whole, even though they have their own essential nature and field of operation; similarly, the individual words fails to perform their function if they are stripped from the sentence.

It is interesting to note that there is considerable evidence that the process of learning a language begins at the level of sentences and not through isolated words. A child learns language by observing the linguistic utterances and their corresponding actions. The initial cognition of the child is the cognition of the whole sentence and its meaning without cognising the internal distinctions such as words and their specific meanings. The internal distinctions of the words and their meanings are known subsequently with the application of the method of agreement and difference.[25] Consider

---

24. *The Vākyārathamātṛkā, of Śālikanātha Miśra with his own Vṛtti,* p. 1.

25. 'The denotative power (*śakti*) of the words is ascertained by (observing) the difference of the process of inclusion and exclusion (*avapa* and *uddhara*) in the usages subsequent to the hearing of sentences by elderly persons'. *Ibid.*, 6, p. 4. Similar argument we find in Nyāya texts such as *Tarkasaṁgrahadīpikā* and *Siddāntamuktāvalī.* However, they do not subscribe to *anvitābhidhānavāda.*

this example: A child observes an elder speaking to the other — 'Bring the car' and the latter's corresponding action. At this stage, the child cannot differentiate the corresponding meanings of the different words occurring in this sentence. The child can only cognise the non-differentiating relation between the whole sentence and its related action. Later, the child hears somebody saying to another — 'Park the car' and observes the latter parking the car. The child compares these two sentences and comes to know that the term 'car' refers to a particular kind of motor vehicle. Similarly, the child learns to connect the words 'bring' and 'park' with their corresponding actions. Thus the initial cognition of the child is the cognition of the whole sentence and its meaning. The cognition of the internal distinction of the words and their meanings in a sentence is grasped subsequently. Thus, if the process of learning a language is possible only through the use sentences and not through unconnected words, then the meaning of a word cannot be known in isolation.

Further, though the meaning of the individual words are cognised by analysis involved in the application of the joint method of agreement and difference, the meanings must not be considered as simple unrelated facts. The meanings of the words, for *anvitābhidhānavādins*, are concepts, which are universal in nature and are always understood as related with one another. To quote Ganganath Jha,

> — 'while the cognition pertains to the class, the action laid down pertains to the individual'. The same view is accepted by Prabhākara, who hold *anvitābhidhānavāda* theory, according to which the denotation of the word is obtainable only through its connection with some particular action; and as each sentence would naturally pertain to some individual thing, this theory would appear to lend support to the *Individualistic* theory.[26]

The relation between the universal and the particular is similar to

26. Ganganath Jha, *The Prābhākara School of Pūrva Mīmāṁsā*, Motilal Banarsidass, Delhi, 1978, p.153.

that of an attribute and substance. Just as an attribute cannot be cognised without a substance in which it resides, similarly the universal cannot be cognised without the particular. The universal that is denoted by the word also denotes the particular in a sentential structure, as there is an inseparable relation between them in respect of both knowledge and existence. The sentence-meaning for *anvitābhidhānavādins* is directly denoted by the primary denotative power of the related words and not through secondary denotation (*lakṣaṇā*) as held by *abhihitānvayavādins*. However, secondary denotation is resorted to only when the direct denotation of a word does not consist with the other words of the sentence or with the intention of the speaker.

Thus, for *anvitābhidhānavādins*, the sentence has a unitary meaning of its own and the constituent words of a sentence possess meaning only as they are related to this unitary sentence-meaning. We know the meaning of a word only when we know how it is used. A word may stand in relation with another word in a sentence and may appear in another sentence in relation with some other word, but it is certain that it must stand in some relation with some word or other. The status of the individual meaning of a word is trivial outside the structure of a sentence. With the theory so construed, it remains to be seen how *anvitābhidhānavādins* handle various objections to their view.

The basic argument against *anvitābhidhānavāda* is that if the first word of a sentence conveys it meaning as being related with the other words, then the other words in the sentence are superfluous, as their function has already been performed by the first word. In that case, only one word should always be sufficient to make a sentence. A possible defense that could be given to such a criticism is that the subsequent words help in restricting the meaning indicated by the first word as related to the next word and the next word with the following and so on. Here an analogy of a machine is appropriate. A machine consisting of various parts is made to perform a particular work. Each part is essential and has its own definite function in completing the work for which the machine is made. However, each part at the same time can do its function only in association with the distinct functions of the other parts. Similarly, a word as a part of a sentence can mean its meaning only in so far as it and its meaning are respectively related to other words and their meanings to generate the unitary meaning of the sentence. Hence, all the words in the sentence are equally important in contributing to the emergence of the sentence-meaning.

Another objection against *anvitābhidhānavāda* is that it involves the fallacy of interdependence (*anyonyāśraya*). If the words do not have independent meaning of their own, and always have their meanings interrelated, then the cognition of the meaning of the first word of a sentence depend on the other word/words of the same sentence and the meaning of the other word/words of the sentence depend on the first word of the same sentence. On this view, for instance, in the sentence 'Bring a pot', unless the word, 'pot' conveys its sense, the word, 'bring' is not to be understood; but until the word, 'bring' conveys its sense, the word 'pot' cannot be understood. *Anvitābhidhānavādins* respond to this objection by stating that the words of a sentence are related in a sequential order. In a sentence, the first word-meaning is related to the second word-meaning, the second word-meaning to the third one and so on until the sentence is complete. The meanings of the preceding words in a sentence fulfil the conditions of expectancy and proximity with the succeeding words. As the words are manifested in a sequential way, the fallacy of interdependence is a far-fetched assumption.[27]

Yet, another possible objection to *anvitābhidhānavāda* is from the impossibility of knowing the infinite correlates of a word and as a consequence failure to comprehend the meaning of new sentences. According to *anvitābhidhānavāda* a word always conveys its meaning only in relation to the meaning of other words of a sentence. A word may stand in relation to another word in a sentence and may appear

---

27. Thus all the words speak of (convey) all meanings related by their own meanings (coming) to be proximate through recollection and as such there is no (involvement) of the fallacy of mutual interdependence. *The Vākyārathamātṛkā, of Śālikanātha Miśra with his own Vṛtti, op.cit.*, p. 32.

in another sentence in relation with some other word and so on. Thus, a word may occur commonly in an infinite number of sentences along with its relation with infinite number of words. A word 'car' may be used in different sentences with its relation with infinite number of words such actions as bringing, parking and driving, such attributes as white, large and such substances as iron, etc., to name few. In such a case, it is impossible to know the meaning of a word 'car' as it has infinite correlates. Consequently, we may not be able to comprehend the meaning of a new sentence containing the word 'car' in relation to another word which was not grasped before. The response to this objection is simple. When we have mastered sufficient stock of sentences, we proceed to the level of word-meanings through the process of inclusion and exclusion and in the process we realise a general law of syntax, namely, any word communicates its meaning only in association with other word or words which are expected, proximate and compatible. Once this law is known comprehending the meaning of new sentences is not difficult.

Among the three theories discussed above *anvitābhidhānavāda* adopted by the Prābhākara School of Pūrva-Mīmāṁsā seems to be empirically more satisfactory. *Akhaṇḍa-vākyārthavāda,* adopted by the Grammarians, maintain the sentence as the basic indivisible semantic unit and consider word and word-meanings as unreal abstractions of the sentence and sentence-meaning is empirically weak, for we do find sentence as whole consisting of words as parts. *Abhihitānvayavāda* adopted by the Bhāṭṭa School of Pūrva-Mīmāṁsā puts premium on the constituent words and their meanings relegating to the background their mutual relationship. Consequently, the sentence-meaning does not form the primary meaning; it is the secondary one, which we arrive at by a process of relating the different word-meanings. Such a view is untenable, for we resort to secondary meaning only when there is incompatibility regarding the syntactical combination of the primary meanings or with the intention of the speaker and not always. While granting the independent status to words, *anvitābhidhānavādins* deny an independent meaning to the word outside the sentential frame. They maintain that words always acquire meanings only in the context of a sentence. Thus, *anvitābhidhānavāda* differs from both *akhaṇḍa-vākyārthavāda* and *abhihitānvayavāda* by rendering status to the word to the extent of conveying a related word-meaning. This is obvious from the way people learn language. The fact that the words are never used in isolation suggests that the words are meaningful only in sentence. The sentence is a reality over and above the constituent words. However, unlike *akhaṇḍa-vākyārthavāda, anvitābhidhānavāda* is less insistent on the absolute indivisibility of the sentence. What is invariably grasped to start with is the primary meaning of a sentence as whole, and the meanings of the constituent words are located if necessary, although their functional value would be insignificant. Thus, *anvitābhidhānavāda* seems to be the most convincing theory of semantics in Indian philosophy.

The Contributors

V.N. Jha is Director, Centre of Advanced Study in Sanskrit, University of Pune, Pune.

John Vattanky is Professor, De Nobili College, Pune

A. Ramamurthy is retired Professor, Department of Philosophy, University of Hyderabad, Hyderabad.

R.C. Pradhan is Professor, Department of Philosophy, University of Hyderabad, Hyderabad. Currently Member Secretary, ICPR, New Delhi.

P.R. Bhat is Professor, Department of Humanities and Social Sciences, IIT, Bombay.

Tandra Patnaik is Professor, Department of Philosophy, Utkal University, Bhubaneswar.

Amitabha Dasgupta is Professor, Department of Philosophy, University of Hyderabad, Hyderabad.

Brinda Sen is Reader, Department of Philosophy, Victoria Institution (College), Kolkata.

Raghunatha Ghosh is Professor, Department of Philosophy, University of North Bengal, Darjeeling.

Prabal Kumar Sen is Professor, Department of Philosophy, University of Calcutta, Kolkata.

S. Panneerselvam is Professor, Dr. S. Radhakrishnan Institute of Advanced Studies in Philosophy, University of Madras, Chennai.

Mohini Mullick is retired Professor, Department of Humanities and Social Sciences, IIT, Kanpur.

K.S. Prasad is Reader, Department of Philosophy, University of Hyderabad, Hyderabad.

Index